Luminos is the Open Access monograph publishing program from UC Press. Luminos provides a framework for preserving and reinvigorating monograph publishing for the future and increases the reach and visibility of important scholarly work. Titles published in the UC Press Luminos model are published with the same high standards for selection, peer review, production, and marketing as those in our traditional program. www.luminosoa.org

D1565071

UNIVERSITY OF CALIFORNIA SERIES
IN JEWISH HISTORY AND CULTURES

Edited by

Todd Presner, Ross Professor of Germanic Languages
and Comparative Literature, UCLA
David Myers, Professor and Sady and Ludwig Kahn Chair
in Jewish History, UCLA

In partnership with University of California Press's Luminos program, the University of California Series in Jewish History and Cultures publishes cutting-edge scholarship in Jewish studies, with a particular ability to highlight work that relies on digital media. The series promotes interdisciplinary work that opens new conceptual and methodological horizons and has the potential to make a broad impact on diverse fields of study.

Golden Ages

Golden Ages

Hasidic Singers and Cantorial Revival in the Digital Era

———

Jeremiah Lockwood

UNIVERSITY OF CALIFORNIA PRESS

University of California Press
Oakland, California

Suggested citation: Lockwood, J. *Golden Ages: Hasidic Singers and Cantorial Revival in the Digital Era*. Oakland: University of California Press, 2024.
DOI: https://doi.org/10.1525/luminos.175

Cataloging-in-Publication Data is on file at the Library of Congress.

ISBN 978–0–520–00000–0 (pbk. : alk. paper)
ISBN 978–0–520–00000–0 (ebook)

32 31 30 29 28 27 26 25 24 23
10 9 8 7 6 5 4 3 2 1

CONTENTS

ACKNOWLEDGMENTS

"There is more than one golden age." Early in my research, elder cantorial peda-gogue Noah Schall offered these words to me in response to a question in which I casually referred to the cantorial "golden age," as if such a banal periodization could offer a transparent description of any moment from the vast terrain of can-torial histories, geographies, and personalities. His terse response suggested to me that every participant in the cantorial world and every deep listener to the archive of old cantorial records would have their own concept of what constitutes the peak of Jewish creativity or holiness. And that each of these many viewpoints on the past would be formative to very different approaches on how to go about the work of being a cantor in the present day. Different golden ages are created by each cantor who looks at the past and transforms it, bending it to serve their needs.

Schall was just one of the many figures, including sage-like cantorial elders, academic mentors, colleagues, musical collaborators, and friends, who helped me along the more than six years of research and writing that produced this book. This project encompasses many faces of my life, drawing on a family legacy, my music career, and my work as an academic. While I began my work with Hasidic cantors as a graduate student at the Stanford University Graduate School of Education Concentration in Education and Jewish Studies, the project extends back to my childhood, and really before my birth to several generations of cantors and musicians in my family.

I would like to begin with thanks to Ari Kelman, my thesis advisor, who brought me out to study at Stanford, believing in my potentials as a scholar despite my lack of experience in academic institutions, and putting me to work almost from the first day as an active participant in a series of research projects that helped me develop skills as an ethnographer and scholar of American Jewish life. I am grateful to the Jim Joseph Foundation that funded my graduate studies with Ari, and to the Taube Center for Jewish Studies at Stanford that provided material support for my research, including funding my production of the album *Golden Ages: Brooklyn Chassidic Cantorial Revival Today*. My colleagues in the Concentration in Education and Jewish Studies, Ilana Horowitz, Abiya Ahmed, Marva Shalev Marom, Matt Williams, rafa kern, and Hannah Kober were stimulating collaborators on Ari's numerous projects over the years. At the Graduate School of Education I was deeply impacted by scholars, including Raymond McDermott, Shelley Goldman, Brigid Barron, and Lee Shulman.

Outside the GSE, I was grateful to find a second home at Stanford in the music school, where I worked extensively with both Anna Schultz, taking all the courses she offered there and serving as her teaching assistant, and Charles Kronengold. My colleagues in the music school, Ioanida Costache and Jonathan Leal, were valued friends from whom I learned a great deal.

In the wider Stanford Jewish studies community, I studied extensively with Gabrielle Safran, and was greatly touched by the energy Steven Zipperstein bestowed on me, both in his research seminar and in subsequent years as an insightful mentor. Charlotte Fonrobert was a knowledgeable and kind guide as director of Jewish studies during most of my years at Stanford; I am grateful to Linda Huynh and Annie Altura who helped run Jewish studies with intelligence and patience. Shoshana Olidort and Jake Marmer provided moments of conversation and connection in a social world on campus that could get pretty wonky with isolation.

During my years at Stanford, my closest friend, interlocuter, and music collaborator was Jewlia Eisenberg. I discussed every aspect of this research project with her nearly daily for years; it was one among countless streams of thought we had running together. Her death in March of 2021 was a tragic loss for the worlds of music and new Jewish culture and has deeply impacted my life, leaving traces that I am not sure yet how to understand and how to live with. Placing Jewlia in this list of acknowledgements feels woefully inadequate, but it would be much worse to not name her.

My New York people have been the thorough line in life who have provided support and love during my time in California and with whom I have joyfully reunited full time in the last year. I give great thanks to bandmates and musical collaborators Ricky Gordon, Ernesto Gomez, Stuart Bogie, John Bollinger, Jordan McLean, Yuli Yael Be'eri, Timothy Allen, Nikhil Yerawadekar, Matt Bauder, and Kenny Warren. My parents, Sherry and Larry Lockwood, my uncle and aunt Cantor Josh Konigsberg and Meri Glasgall, and my extended world of cousins, especially Cantor Zachary Konigsberg and Phyllis Sussman and their family, are all central to my life and this work. My grandparents, Cantor Jacob Konigsberg and Geta Frumit Gittel Roth Konigsberg, are deeply missed—the sense memories of their home, the experiences of singing and eating around their table, are ingrained into this project.

As the preponderance of the title "cantor" before names on this list of acknowledgements indicates, I have lived my life with Jewish music. In the year since I moved back to New York after finishing my PhD, my cantorial circles have continued to grow. I have been blessed to spend time with a number of important elder cantors. I have spent the last year singing in the choir of Young Israel Beth El of Borough Park supporting Cantor Benzion Miller. Cantor Mayer Boruch Kohn has granted me several interviews. I spent much of 2021 working with Cantor Robert Kieval of blessed memory in the home he shared with the wonderful Gayna Kieval, working on assembling an archive of his legendary music manuscript collection. As the lead researcher for the Cantorial and Synagogue Music Archive project, overseen by Cantor Matthew Austerklein and the Cantors Assembly Foundation, I had the opportunity to work with Cantor Kieval before he passed away. I have also been working with Cantor David Lefkowitz.

I give thanks to friends in the Yiddishist and Yiddish music scenes in New York, including Cantor Rachel Weston, Judith Berkson, YIVO sound archivist Eleonore Biezunski, Jake Shulman-Ment, Pete Rushefsky of the Center for Traditional Music and Dance, Anna Elena Torres, Alex Weisser and Eddy Portnoy at YIVO, Sarah Gordon, Frank London, and author and critic Rokhl Kafrissen, who offered valuable feedback on parts of this manuscript. In other circles in the academic world, I gratefully acknowledge mentors and colleagues who have offered a range of guidance and friendship, including Jonathan Boyarin, Ianna Hawkins Owen, Margaret Olin, and Jessica Roda. Scholars who have laid foundations in the fields of American Jewish music and ethnography have generously provided feedback and guidance; these include Judah Cohen, Mark Slobin, Nathaniel Deutsch, Kay Kaufman Shelemay, and Jeffrey Shandler.

Mark Kligman and the Milken Center for Music of the American Jewish Experience at UCLA provided support for a variety of my research and writing projects as a research fellow in my first year out of graduate school. My work is currently being supported by a fellowship at the Yale Institute of Scared Music. I am filled with gratitude to Martin Jean, the director of the ISM, Eben Graves, the fellows advisor, Kristen Forman, outgoing assistant to the director, and to my cohort of fellows, especially my brilliant officemate Ephrem Aboud Ishac.

My sons Moses and Jacob have had the unusual experience of growing up with cantorial music as the soundtrack to their childhood. They seem to be unharmed by that aspect of their upbringing. Every day with the boys is a blessing and I am grateful that I have been able to do this work while raising my family. Their mother, Shasta Lockwood, and I have continued to work together as parents through the last years of the pandemic and other challenges of a more personal nature;

I thank her for enduring the hassle and pain my distractions and obsessions have caused her.

Finally, I wish to thank the artists whose voices are at the center of this project. The cantors who participated in this project opened a window into worlds of creativity and constructive uses of the past that have inspired me and transformed my life. Thank you to Yanky Lemmer, Yoel Kohn, Shimmy Miller, Zevi Steiger, Aryeh Leib Hurwitz, Yisroel Lesches, David Babinet, David Reich, Shulem Lemmer, Zev Muller, Yoel Pollack, and Yossi Pomerantz. I am hopeful the artists will find a reflection of themselves and their work that they recognize in these pages.

Introduction

"I didn't know what I was craving until I found it"

So, once before Passover I was cleaning out the laundry room. There was a lot of old tapes. Real brown and dusty. And I found a tape from a cantor, Ari Klein.[1] So, I listened to it. And I fell in love immediately. I loved it. And from there on you grow into it. And then I started going to the store and buying, every dollar that I had I would spend. And I collected over the years. There was a store on Lee Avenue, Lee Avenue Photo. And when I completed purchasing their entire stock, I started taking the bus to Borough Park, Mostly Music.[2] They had even more, larger selection. I was sent out to do a lot of errands. All the change I had I got to keep. So, with that I purchased tapes.

—DAVID REICH, INTERVIEW, JANUARY 15, 2019[3]

David Reich is a thirty-eight-year-old Hasidic man, born and raised in the Satmar Hasidic neighborhood of Williamsburg, Brooklyn. His life is typical of many men in his community; he is the father of a large family and makes his living running a business as a retail distributor supplying other businesses mostly focused within the Hasidic Brooklyn enclave. He is also a committed and passionate fan and performer of "golden age" recorded cantorial music, a style of Jewish sacred music that reached its peak of popularity in the first half of the twentieth century, decades before he was born. This style is not associated with the Hasidic community and in fact is not popular or particularly well-known or understood in any segment of contemporary Jewish America—Orthodox, liberal, or otherwise.

   In this anecdote, Reich offers a picture of his musical engagement as having emerged from a single, life-altering moment of discovery. For Reich, this moment of aesthetic awakening was transformative, leading toward a path of immersion in an archive of old records.[4] Reich's knowledge of the recorded style of cantorial music and his skill as a performer in this style place him in a community of Hasidic musicians for whom cantorial music has taken a central place as a frame for creative endeavors and constructing identities as artists.

1

This book offers a cultural history of a tiny musical subculture within contemporary Orthodox Judaism in New York City. Yet in the telling, the story of the musical lives of *Hasidic cantorial revivalists* implicates lineages and contexts that resonate beyond their corner of the world. The story of these cantors raises broader theoretical concerns and methodological questions about how considerations of aesthetics can offer insight into histories of social change. Hasidic cantorial revivalists are one of many groups in the contemporary world to redress perceived social and aesthetic limitations in their community through recourse to an image of the past. Their story contributes to a literature on the role of music as a key to understanding processes of social change, especially in the American Jewish community.[5]

Cantorial records of the early twentieth century document a style of Jewish music that is based on older strands of folkloric prayer sounds arranged and composed in an aestheticized form and decontextualized from their role as ritual in the synagogue. This style is at one and the same time understood by cantorial music fans as a folkloric, primitivist aesthetic that harkens back to Eastern European traditions, but one that is also deeply influenced by Western classical music and opera. It is this doubleness, this spiritual and musical paradox in the sound world of early twentieth century cantors, that continues to intrigue and present opportunities for aesthetic exploration for artists in the twenty-first century. Gramophone-era records present a musical world that includes more than sound alone: the records preserve a unique style of Jewish musical aesthetics, but they also suggest a conception of the cantor as a form of Jewish personhood, an identity grounded both in ritual knowledge and musical expertise. Old records offer testimony of the existence in the past of an approach to prayer that was lent its specific sociality by the experience of music performance and listening. Gramophone-era cantorial culture presents Hasidic cantorial revivalists with attractive and novel enticements: a distinctive musical style, an identity category of the charismatic Jewish sacred music artist, and an approach to prayer characterized by an aesthetic listening experience. All three of these signature elements of cantorial culture are absent from the contemporary Jewish life that is familiar to Hasidic singers.

This book explores how Hasidic cantorial revivalists learn the musical style of gramophone-era cantors and then what they are able to do with this knowledge, working within the affordances and pushing at the limitations of their social worlds. It is a story of adventurous exploration of the archive, imaginative expression of a sensorium of novel aesthetic experience, and tentative, furtive steps toward building a sonic future based in the experience of listening to the past. On a practical level, Hasidic cantorial revival always involves work of cultural translation and recontextualization of sounds and ideas across boundaries of time and identity. The Hasidic singers studied here are, for the most part, performing their revivalist style of singing in non-Hasidic spaces. The key challenge of their journey as artists involves finding a place for their musical endeavor, usually working outside the separatist religious community in which they have lived their lives.

The contemporary cantorial revivalists of Brooklyn were born into Hasidic enclave communities that have their foundational roots in the eighteenth century in the Russian Pale of Settlement and Poland. The founder of the modern Hasidic movement, Israel ben Eliezer (ca.1700–60), referred to as the Baal Shem Tov (Hebrew, the master of the good name) was a populist leader who sought to revolutionize the religious life of Jews by democratizing access to the Jewish mystical tradition. The revitalized spiritual experience championed by the Baal Shem Tov and other early Hasidic leaders was achieved through storytelling, ecstatic dance, and music. While Hasidism began as a revolutionary movement in Orthodox Judaism with an anti-establishment cast, by the early nineteenth century the leaders of Hasidism had consolidated authority into hereditary courts led by charismatic rabbis referred to as *tsadik* (Hebrew, righteous one, pl. *tsadikim*) or *rebbe* (Yiddish, a familiar term for rabbi). Hasidic courts functioned both as religious sects and as the centers of political and social life. Hasidic rebbes were vested by custom and fortified by institutions with a broad array of forms of authority over the spiritual and practical lives of their followers.[6]

Forms of radical pietism established by the first generation of Hasidic leaders were formalized into religious practices that were adhered to with increasing strictness by subsequent generations of Hasidim. Today, Hasidic Judaism is associated with a dedication to the preservation of Jewish life ways and customs in the context of modernization and assimilation. The artists whose work I profile in this book were raised in the Belz, Bobov, Satmar and Lubavitch communities, all sects named for their places of origin in Eastern Europe. While there are important cultural differences between these groups that I will address in the context of discussions of the cantors and their music, these Hasidic communities share in common a separatist orientation, a focus on religious life, and conservative attitudes that have a controlling influence on approaches to education and expressive culture.

The Hasidic singers involved in cantorial revival are not bound exclusively to the separatist communities in which they were born; their professional lives especially are characterized by movement between social worlds. Contemporary Orthodoxy in the United States can be broadly divided into two main categories—Modern Orthodoxy and separatist Orthodoxy. Hasidism falls into the latter category. Other branches of separatist Orthodoxy include groups referred to as Litvish or Yeshivish, terms that convey the centrality of traditional Jewish textual learning to the community. Litvish and Hasidic Jews are often grouped together under the umbrella term Haredi, a word used in Israel to connote separatist Orthodox Jewish communities. Hasidism is perhaps the separatist Orthodox group that is most broadly recognized in the United States with its enclave communities, its use of the Yiddish language in daily life, and its distinct forms of dress frequently depicted in popular media. In contrast, Modern Orthodoxy is a religious movement that seeks to synthesize stringent religious observance with integration into the modern nation state. Modern Orthodoxy is more culturally aligned with non-Orthodox Jews and the "mainstream" of American society in terms of dress, English language use, and educational and professional norms. The American Jewish community is also represented by "liberal Judaism," a broad category that includes the Conservative and Reform denominational movements, as well as many American Jews who do not affiliate with any religious group. For the Hasidic cantorial revivalists profiled in this book the non-Hasidic communities that play the most significant roles are Modern Orthodox, who look to more stringently religious Jews for ritual leadership and who sometimes employ Hasidic Jews as cantors, on the one hand, and secular Jews and Jews in the liberal denominational movements, who interact with Hasidic cantorial revivalists in the realm of concert performance, on the other.[7]

Learning about cantorial music offered David Reich multiple streams of new and exciting activity that stood outside the norms of his life. Studying the music helped him develop a set of practices as an artist, cultivating knowledge about performance in an arcane domain. His love of old records thrust him into the role of an archivist. David sought out knowledge from sources that lay beyond his typical sphere of activity. He found sites for accessing the music he wanted in out-of-the way places, devoting resources of time, money, and mental energy to forming the collection he would need to become an expert in his desired area of expressive culture. David cultivated a new set of understandings and values based on his own musical judgements and desires. He began to develop a critique of the prayer life of his community based not in the norms of rabbinic authority but rather in his own judgements formed along lines of aesthetic impulses, guided by musical desires and his newfound identity as an expert in Jewish liturgical music of the past.

> I grew up in Brooklyn, Williamsburg. I always loved music. I grew up with a lot of music. We listened to Mordechai Ben David, Avraham Fried, you know the usual, Mendy Werdiger [Ben David, Avraham Fried, and Mendy Werdiger are three of the major stars of Orthodox Jewish pop music]. No *khazones* [Yiddish, cantorial music] . . . I didn't know even that khazones exists. There was nobody, we didn't have any khazones cassettes at home.

A style of music often called Orthodox pop is what Hasidic participants in this study refer to as "normal music." Starting in the late 1950s and early 1960s, singer-songwriters in the Orthodox community such as Shlomo Carlebach and Ben Zion Shenker released albums of original songs in a quasi-traditional, or neo-Hasidic style.[8] While Carlebach and Shenker were both associated with Hasidic communities, their music resonated beyond the Hasidic world and was embraced by all branches of Orthodoxy, and eventually by liberal Jewish denominations as well. Carlebach's work was particularly forward-minded in embracing aesthetics of the folk music movement; in fact, he performed in the same New York nightclub circuit as Joan Baez and Odetta. At the same time, a push to preserve the traditional repertoire of older Hasidic *nigunim* (Hebrew, melodies, here referring to paraliturgical wordless songs) led to the production of a series of albums of Hasidic choirs and soloists.[9] These Hasidic music efforts laid the groundwork for a new style of recorded pop music in the late 1960s and early 1970s, pioneered by Mordechai Ben David and Avraham Fried, the two most notable names in the emerging genre, both of whom are Hasidic Jews. Ben David and Fried embraced sounds of pop, especially disco, to formulate a new Orthodox music style. A new crop of Orthodox pop stars, often drawn from the Hasidic community, arises on an ongoing basis. While Orthodox pop originated with artists in the Hasidic community, its popularity crossed boundaries between separatist Orthodox and Modern Orthodox communities. Orthodox pop is relatively unknown to liberal and secular Jews.[10]

The new pop sound was broadly embraced by separatist Orthodox Jews. Noted Talmudic scholar Haym Soloveitchik characterized the development of Orthodox pop as part of a general move away from aurality in Orthodox life toward an increasing focus on text, leading to a shift away from what he considered to be traditional Jewish life.[11] According to Soloveitchik, the appropriation of pop sounds reflected a surprising abandonment of Jewish customs in an Orthodoxy that purported to be devotedly preservationist and opposed to change. In the decades since Soloveitchik wrote, pop has become further entrenched in the community. The pop sound—based in the timbres of synthesizers, drum machines, and electric guitar, and employing stylistic elements borrowed from radio pop and adult contemporary genres—forms the public soundscape of separatist Orthodox Jewish neighborhoods, heard in restaurants and stores over PA systems, played at weddings and at celebrations presided over by prestigious rabbis and listened to by families on car stereos.[12]

In the separatist Orthodox context, where pop music is a normative style of performance, cantorial music bears a liminal status as an art form that is partly familiar through elements of shared vocabulary with synagogue prayer but not fully integrated into communal life. Cantorial music is intermittently brought to the fore of mainstream Hasidic culture through new reissue projects or performances by a handful of international cantorial stars (some Hasidic Jews from Israel) but is generally considered an underground niche style and in some cases, as in David Reich's story, was essentially an unknown.[13]

The performance of prayer in Hasidic synagogues has its own conventions and is typically led by nonprofessional singers. There are a handful of professional *bal tefiles* (Hebrew, prayer leaders) working in the Brooklyn Hasidic community whose work is sonically different and bears a different set of associations from the cantorial sound aspired to by the revivalists I focus on in this book. The revivalist sound is primarily structured around styles of performance that are preserved on old records; it is characterized by a distinctive repertoire of musical techniques and usually involves professional vocal cultivation. In contrast, bal tefiles are characterized by a more rough-hewn vocal sound and a less prominent display of the motivic vocabulary of cantorial performance, as demonstrated on classic recordings.

I use the term *Hasidic cantorial revivalists* to distinguish the primary subject of this work from other prayer leaders in the Hasidic community. The revivalist sound can be understood as drawing from a professionalized musical form that is primarily known through mediated sources. Hasidic cantorial revival is an arcane musical field in tight dialogue with a temporally removed object of study and desire, in contrast to bal tefile prayer leading, which is a well-understood musical practice that many members of the community have some access to as performers.

While Hasidic cantorial revivalists sing mostly outside their birth community, and Hasidic bal tefiles are heard almost exclusively within the community, nigunim repertoires have a life both within and outside the Hasidic community. Nigunim, a specialized repertoire often sung without words and distinct from the prescribed prayer texts that khazones is yoked to, are sung as a paraliturgical devotional repertoire at Hasidic community events. Both older nigunim and new songs influenced by nigunim repertoires have been adopted by liberal Jewish communities, adapted to local musical styles as a popular devotional music form, and are frequently used today in prayer services.

The musical style documented on classic cantorial records is distinct both from what is heard in Hasidic prayer houses and from the pop sounds of the Orthodox Jewish music industry. Not just repertoire and musical style are different; pronunciation of Hebrew prayer texts is different from the norms of present-day Hasidic practice. Hasidic Jews in Brooklyn today generally pronounce Hebrew prayer texts with what is commonly referred to as Polish or Hungarian accents, regional variants that correlate to the origins of different Hasidic communities in Europe. However, Hasidic cantorial revivalists imitate the pronunciation of gramophone-era cantors in their cantorial performance, who employed a "standardized" Ashkenazi pronunciation that is described by Hasidic Jews as "Litvish" (Lithuanian). Another important influence on norms of golden age cantorial pronunciation is likely the prestigious central European cantors who set standards for the modern cantorial style.[14] Embracing the Hebrew pronunciation of early twentieth century cantors places Hasidic cantorial revivalist performance in a special aestheticized terrain, one that is neither Hasidic nor representative of common practice in Modern Orthodox shuls and that occupies a position that is also far removed from the practices of liberal movement synagogues, where Modern Hebrew phonology is the norm.

And yet Reich's listening experience was not a complete rupture, sealed off from the rest of his religious life and his enculturation into Hasidic life. The texts being sung on old cantorial records were drawn from an intimately familiar body of liturgy that Reich knew from a lifetime of daily prayer. Furthermore, the Satmar community does include cantors in some important communal events, such as the annual celebration of the Satmar Rebbe's freedom from Auschwitz and a mass community event held each year for Chanukah that has been conducted since the days before the immigration of the community to Brooklyn in the mid-twentieth century. These events connect to the community's European past, calling on the sounds of cantorial singing as a signifier of heritage.

The cantorial sound David heard on that first record was novel but not entirely unfamiliar—it is a constitutive part of the ambient Jewish culture that feeds a variety of contemporary styles and vocal music approaches. Reich told me that part of what drew him to the sound of cantorial records was that the music reminded him of a track on a record by Hasidic pop star Avraham Fried, the song "Emes" from Fried's 1988 album *We Are Ready*, which came out when Reich was a boy. The track contains a lengthy section in which Fried mimics the sound of an old cantorial performance, muting the drum machine and synthesizer that dominate the song in an extended breakdown to the spare texture of voice and organ heard on many cantorial records. The dance beat that predominates on the track, and in most of Fried's music, comes to a halt, embracing the lugubrious nonmetered rhythmic quality of cantorial recitative. Reich had taken note of this remarkably different musical style. When he first heard the cassette of Ari Klein, he was grateful that "I can finally have a full cassette of this stuff." While Reich had never been taught about cantorial music, his enculturation in the Orthodox Jewish world offered him clues about the existence of other Jewish musical worlds, priming him for the experience of discovering cantorial music.

> So, I developed into it. I started going to the store and buying, every dollar that I had I purchased tapes. I started out, you know, with Yossele Rosenblatt [1882–1933] and then I moved on to Shia [Yehoshua] Wider [1906–64], and then Moshe Koussevitzky [1899–1965], Mordechai Hershman [1888–1940]. I was getting into it. And then Moishe Oysher [1906–58]. It was a journey. It was a big part of my childhood.

Reich uses the Yiddish term *khazones* to refer to cantorial music, invoking the musical knowledge of the *khazn*, or cantor, as its own distinctive musical category. Throughout this book, I use the term *khazones*, as Hasidic cantors do, to refer to the cantorial art music documented on gramophone-era recordings.[15] Unlike the more general term *cantorial music*, which can connote a variety of styles and historical contexts of professionalized Jewish liturgy, *khazones* references the sacred music of Yiddish-speaking Jews. *Khazones* is historically linked to the Eastern European cultural context and the secondary diaspora of Yiddish speakers in the United States and internationally. Despite the profile of the Hasidic community as the champions of the Yiddish language and of Eastern European Jewish tradition, the historical memory of the community is highly selective, as its musical life makes clear.

The archive of old Jewish records offers Hasidic singers testimony about the existence of a world of star cantors who straddled the line between achievement as secular artists and sacred ritual leaders. What is now called the "golden age" of cantorial records (roughly 1901–50) emerged against a backdrop of controversy, musical rebellions, and a Yiddish culture pulsating with literary experimentation and political radicalism. Gramophone records made by star cantors were sold in the hundreds of thousands to a listening public on both sides of the Jewish Atlantic world—in America, Poland, and Russia. The "gramophone era," a term I will use in this book to describe the period of cantorial music as a popular music phenomenon, introduced the work of a small cohort of star cantors to a mass listening public. Jewish listeners were parched, thirsting for a sonic representation of themselves and their community.

During the nineteenth century, cantors serving elite urban synagogues embraced a new style of Jewish choral music influenced by European classical music and German romanticism. Working under the influence of Salomon Sulzer (1804–90), the first state sanctioned *Oberkantor* of Vienna, cantors throughout Europe embraced the "Vienna rite" sound, which was focused on trained choirs singing newly composed music for Hebrew prayer texts.[16] The Hasidic community never adopted Sulzer's liturgical reforms, instantiating a sense of Eastern European small towns as a bastion of older strands of Jewish music. The music of the phonograph-era cantors offered a populist response to the "choral" repertoire. The "new" cantorial sound of the early twentieth century was described in romanticized terms by cantors and their supporters as a revival of the folkloric roots of sonic Jewishness—characterized by the work of small-town *bal tefiles*, Hasidic devotional music, and the noisy heterophony of *davenen* (Yiddish, chanting prayer texts). This primitivist aesthetic was in turn reconfigured as an art music influenced by opera and performed by dramatic virtuoso singers. The conception of cantors as champions defending the sacred Jewish past against sonic assimilation is a crucial element in the mythology of the golden age that appeals to contemporary Hasidic singers.

The cantorial gramophone era was initiated by the popular discs made by Gershon Sirota in Warsaw and Zawel Kwartin in Vienna. Sirota and Kwartin were the first international stars of Jewish music.[17] Their records played a niche role in the era of early phonograph stars who were drawn from the opera world. As the historian of the phonograph Roland Gelatt noted, the sound of trained voices was particularly well-suited to the limited sound spectrum of early recording technology, bringing classically trained vocal artists to a broader level of stardom.[18] This cultural phenomenon swept up cantors in its moment. The first decade of cantorial records established the concept of the star cantor on a mass scale.

Cantors were popular music stars; some of the most successful performers were known to be nonreligious in their private lives or to have nonconforming identities associated with the world of the arts. Fandom of cantorial music was not limited to the religious; both religious and nonreligious Jewish people, men and women, secular and leftist Jews, coconstituted a listening public that avidly consumed cantorial music. Cantorial records united Orthodox and secular Jews into what Ari Kelman calls an "acoustic community," bound together by a shared set of listening habits and musical desires.[19] The archive of commercial cantorial records offers contemporary Hasidic musicians testimony to the diversity of Jewish experience across time. Records preserve traces of a culture of sacred performance that made room for a form of personhood barely known in the Orthodox Jewish world today—ritual leaders who were also skilled creative artists. The listening community for khazones connected ritual musicians to a broad and musically well-educated public that was knowledgeable about classical music, as well as cantorial performance. This internally diverse Jewish milieu is foreign to the current landscape of Hasidic Judaism in which secular arts education is discouraged and contact with secular or acculturated Jews is limited.

The center of cantorial recording moved from Europe to New York City after World War I. The golden age records of the 1920s made in New York moved further from the "elite" choral synagogue styles of the major European metropolises, instead offering performances that were intended to evoke the culturally intimate sounds of Jewish liturgical folklore. Performances on record were tailored to the time limitations of 78rpm records, sculpting tightly scripted representations of cantorial prayer leading. Cantors such as Kwartin and Yossele Rosenblatt wrote pieces that expertly manipulated the dramatic potentials of their tenor voices, framing compositions around virtuoso melismatic passages that were considered to be the signatory sonic gesture of Eastern European cantors. Frequently, their compositions would climax in the highest vocal registers, executing a devastating emotional impact.

The careers of recording star cantors offer Hasidic singers a tantalizing vison of lives that bound together musical mastery with a successful ability to connect to an audience. Hasidic cantors are motivated by the desire to recreate such successes, even in the face of overwhelming evidence that their style of Jewish sacred performance will not be embraced by any of the institutions of contemporary Jewish life and that their conception of aesthetics and musical value is considered suspect in their own birth community.

> When I was a kid, I used to love classical music, but I had to find my way around—I would record from 106.7, the classical station, and put "lecture from Rabbi" on it [i.e., intentionally mislabel the cassette tape], so this way I could have it in my room. They wouldn't have been happy if I was listening to non-Jewish music.

For young musicians in the Hasidic community, communal focus on norms of piety and bodily comportment extend to what forms of music can legitimately be engaged with, for listening or performing. In David Reich's family, non-Jewish European classical music might not have been considered acceptable, but Orthodox pop was. David and several other participants in this project described a Hasidic home life in which old cantorial records were practically unheard of. But David's musical experience is not easily generalizable. The Hasidic Brooklyn community contains a variety of approaches to music and heritage, including families with cantorial lineages and musically conservative households that maintain a ban on pop music, giving musical styles that are perceived by some as more traditional an opportunity to take hold.

Yoel Kohn, whose father Mayer Boruch Kohn is a well-known *bal tefile* in the Satmar community, was discouraged from listening to Orthodox pop. His father loved old cantorial music and disparaged newer styles; however, the elder Kohn had specific parameters for what was acceptable even in classic cantorial music. For example, Yoel's father always fast-forwarded through the part of the cassette tape of *Zawel Kwartin Sings His Best Cantorial Works* when Kwartin's 1928 recording "Moron D'vishmayo" appears on the anthology. "Moron D'vishmayo," with its chordal sequence lifted from European art music sources and operatic declamatory style, sounded to Mayer Boruch Kohn like "church music." How Mayer Boruch Kohn gained his sense of what church music sounds like is unclear—but the music did not "sound Jewish" to his ears, and thus was liable to censorship.

Yanky Lemmer and his brother Shulem Lemmer, both of whom are professional singers, told me that their father, a passionate fan of old cantorial records, forbade pre-World War II Yiddish songs because they were written by nonreligious Jews and expressed anti-Orthodox messages. This experience of the Lemmer brothers accords with Asya Vaisman's ethnography in the Hasidic community that shows how older repertoires of Yiddish song, associated with secular Jews, have largely disappeared among Hasidic women. These older repertoires have been replaced by more recent songs written by current artists in the familiar Orthodox pop vein.[20]

In the Hasidic milieu, religion and religious power-holders influence all aspects of life, including the musical life of the community. Attention to hierarchies of power are important considerations in analyzing contemporary Hasidic life. Hasidic communities in Brooklyn today are explicitly organized around faith in the divine origin of Jewish law, a selective conception of traditional lifeways and the authority of rabbinic leaders. This faith is visibly expressed through public displays of piety, ritual observance, sartorial conformity, communal foodways, the study of sacred texts, sharply segregated gender roles, and a communally disciplined approach to heterosexual family life. According to sociologist Samuel Heilman, the Orthodox community is in the grips of a fifty-year "slide to the right" that places continuously expanding strictures on the personal life of members of the community.[21] Anthropologist Ayala Fader's ethnography in the Hasidic community emphasizes how a culture of religious discipline shapes "bodies and minds to serve God rather than any modern form of authority."[22] A profusion of interest in the Hasidic community in recent years has permeated popular culture, with memoir literature, film, and television representations of the Orthodox world accentuating the repression of sexuality and individual expression. These popular works purport to represent Orthodoxy to the liberal world, comfortably reifying the image of nonliberal religion as oppressive in comparison to the presumed "freedom" of liberal society.[23]

Recent ethnographic scholarship on Orthodoxy has taken a varied view on the construction of agency in the community. Earlier anthropological assessments of nonliberal religious communities highlighted the distance between authority and individuality, analyzing behaviors in terms of resistance and compliance. New approaches, building on what Sabah Mahmood refers to as expressions of "agency without resistance" in nonliberal religious movements, suggest that self-expression is not uniformly incompatible with communally enforced religious beliefs.[24] Not surprisingly, some of the most fecund new perspectives on Orthodoxy have emerged from scholarship on women's experiences, a historically overlooked area of research. Orit Avishai, in a study of women's ritual lives in Orthodox communities, offers the analytic rubric of "doing religion" to explore how performance of ritual law can contribute to an active construction of identity and self, challenging normative evaluative approaches to religious authority as necessitating submission. In a study of reproductive decision-making strategies among Orthodox Jews, Lea Taragin-Zeller argues for the power of ethnography to reveal the interdependence of rabbinic authorities and the communities they guide; she documents a fluid dance between agency and submission in the coconstruction of a religious community. And recent work by Jessica Roda suggests that a newly emergent engagement with Orthodox pop music by Hasidic women is creating new opportunities and identities as artists. Although Roda and I worked separately, her ethnography closely parallels the research I have conducted with Hasidic men in considering the role of music as a nonconforming creative practice within separatist Orthodoxy; our research projects also share a recent time frame and geographic location in New York City. These studies, and others, highlight the role of discourse as a means of constituting an ethical self in the context of a highly structured and rule-based religious system. Recent anthropological research in the Orthodox community is increasingly attuned to the ways in which a conception of values and valorized practices is coconstructed by authorities and members of the community.[25]

While their aesthetic orientation places Hasidic cantorial revivalists on the fringe of their community in terms of their interests, I have not found that resistance to authority is an explicit motivation for the artists who participated in this study. Hasidic singers drawn to cantorial music stretch the boundaries of acceptable behavior, but they do so to cultural and aesthetic ends that are not geared toward an overthrow of authority or a rupturing of their identities as Hasidic men. Scholars of separatist Orthodoxy have made recourse to Foucault's image of the panopticon to describe a society in which hierarchies of power and rules of conformity are maintained through public discipline and surveillance.[26] While this description of Brooklyn Hasidic life may contain some truth, it is inadequate as a rubric for analyzing and theorizing the creative lives of members of the community. More problematic for this study, a Foucauldian approach tends to gloss over the possibility of intellectual integrity for artists and intellectuals whose creative work takes place within the structure of religious authority. As Hussein Ali Agrama has argued, ethical agency is not a unique characteristic of the Western liberal milieu.[27] By extension, the ethical and intellectual probing characteristic of artistic creativity is not dependent on the overthrow of tradition and the adoption of a liberal sensibility.

As anthropologist Dorothy Holland has noted, projects of personal development are constructed within the confines of historically contingent identities and communities. Rather than being comprehensible exclusively through a lens of resistance to the social settings individuals are born and enculturated into, "the development of self-understandings (identities) on intimate terrains . . . [are] an outcome of living in, through, and around the cultural forms practiced in social life."[28] Hasidic cantorial revivalists are challenged by an aesthetic need that they address through the prism of the social norms they have been educated in, grasping on to a recognizably Jewish art form with a basis in religious ritual and sacred texts. That their musical expression is sometimes perceived as a form of rebellion against religious norms is a source of pain and tension in the lives of Hasidic cantors; indeed, this places serious limits on their ability to imagine futures for their music. Piety, on the one hand, and skepticism about rabbinic authority, on the other, are two extremes along a spectrum of responses to the strictures of Hasidic life. Hasidic cantorial revivalists dance along this spectrum, responding to the pressure to conform to communal norms in ways that are contingent, contextual, and geared toward finding ways to reconcile their desires as musicians with the rules of communal life.

> There are opportunities that come along that allow me to express myself in music. There's opportunities—there's no plan . . . There's always a love for it. I was born with a love for it, but I didn't know what I was craving until I found it. When I found it, I was, *oh, this is what I like.*

Singing khazones is a project of aesthetic self-cultivation that takes place within the confines of the Hasidic community. The singers who participated in my research are passionate about memorializing and perpetuating the music of the cantorial golden age, but are in some ways surprisingly quiet about the specifics of the cultural milieu they revere. Cantors of the phonograph era were often secular or secularizing Jews whose work was consumed on mass-mediated records that blurred the line between sacred and secular experience. Golden age recorded cantorial music addressed listeners with a form of sacred music that placed aesthetic beauty on the same level as the religious mandate of prayer, an inversion of the normative values of the Hasidic community. Hasidic singers play with these contradictions through evasion and context-specific compromises.

The commodified and aestheticized version of Jewish prayer associated with old records continues to be critiqued for its perceived transgressions against the purity of synagogue prayer experience and the displacement of the sacred into "immoral" settings. These criticisms and the dents they can make in the reputations of singers place limits on the kinds of performance opportunities that Hasidic cantorial revivalists pursue. As I learned while following the careers of the artists profiled in this book, and especially when trying to produce concerts, Hasidic cantors are careful and strategic about when and where they will perform, and mindful of the criticism they may encounter from members of their birth community or their own families.

For example, Yoel Kohn foreswore any performance opportunities outside the Hasidic community in deference to his father's wishes—that is, until he broke with the community completely a few years ago. Yanky Lemmer has had to sustain online disparagement of his performance activities. In both these cases the defining issue was gender and the perceived immorality in performing for audiences with mixed-gender seating. Because cantorial performance brings Hasidic singers into contact with audiences outside their birth community, the potential for violating rules of behavior is greatly increased. For Hasidic singers, pursuing khazones is a disruptive act; the history of cantors as artists who pushed boundaries and social norms in their pursuit of an aesthetic vision resonates in the lives of Hasidic singers who are working in the context of a bounded world of religious ethics.

. . .

My research with Hasidic cantors began in the summer of 2015, when I drove out to Swan Lake, New York, a small town in the Catskill Mountains, to meet Cantor Yanky Lemmer for the first time. Lemmer and his family were vacationing in a bucolic bungalow resort of the variety that is patronized exclusively by Hasidic Jews from Brooklyn. I was already a fan of Lemmer from his YouTube videos and was aware of his prestigious cantorial position at the Lincoln Square Synagogue in Manhattan. Before starting the interview, Lemmer ran in to his bungalow and came out with a pile of 78-rpm records. The records were mostly missing dust jackets and were bundled together in a flimsy plastic shopping bag. Some of these records were a hundred years old. Yanky explained that these were a few loose ends from his collection that he had brought on vacation. He pulled out a record of Gershon Sirota. This particular disc was a later American reissue of a recording made by the famed Warsaw-based cantor in Europe before World War I. Then Lemmer went back inside and came out with an even more fanciful treasure. It was a hand-cranked Victrola, the size of a suitcase. He had bought it at a vintage electronics show in New Jersey.

As he set it up and started to crank, a gang of little boys streamed over from a nearby field to see what was happening. Lemmer spoke to the children in Yiddish, showing off his unusual possession. He let one of the boys give the crank a few turns. The Victrola had no volume control knob; its only settings were on and off. The needle lowered down onto the record and I was immediately impressed by how loud and clear its sound was. The presence of the hundred-year-old record by Gershon Sirota, the famed Warsaw cantor, piping out of the resonant horn was vibrant and traced an arc of excitement through the air.

At this first meeting with Lemmer, he described to me the interest in cantorial music among Hasidic singers:

> There is a very interesting phenomenon right now that Hasidim are more interested in khazones than any other sect . . . So I'm not exactly sure [when that started], but probably with the . . . sort of with the demise of Yiddish culture. Plus, the explosion of access to media, there had to be something for Hasidim to grab onto. It couldn't be whatever was left of Yiddish culture because a lot of it was secular or profanity, in a Hasid's view. Heretics wrote the stuff, stuff like that. They had to hang onto something. They couldn't hang on to classical music because, oh it's *goyish* [Yiddish, non-Jewish]. So, we went to khazones. And khazones is the most pure form. (Yanky Lemmer, interview August 9, 2015)

In his introduction to the scene of Hasidic cantorial revivalists, Lemmer outlined some of the tensions that would guide me in my research for the next few years. He presented a series of dualisms that drew attention to their fragmentariness, gesturing at a picture of a nebulous *something* that Hasidic singers find in the cantorial legacy and seek to make their own: cantorial music is specifically Jewish, yet it holds a similar allure to the high aesthetic of forbidden non-Jewish European classical music; it is a product of a predominantly Yiddish-speaking world nearly destroyed by the Holocaust (never mind that Yiddish was the native language of almost everyone at the bungalow colony that day), yet it manages to escape the castigating glance of contemporary Hasidic Jews who decry the secularism of much of early twentieth century Jewish culture; it is "the most pure form" (of what, exactly? of Jewish music? of prayer? of modern Yiddish culture?), and yet it is something that is outside the norms of the conservative and preservationist Hasidic world that members of the community have discovered because of newly acquired access to digital media. Enticed by these attractive paradoxes, Hasidic singers look to the canon of classic cantorial records for pathways toward an elevated aesthetic out of which they can constitute an identity as artists and ritual leaders.

In the Hasidic community, the culture of old cantorial stars is viewed with some suspicion. A recent article about Jewish records by a Hasidic author that appeared in the Yiddish-language *Forverts* newspaper repeats accusations against cantors that could have been written a century ago:

> I am, however, not convinced of the holiness of khazones. The real source of the singer, their vocal sound, with their rich, purposeful voice, comes from Italian opera—the pop music of the old days. It is true, people didn't idolize cantors with the same coarse wildness as they idolized the "pop stars," but that doesn't mean the source of khazones is holy. And who were these khazonim of the cantorial golden age? Were they *tsadikim* [Hebrew, righteous men]? It's well known many of the khazonim were pure *goyim* [Hebrew, non-Jews], "hot boys." Not for nothing did the rabbis teach that music can draw one down to hell. Such well known cantors as Zawel Kwartin, Mordechai Hershman, Pinchik, Samuel Malavsky didn't even wear a Jewish beard, barely kept the Sabbath, and perhaps other transgressions.[29]

The author of this article exhorts against the greats of cantorial music, echoing the century-old claims that recording star cantors of the golden age had one foot planted in the secular world. The argument that cantorial records bring the Jewish sacred into unholy proximity with commercial secularism is relevant in the contemporary Hasidic community. As Yanky Lemmer explained to me, "Look when I grew up, this was the narrative. The *khazonim* [Hebrew, cantors] of the golden age they were all *fray* [Yiddish, free, not religious] and *goyim, mamish* [Hebrew, an intensifier], they didn't mean a word they said, blah, blah, blah . . ." In the eyes of some members of Yanky's birth community the ethical profile of cantorial records and the artists who made them are still under scrutiny.

The work of Hasidic cantorial revivalists and their approach to the cantorial legacy as a contentious art form, pursued by artists despite it being an object of suspicion of impiety, has caused me to reflect on the received narratives that I have taken in, unquestioned, in a lifetime lived among cantors. My grandfather, Jacob Konigsberg (1921–2007), was an important cantor in his generation—throughout the five decades of his career he held prestigious positions throughout the United States, including as High Holiday cantor at the Chicago Loop Synagogue for over thirty years. His recordings are late classics of the genre. He was born as late as one could possibly have been to have still been enculturated in the Yiddish-speaking immigrant milieu in which cantors were a central facet of Jewish popular culture. My grandfather held an attitude of deep contention with organized Jewish communities and could not bend his unflagging commitment to his own nonconformist artistic identity to fit the norms of any institution. In general, he would not step foot in a synagogue if he himself was not leading services, a stance I later learned was not uncommon among "star" cantors. At the same time, he held a deep belief in the truth of the cantorial tradition, the value of its great artists, the integrity and reality of "Jewishness" as a sound that could be recognized and evaluated, even if it could not be defined.

My grandfather first led services as a seven-year-old *vunderkind* in the synagogue in Cleveland founded by his own grandfather. His education as a cantor continued by listening to gramophone records with his uncle Jacob Lefkowitz (1913–2009), also a cantor. My uncle Joshua Konigsberg and my first cousin Zachary Konigsberg all followed the family profession, contributing to a sense of biological continuity associated with the music. Within our cantorial family structure, the *reality* of tradition and the unity of a continuous stream of cantorial knowledge represented in part through bloodlines were accepted as an unquestioned truth.

Despite this belief in the authoritativeness of tradition, I felt there to be a tension in the space between my grandfather's deep antipathy to authority, his maverick position as a permanent outsider, and the master narrative of cantors as upholders of a "truth" about Jewish community and communal sound. I could not name this tension or explore it in historical context. Instead, I adopted a useful narrative about cantors as champions of the primordial Jewish past and their music as a key to a mythic Jewish premodernity. This narrative helped me to describe my own musical creativity, which drew on my grandfather's music and gramophone-era cantors, as a form of musical traditionalism.

At the same time, I was aware that the vision of cantorial authority being rooted in ancient lineages did not coalesce with certain historical facts. Cantorial music is a product of modernity and the figure of cantors as folkloric master artists emerges from discourses of Romanticism, nationalism, and Herderian conceptions of the folk. The key "texts" in the cantorial tradition, as I understood it growing up, were gramophone records, products of mass media and popular culture, not an oral tradition. These paradoxes prompted me to play with the tradition. As the leader of the experimental rock band The Sway Machinery I approached khazones with an agenda of recontextualization, reconstructing sounds I had learned in my family or from old records through techniques of musical bricolage, drawing on more contemporary genres to spin new stories around the music. At the same time, in my early writings about cantorial music, I adhered to a romanticized ideology of cultural purity in my fantasies about the "roots" of my musical heritage.[30]

Becoming acquainted with the work of Hasidic cantorial revivalists and analyzing their musical endeavor as a form of *revival* have helped me gain a needed perspective on the problematic concept of tradition. Hasidic cantorial revivalists use the image of heritage and tradition to create new musical and personal agentic paths.[31] The term *revival* is descriptive of their creative process; it highlights the nonlinear temporality of their work. Their learning process is focused on listening to old records—touching the past through mediated experience—not on biological lineages or forms of musical education that are fostered by institutional structures regulated by elders within the community.[32] Cantorial knowledge marks its possessor as a distinctive kind of person, an artist whose work stretches the boundaries of normative behavior, in the context of a social milieu that ostensibly prioritizes conformity and the maintenance of communal structures.

Revival in the American Jewish musical context invokes the image of the klezmer revival, a major music scene that has evolved over the period of the last forty years. In addition to igniting music scenes and star artist careers internationally, the klezmer movement also produced important theorists of revival such as Barbara Kirshenblatt-Gimblett and Mark Slobin. Starting in the late 1970s with the work of young urban secular Jewish musicians who were the children and grandchildren of Yiddish-speaking immigrants, older sounds of Jewish instrumental wedding music inspired the construction of a new genre of music. Klezmer has been discussed by musicians and critics as a form of heritage reclamation in the context of rapid acculturation. Early artists in the klezmer scene saw their work as a form of resistance to the totalizing effects of the immigrant embrace of capitalist American culture through recourse to an image of the Jewish past. Their new-old Jewish dance music would produce a "structure of feeling," creating a suture across the divide of generations and the amnesia of assimilation.[33]

The Hasidic cantorial revival parallels the freshness and youthful excitement of the early klezmer revival, but it functions in a radically different American Jewish milieu. The embrace of khazones speaks to the cultural knowledge and experience of separatist religious communities and the focus of Hasidic Jews on liturgy and prayer as integral to Jewish heritage. While klezmer players of the 1980s sought alterity from the American mainstream, Hasidic cantorial revivalists today are pursuing an aesthetic path that will offer them aesthetic and creative freedoms within the context of a community that has achieved a separatist lifestyle, at least in its official discourse and public profile. What is operational for Hasidic cantorial revivalists is the fact that their community places restrictions on forms of individual freedom other American Jews take for granted. While reclamation of heritage is an important motivator for cantorial revivalists, the challenge that is specific to Hasidic cantorial revivalists is the need to articulate an artist's identity that can still manage to function within the framework of separatist religious life. With a startling insight into the complex history and aesthetic modernism of khazones, Hasidic cantorial revivalists have staked their intervention into Jewish heritage around the figure of the golden age cantor.

My engagement with the work of this cohort of singers emerges from an activist stance in relationship to the preservation of khazones. I hold a deeply rooted sense of reciprocity with the cantorial legacy, and a concern with the aesthetics of prayer in the contemporary American synagogue. In my own music, I have attempted to tell a story about the radicalism of Jewish liturgical music; I understand cantorial performance as a site where boundary-crossing between communities can be achieved and in which conceptions of the sacred and the aesthetic are gloriously blurred. Furthermore, in my music and scholarship I am motivated by a methodological approach that seeks transformative experience in the voices that can be reclaimed from the archive. The special quality of research that is based in communication with dead artists from earlier generations has a transformative impact on the methods and outcomes of archival delving. I understand Hasidic cantorial revivalists as embodied research practitioners whose methods of reanimating sounds from the archive of old records has lent them unique powers to vivify and illuminate the meaning of cantorial history.

The innovative approach taken by these singers to animating the archive has been instrumental in shaping my own ethnographic practices during my work on this project. Throughout the years of my research, my use of traditional methods of participant observation have been enhanced and transformed by working with learning practices inspired by the cantors' own approaches. I have cultivated a practice of embodied research through deep listening and embodied transcription of old recordings that is modeled on descriptions of learning the cantors have told me about in interviews. Experimenting with their approaches to music-making has played a role in helping me access their musical worlds and their conceptions of the meaning of the music, and to enter into a phenomenology of the learning experience.

I have approached this research project from the stance of advocate and, at times, musical collaborator. Over the course of the years of this project, I have produced numerous performances with the cantors nationally and in Europe and produced an album of their music. My goals in working with the cantors have extended beyond a purely academic engagement. In producing the concerts and album project, I have sought to make space for their music in environments, such as universities, academic conferences, and even rock clubs, that expand the reach of their work. I am keenly aware that my presence in the cantorial revivalist scene furthers my own agenda of experimentation and aesthetic independence from the normative—I am comfortable with the discomfort of my blurry role in relationship to the "object" of my study, an area of fluidity, creativity, and exchange that is subject to the vicissitudes of music careers, communal restrictions, and the affordances of chance and luck.

My desire to understand and support the work of the cantors has, on occasion, led to conflict about the meaning of the work they are undertaking. The narrative I have arrived at in describing their work has, at times, been in contention with the self-understanding of the cantors. This is particularly relevant to the use of the term *revival*. For most of the cantors I worked with, *revival* holds a questionable valence that they could not embrace, largely because their career experiences have been characterized by marginalization and precarity. I find the term *revival* to be useful to describe the ideologies that support the work of artists who work with heritage art forms. *Revival* speaks to the repair that the cantors seek by bridging across time to find a model for contemporary aesthetic and social needs.

What I have sought to communicate in this book is the energy and intellectual vibrancy of their work that has been undertaken in the face of frequent rejection and commercial failure. For the cantors, the implied optimism in the image of life renewed rang false. My enthusiasm for their music is driven by what I perceive as the undercurrents of utopianism that resonate in the choice to pursue nonconforming aesthetic pathways. For the artists this perspective does not adequately account for the social and economic aspects of their undertaking, which are persistently and naggingly present in their creative lives. I have sought to balance my critique, based on ethnography, with the self-understanding of my research participants in the presentation of their stories.

The work of Hasidic cantorial revivalists lends a perspective that revises conventional narratives about Jewish liturgical music. Their performance style presents khazones as a meditative listening genre; their approach to the music invites a deeper inquest into the mediated listening habits associated with early twentieth-century sacred gramophone culture. The invocation of cantorial repertoires as the basis for nonconformist art practices demands a reappraisal of contemporary professional cantorial ideology that has sought to establish an association of cantors with an ideology of conservative cultural maintenance, characterized by normative conceptions of tradition. The exploratory approach to the archive of cantorial records and revival of music from a period characterized by intense musical creativity and competing stylistic approaches undermines the contemporary professional cantorial concept of a totalizing "correct" prayer performance, dependent on institutions for its faithful reproduction.

The musical lives of Hasidic cantorial revivalists point toward the internal diversity of historic forms of Jewish prayer sound. The sound worlds of the past they animate and the heterogeneity of musical forms they access raise new questions about how the current norms of Jewish prayer music have come into being, and what social structures and hierarchies music in the synagogue supports. Hasidic cantorial revivalists turn to an early twentieth-century aesthetic that renews questions about the representation of Jewish collectivity through sound. Their celebration of the khazones aesthetic highlights the shifts in the contemporary music of the synagogue away from Jewish particularism. Over the course of the twentieth century, synagogue musical traditions have emerged in the United States that downplay virtuosic soloist vocal performance. This development is typically discussed in terms of a democratizing move from performance to participation, with professional cantors sometimes pegged as being resistant to progress.[34] Such an approach bypasses discussions of Jewish aesthetics and the role of sonic particularism in establishing collectivity and supporting an ethos of mutual aid, a conception that was central to the way khazones was discussed and consumed in the period of its greatest popularity.

Hasidic cantorial revivalists intentionally harness their talents to an art form that they understand as representative of Jewish prayer and a lineage of sacred artists. Theorizing agency as intrinsically yoked to resistance is inadequate to the task of analyzing their cultural productivity. Instead, I have come to understand the Hasidic cantorial revival as a kind of local contentious practice, inclined toward imagining and reconstructing sounds of Jewish collectivity and building identities through reference to this sound.[35] Singers who seek to redress the perceived aesthetic and spiritual limitations of their community by becoming cantors do not choose this liturgical music idiom because they are trying to dismantle the authority of sacred tradition. On the contrary, they believe that their work, which engages both textual and oral/aural traditions, holds a greater truth in representing the potentials of prayer to express interiority and sophisticated frameworks of emotional engagement. Hasidic cantorial revival is resistant not to Hasidic Judaism, per se, but to binaries in Jewish experience between conceptions of performance and ritual, and between the vast creative potentials in the archive and the muted reception of audiences.

Opportunities for the kinds of activities that would substantiate and legitimize a cantorial revivalist economy are extremely limited. The absence of a clearly defined community of reception complicates the work of revival and draws attention to the utopian quality of their creative longings and the uncertainties implicit in devoting a lifetime to an art form that lacks an audience. None of the cantors

I spoke to, even those with conspicuously successful careers, make their living exclusively from singing khazones. Hasidic cantors are keenly aware of the limitations on achieving conventional career success from their musical ambitions, and yet they are strikingly committed to their work. At the core of this book is an impulse to understand the means and ends of cantorial revival and its position that lies between religious act, self-disciplined art practice, and rebellious boundary pushing at the norms of American Jewish life.

· · ·

The chapters of this book are organized around communities in which music-making takes place. The chapters move along a spectrum of intimacy—from experiences of private record-listening and archival-delving, to public spaces of ritual and performance. The communities structured by cantorial revival can be virtual, connecting musicians to golden age artists across divides of time and across digital space, or they can take place "in real life," in physical spaces that are shared by cantors and their listeners. The work of Hasidic cantors hinges on the multiple meanings that emerge from the experience of animating the archive through performance; the relationship of singers to the Jewish sonic past gives them special affective powers, but simultaneously places limits and skeptical expectations on what public spaces their work can legitimately occupy.

In chapter 1, I explore how early twentieth century cantorial records have come to offer the framework for a musical practice in the present day that expresses nonconformist artistic impulses. I offer a history of cantorial records as a prehistory of the present-day revival, focusing on the history of contention and controversy that surrounded innovative technologies and sacred sound. Cantorial recording stars embraced a new technology that was condemned by critics as undermining the cultural coherence of Jewish liturgy by decontextualizing ritual sound from its place in the synagogue. At the same time, records offered an "imagined ethnography" of the Jewish past that was recognizable and desired by a mass Jewish listening public. I suggest that these popular intellectual currents—of chastisement, on the one hand, and utopian aspiration, on the other—inform the way cantorial music operates on the imagination and aesthetic desires of contemporary Hasidic cantors. I offer a further contextualization of today's Hasidic cantors with an historical outline of the relationship of cantors to Hasidic Judaism. The chapter concludes with an ethnographic account of how records are used in learning practices.

Chapter 2 explores how Hasidic singers develop the skills needed to facilitate working in a synagogue as a professional cantor. For singers who aspire to attain pulpit positions, a learning pathway is needed to bridge the gap between performing music learned from old cantorial records and the ritual norms of the contemporary synagogue. Over the course of the twentieth century, professionalized American cantors working in training seminaries have developed an ideology about what melodies and modal improvisatory forms are appropriate for each textual segment of the liturgy, referred to as *nusakh hatefilah* (Hebrew, manner of prayer). In order to learn the style of prayer music employed in synagogues that hire professional cantors, singers from Hasidic backgrounds must find instruction. Noah Schall, a nonagenarian cantorial pedagogue who had personal relationships with famed cantors of the gramophone era, offers lessons in nusakh and has taught several of the cantors who participated in my research. For singers from Hasidic backgrounds, Schall's instruction provides access to musical skills, ideological indoctrination in "correct" nusakh, and enculturation in the community of professional cantors. An exploration of Schall's sacred music ideology will illuminate how his instruction helps revivalists move along a learning path from interpreters of old records to performers of the prayer-leading style associated with professional cantorial practice, adopting Schall's ideology of nusakh as a key element in their cultivation of a cantorial musical disposition. In keeping with their immersion in the archive, revivalists utilize their instruction in Schall's idiosyncratic and nuanced approach to the music of professional cantorial nusakh as a way of interpolating sonic artefacts of golden age records into their work as prayer leaders.

In chapter 3 I discuss how Hasidic cantorial revivalists construct services in synagogues where their soloist cantorial repertoire based on old records is not a normative part of the culture of prayer. As is also the case for cantors across Jewish American denominations, there is a disconnect between the knowledge cantors have when they are initially employed by congregations and the musical skills they implement in the actual services they lead, requiring them to attain new forms of expertise on the job. In this chapter I will discuss the four main musical categories that inform Hasidic cantorial revivalist conceptions of prayer leading: (1) The prayer music they are enculturated in from their upbringing in the Hasidic community; (2) The prayer-leading style associated with gramophone-era cantors; (3) The professional nusakh associated with published anthologies of cantorial music that are taught in cantorial training institutions; (4) The most dominant form in the contemporary synagogue, the folk-pop participatory music that has become ascendant in the past fifty years and that all contemporary cantors must reckon with in their prayer leading. Hasidic cantors undertake a self-directed program of study of classic cantorial records in order to address personal aesthetic desires. In their congregational jobs they are expected to perform in a liturgical style that is removed from this area of expertise. Across American Jewish communities, cantors must cultivate a repertoire tailored to local tastes, usually geared toward facilitating group singing; this well-established phenomenon of synagogue life plays out in distinct ways in the musical careers of Hasidic cantors. While cantorial revivalists may be hired for their unique access to an archive of sacred Jewish music, in practice they are required to fulfill the normative musical expectations of the current American synagogue.

Chapter 4 will explore the sites in which Hasidic cantors perform their historically informed concept of cantorial sound. While synagogues are by and large inhospitable to a prayer-leading style that draws on the style of classic cantorial records, performances outside synagogues provide opportunities to experiment with musical content by forming temporary communities organized around cantorial revivalist musical practices. I will discuss three main sites for Hasidic cantorial performance: the internet, the concert stage, and the *kumsitz* (Yiddish, music-making party), attending to how cantors utilize the potentials of each of these music-making spaces to cultivate their artistry and connect with a listening public. Although the normative definition of a cantor is a ritual functionary in a synagogue, for performers interested in historically informed styles of Jewish sacred music contemporary synagogues are not welcoming of their work. I argue that in nonritual performances the cantors are able to articulate a philosophy of sacred listening that is no longer legible in most American synagogue spaces.

Interspersed into the chapters of the book are three interludes that offer portraits of some of the cantors I worked with during my research. These interludes are intended to provide a window into the lives and careers of living artists whose work involves struggle, sacrifice, and moments of profound achievement. The main body of this book is structured by arguments I have constructed that place revivalists in conversation with the archive of old records and the history of American Jewish life. The ethnographic interludes sketch some of the texture of creative life, touching on elements of artists' stories that do not fit easily into a narrativized version of their work or that foreground their priorities and interests over my own investment in creating a linear argument. By attending to the words and experiences of cantorial revivalists, I hope to draw the reader into deeper communication with the elements of surprise and paradox that animate the story of these wonderful artists.

The nonconformist undertaking of Hasidic cantors is geared toward a style of music-making and a form of ritual community that do not currently have a home in any of the worlds that are available to the artists. Whether intentionally or not, cantorial revivalists are inventing a musical community that echoes the unregulated expressiveness of Jewish liturgical popular records of the golden age. Their unmethodical and idiosyncratic movements in this direction cut against the grain of social norms of contemporary Jewish ritual practices. By attending to intimate dialogues of artists with the archive, I hope to shed empathetic light on their idealism, their creativity, and the power of their explorations to achieve transformations in their own personhood and in the communal experience of sacred listening.

Animating the Archive

Old Records and Young Singers

Zevi Steiger knew that he was different from other young men: sensitive and attuned to music and emotion, he sometimes got into trouble in Yeshivah for his chronic lateness, despite being an excellent student academically. As he told me, "Later I learned I'm not the only one. There are a lot of people who are creative, who are into art and stuff like that, that have difficulty with that." Listening to old cantorial records and learning to sing the pieces he loved was the signal manifestation of his burgeoning creative identity.

Yanky Lemmer, the most commercially successful cantor among the participants in this study, told me that among his friends growing up, "they were into music but not khazones. I was the only oddball." Being a fan of cantorial music was a marker of his nonconformity.

Yoel Kohn connects his love of khazones to a period of disaffected youth when he was "bored out of his mind"; when he was desperate for an aesthetic outlet that could express his developing world of feeling. Speaking about his cohort of young Hasidic cantorial revivalists, he said, "That's part of what made us. We were all sort of artistic. We were deprived. We had no outlets. We had to focus inside. We had to become introspective in order to achieve any sort of artistic or creative outlet, any sort of creative climax."

Shimmy Miller similarly described khazones as part of the emotional turbulence of a sensitive youth striving to define an adult identity. "It's like it's part of the transformation . . . It's just part of the chronological order of things . . . You're a teen. You have all kinds of things on your mind . . . So I started getting into listening to khazones, mainly old khazonim." In another conversation with Shimmy, I asked him to elaborate on what it was about khazones that attracted some young Hasidic singers to this as their genre of choice. "They feel pulled to it. It's just an art form. You have something you're interested in, right? What drew you to khazones?"

This moment of ethnographic reversal felt significant to me—Shimmy was cautioning me against essentializing Hasidic musicians by ascribing a meaning to the Hasidic cantorial phenomenon that was qualitatively different from the aesthetic desires of other artistically inclined people, those without "marked" identities. Shimmy was advocating for his right to what philosopher Édouard Glissant calls *opacity*[1]—he was claiming the right to pursue abstraction and pure aesthetics that is often denied to people who have "visible identities" and who are expected by outsiders to represent their collectivities, not their own agentic desires.[2]

Shimmy was also drawing my attention to the fact that Hasidic cantorial revivalists have ascribed a surprising meaning to khazones: they understand century-old records of Jewish sacred music as an art form, along the lines of other music styles, that can illuminate an artistic path of nonconformity and self-discovery. These Hasidic singers share in common a conception of khazones as a genre that is appropriate for use in grappling with their world, defining a nonconforming social stance, and coming to terms with feelings of personal difference from the norm. Rather than viewing the music as primarily a conservative retention of an old form of Jewish religious practice, we should understand that khazones serves as a genre of performance and creative practice. This conception of the social potentials of the genre push against a strictly conceived binary between religious authority and conceptions of creativity. The engagement of Hasidic cantorial revivalists with khazones suggests a novel way of looking at the history of the music. It raises the question, what qualities inhere in gramophone-era cantorial music that make it appropriate as the basis for a nonconformist musical practice?

Conventional descriptions of cantorial music found in professional journals such as the *Journal of Synagogue Music* (*JSM*) tend to focus on the sacred function of the music and its role as a lever of cultural continuity. Samuel Rosenbaum, a Conservative cantor and frequent contributor to the *JSM* in the 1970s, expressed the opinion that "Hazzanut is a sanctity of Jewish life. It is intimately and eternally bound up with the mystical, mysterious process which we call prayer. It is both the message and the medium of the mirror to which we hold up our souls . . . It is the light by which we may, in a rare moment of incandescence, catch a glimpse of Him who is the Hearer of prayer."[3] Rosenbaum's stylized, sanctimonious, nearly Christologized view of the cantorate is echoed across writings about Jewish liturgical music. In the more conventionally phrased words of Josh Breitzer, the current cantor of Beth Elohim, a Reform synagogue in Brooklyn, "cantors are the vessels of Jewish musical tradition and innovators of public prayer. They lead worship, teach across the generations through melodies new and old, and help Jewish communities envision and enrich their spiritual lives."[4]

Cantor Breitzer's description of a cantor's work reifies a commonly held conception of cantors as preservers of religious tradition and communal stability.

His description is also reminiscent of the popular understanding of the separatist Hasidic community: both cantors and Hasidic Jews are described from within and by outsider observers as being conservationist and concerned with cultivating holiness and piety. Definitions of cantorial music that focus on community maintenance and conventional expressions of public piety do not fit easily with the use of the music as a form of musical rebellion or an outpouring of adolescent angst. For Hasidic cantorial revivalists, khazones is a means toward framing an identity as an artist that is at odds with the cultural norms of their birth community, as defined by rabbinic leadership, and in opposition to the sounds of most contemporary synagogue life in America. Rather than being a means toward maintaining the boundaries of the community or the decorous sanctimony of tradition, cantorial music offers Hasidic singers a path toward an individualist pursuit of aesthetics and a heightening of experience beyond the norms of institutional life.

Thinking about the cantorial tradition as a site of contention over values and practices of identity formation encouraged me to take a deeper look at the history of cantorial music. In the following discussion of cantorial history, I explore the ways in which cantors have been embedded at the juncture of debates about creativity, modernity, sacred experience and the corruption of tradition. I focus here on the recorded cantorial legacy of the early twentieth century that forms the backbone of contemporary cantorial revivalist practices. Working with the revivalists' conception of cantorial music as a centripetal force acting on my reading of the historical record, I approach the archive of documentary evidence about the gramophone-era golden age with new questions about the controversial role of cantors in popular culture.

In this chapter, I approach the history of the golden age as a prehistory of its own revival, spotlighting those aspects of the story that are most germane to understanding the work of young Hasidic cantorial revivalists. My initial findings suggest that the music of the cantors of the gramophone era reflect the period of radical social change in which they worked. Recording star cantors occupied a nebulous place between the synagogue and popular music performance. Although they themselves were stars of new forms of media, they represented a style of Jewish prayer music that was meant to evoke the sounds of a disappearing Jewish folklore situated in the past. Cantors performed a theatrical version of premodernity, tailored to exploit the potentials of the most modern technologies.

Cantorial records present an *imagined ethnography*, offering a Jewish popular culture parallel to contemporary trends of musical nationalism that employed academic folklore and anthropological research to try to establish national music styles. The creativity and innovation characteristic of gramophone-era cantors served the goals of building national identity in an era of heightened nationalistic and collectivist sentiment. In this respect, cantors fit into the "invented tradition" musical nationalist trends of the early twentieth century.[5] At the same time, cantors were deeply immersed in a set of musical practices with textual and musical lineages that precede the efflorescence of musical nationalism and that reflect the experience of Jews as a marginalized and minoritized population occupying a tenuous and fringe position in European society. The work of cantors emerges from historically embedded lifeways, which defy a binary assessment of "invented" or "authentic." What Michael Herzfeld calls "culturally intimate" practices are understood as representative of collective identity by members of a group.[6] Unlike some of their better-known contemporaries among urban conservatory-trained composers who were invested in the idea of folklore, perhaps best represented by Bela Bartok, cantors drew on their personal learning experiences in cantorial choirs and enculturation in small-town Jewish life to create a version of Jewish tradition that would be recognizable to Jewish audiences and that would retrospectively form a sense of what the past sounded like.

Cantors sought to illuminate a thread of folklore they felt themselves to be intimately connected to and therefore had the right to manipulate and transform through their creative endeavors. Both fiercely competitive in their pursuit of marketable originality *and* committed to preserving a conception of tradition, cantors were both custodians of the past and inventors of a broadly disseminated sonic representation of Jewish musical heritage. The work of recording star cantors was revered by fans, consumed by a mass audience, and simultaneously castigated as a corruption of tradition. The uses of the gramophone-era style by present-day Hasidic cantorial revivalists as a nonconformist art practice reflect the conflicting meanings and motivations that accompanied the music in the period of its production.

Following a discussion of the gramophone era of mediatized cantorial music, I will offer an outline of the role of cantors in the Hasidic context. Just as the musical innovations associated with the new technology of the gramophone heightened tensions already accruing around the figure of the cantor, the Hasidic community has its own history of castigation of the figure of the cantor. A perusal of teachings about music by Hasidic leaders and examples drawn from the cultural history of the movement illustrate how rabbinic leaders in the Hasidic community took a variety of attitudes toward the artistry of cantors. Alternating between condemning cantors for their excessive emphasis on aesthetics and embracing symbiotic relationships with cantors to further the charismatic draw of the Hasidic movement, leaders of the Hasidic community were ambivalent in their stance toward khazones. The multiplicity and contingency of attitudes around music and cantors in Hasidic contexts are strikingly similar to the range of attitudes and debates expressed in discourse among cantors and in the larger Jewish world. While attitudes toward cantors held by Hasidic leaders fit into larger dialogues in other Jewish contexts, they are inflected by the power dynamics and conservative focus on the maintenance of cultural norms that are specific to the community.

Finally, I will end the chapter with an ethnographic description of an intimate use of an old cantorial recording in the private study of a contemporary Hasidic cantor. By zooming in on one example I will demonstrate how cantors use golden age recordings as objects of reflection, pedagogy and performance. Records have a transformative effect on the body of young singers, as they allow the recorded voices of dead cantors to resonate in their bodies, training and transforming the musculature of their vocal apparatus. In this way, the frozen recorded sound of the archive is animated into an intimate form, embodied in its presence in the work of living artists.

In the interior space of deep listening and learning, Hasidic cantorial revivalists imagine themselves identified with a kind of creative personhood that is not at home in any contemporary Jewish community. Old records of star cantors help these singers imagine a life that is yoked to tradition, through sound and text, while making room for nonconformity and creativity. As I argue across the chapters of this book, the cantors are working toward a future in which their nonconforming identities as artists and prayer leaders will coalesce with the emergence of new forms of community in which artists can function as ritual leaders and arbiters of sacred experience. This figure of the artist-ritualist, rooted in the stars of the imagined cantorial golden age, is not currently recognized in any Jewish American community.

WHAT IS THE CANTORIAL GOLDEN AGE?

The term *cantorial golden age* calls to mind a body of Jewish liturgical records produced by commercial record labels between 1901 and roughly 1950, primarily, but not exclusively, in Europe and the United States documenting the work of Eastern European cantors. The style documented on these records is often referred to by the Yiddish term *khazones*. During the period of the music's greatest popularity, star cantors sold records in the hundreds of thousands, conducted international performance careers across the Jewish Atlantic world and galvanized a mass listening public of urban Jews with a sound that represented the cultural intimacy of the synagogue.

Classic records of this period purported to document Jewish folklore. Cantors were working in parallel to the efforts of urban Jewish composers and the European nationalist composers who sought to imbue nationalist music movements with motifs gleaned from anthropological research and song collection expeditions to the rural "folk." Unlike figures such as Bela Bartok or Joel Engel, composers who conducted research into small-town European life in search of folk music, cantors had their own training as apprentice singers working with elder cantors to draw on in their construction of new synagogue music. Cantorial records of the gramophone era took on a quality as imagined ethnography, by means of which cantors presented popular audiences with a newly composed representation of the Jewish past. The mediated sound of cantorial records was yoked to the vanishing world of small-town European Jewish life, a milieu that took on a sacred character during the period of urbanization, especially after the widescale destruction of World War I.

Two schema are constitutive of the way the music of gramophone-era cantors is understood by contemporary Hasidic cantorial revivalists, one focused on preservation, the other on creativity. In general, contemporary cantors do not accentuate or consciously draw attention to the tensions between these two images of the cantorial golden age. On the one hand, present-day practitioners tend to believe that the work of golden age cantors was preservationist and rooted in a folklore that largely disappeared after the Holocaust; it is sometimes described by present-day cantors fancifully, as connected to Jewish antiquity. At the same time, they also valorize the creativity of classic cantorial artists, praising their uniqueness and their innovative appropriation of sounds drawn from art music.

For Hasidic cantorial revivalists, as with artists working in other "named-system" revivalist music scenes,[7] the dualism of tradition and creativity is a point of repressed awareness; looking closely at the place of rupture offers a view into the meaning of the work and can be uncomfortable in its exposure of myths. These competing conceptions raise unresolved questions about contemporary cantors' own creativity, and their sense of inadequacy or uncertainty about their creative capacities. In general, they are not composers; rather, they focus on reinterpreting old compositions and, to an extent, on working in an improvisatory style of prayer leading.

For the purposes of this discussion of golden age cantorial music, I adopt the normative claim that recording star cantors were "tradition bearers" who held knowledge of older streams of Jewish liturgical tradition. This is the viewpoint held by present-day cantors who look to old records for clues about what Jewish voices and melodies should sound like. The work of untangling and analyzing the stylistic layering of classic cantorial recordings would be a project unto itself that I refrain from pursuing at this time: it suffices to say that a variety of musical styles and genres contribute to the formation of the gramophone cantorial sound, including opera, operetta, and *Lieder*, in addition to Jewish folkloric sources. The contemporary cantors I discuss tend to rely on an unexamined notion of "tradition," one they see as embodied in recorded khazones. Over the course of this book, I will endeavor to draw attention to the internal diversity that produced what is retrospectively understood simply as "tradition."

The modern cantorial sound heard on classic recordings has its roots in the work of the Viennese cantor Salomon Sulzer (1804–90), the figure most associated with the reform of synagogue music through the introduction of choral music sounds borrowed from European art music and church music. Sulzer was alternately castigated as a disruptive force undermining tradition and celebrated as a preserver of tradition. His work responded to currents in the German-speaking world that sought to adopt the German language and Lutheran hymns into synagogue worship. In contrast, Sulzer was committed to preserving the traditional Hebrew liturgical texts. His anthology, *Schir Zion*, published in 1840, was among the first to publish older prayer melodies, printed alongside newly commissioned pieces by Christian Viennese composers, including Franz Schubert. Sulzer's anthology was followed by an explosion of publishing across Europe of new works by cantors embracing the choral aesthetic, as well as works documenting older prayer melodies that were already seen as endangered and in need of preservation.[8]

According to cantors of the early twentieth century, Eastern European cantors were attracted to Sulzer's innovations, but saw his work as problematic in its rejection of stylistic traits that were understood as deeply representative of Jewish prayer sound. Samuel Vigoda, a recording star of the gramophone era, wrote in his anecdotal book of memoirs:

> And who can tell how far the process of radical transformation of the old but still untarnished typical Jewish motifs would have gone, if not for the counter-revolutionary activities of the East European stalwart representatives of the "Chazzonut Haregesh," [Hebrew, feelingful cantorial music] who stood their ground, like bulwarks manning the ramparts, determined to preserve the precious treasure which had been handed down from the past . . .[9]

As Vigoda and other cantorial authors assert, a perception of an "East-West" divide emerged, with cantors in Russia and Poland styling themselves as preservers of older strands of Jewish sacred vocal music. At the same time, cantors in the urban centers of Eastern Europe embraced the prestigious role of the dignified and prestigious professionalized cantor, as well as embracing many Sulzerian musical innovations, especially the use of four-part choral composition.

Unlike in the Austro-Hungarian Empire, where Jews were experiencing legal emancipation and integration, Russian Jews continued to live in a politically oppressive and volatile setting. The political motivations for musical "assimilation" were more abstract and less clearly tied to practical ends in the context of a system that specifically excluded Jews from participation in the rights and privileges of the state. Instead, Russian Jewish cantors looked to discourses of nationalism to help define a Jewish musical self-conception that was oriented toward achievement in high-status European art music while remaining invested in maintaining Jewish sonic difference. These developments arose against a Russian musical culture in which Jews became increasingly involved as producers and consumers of Western art music.[10] Around the turn of the twentieth century, an ethnographically tinged approach to composition emerged among cantors and choir directors composing for their positions in elite urban synagogues in Eastern Europe.

Russian synagogue music seems to have been influenced by late nineteenth-century trends in the conservatory, where the value of distinctive "national" musical characteristics was championed. Joel Engel, a student of Tchaikovsky, followed in the footsteps of nationalist trends in nineteenth-century art music, claiming ethnography as a key element in the founding of a uniquely Jewish musical concept.[11] Unlike Engel, whose musical enculturation largely excluded Jewish sources and who sought to connect with Jewish sources through anthropological field research, cantors were generally trained in apprenticeship settings with elder cantors or in family musical lineages. Their personal connections to elder cantors and their embodied repertoires served as a source they could leverage into new music. The recorded cantorial archive offers an *imagined ethnography*, new works that purport to represent the past by drawing on popular conceptions of the sound of the collective, and in turn shaping conceptions of group identity through a reified vocabulary of culturally intimate sound distilled through processes of performance and mediatization.

As literary critic Dan Miron has suggested, the image of the shtetl, a Yiddish word for small town, has taken on a quality as a metonym for Jewish premodernity.[12] The aestheticized image of the shtetl in Yiddish literature forms the basis of a retrospective appraisal of the past. Just as the stories of Sholom Aleichem and Y. L. Peretz shaped a Jewish collective memory that threatens to usurp the historical record, cantors created compositions that offered stylized sonic representations of Jewish collectivity. Turning toward a primitivist aesthetic that imagined the future of Jewish music as emerging from its premodernity,[13] cantors looked to melodies and musical forms derived from synagogue oral traditions, small-town Jewish life, and Hasidic Jews for musical elements to be appropriated and aestheticized in musical compositions formally based in Western art music.

Jewish synagogue composers and choir directors such as David Novakovsky (1848–1921) and Baruch Schorr (1823–1904) were at the vanguard of a new, urban cantorial style that consciously sought to integrate older styles of cantorial vocal sounds and techniques into their new and innovative cantorial compositions. Virtuosic soloist vocal techniques, such as the distinctive cantorial coloratura and nonmetered recitative passages, were integrated into choral textures, initiating a new, syncretic synagogue style that was effective as a vehicle for tenor soloists. The cantors of urban synagogues had usually been trained in the cantorial apprenticeship system and held a vocabulary of vocal techniques and repertoires they had learned in an oral tradition context that they could bring to bear in their performances of new compositions.[14]

The technological innovation of the gramophone met cantors at a moment of debate about the appropriate kinds of music Jewish singers should perform and what kinds of sounds should be brought into elite urban synagogues. The first cantor to record was Selmar Cerini (1860–1923), a cantor in Breslau, who made his recording debut was in 1901. Cerini's life story represents the tensions between the synagogue and the allure of Western art music. Over the course of his career, he moved between performing opera roles, which he studied by transliterating librettos into the Hebrew alphabet, and synagogue prayer leading.[15] Cerini's prominence as ground breaker was eclipsed by the massive popularity of Gershon Sirota (1874–1943), the first international recording star of Jewish music. In addition to his best-selling records, Sirota's weekly prayer-leading services at the Tlomackie

Street Synagogue in Warsaw throughout the first two decades of the twentieth century were attended by a congregational audience that routinely numbered in the
thousands. Sirota's tenor was marked by a declarative precision and overpowering
upper register that marked him as one of the great vocal artists of the era and was
compared frequently to opera stars. He was billed at times as "the Jewish Caruso,"
a marketing cliché that appears frequently in Yiddish press accounts of cantors.[16]

Zawel Kwartin (1874–1952) began his recording career in 1907 and rapidly pro-
pelled to success, with records reaching sales of five hundred thousand copies per
year.[17] While Kwartin embraced his role as a star, taking pulpit positions at elite
urban synagogues in Budapest, Vienna, and Saint Petersburg and concertizing
in major concert halls throughout Europe and the United States, he cultivated a
musical style in his compositions that moved away from the choral synagogue
sound. In his autobiography, written at the end of his life, Kwartin asserts that the
most significant influences on his style were the sounds of small-town prayer leaders in his village in Ukraine. Kwartin described his creative work as a rejection of
Western art music. He wrote,

> After a while I started to feel that the modern cantorial repertoire satisfied me less
> and less; I felt ever more drawn to conservation, orthodoxy and tradition. I started to
> search for compositions, recitatives and improvisations that stemmed from the great
> Orthodox cantors of the old traditional form. In Vienna I was successful in finding
> the melodies of Yerucham Hakatan [1798–1891], Nissi Belzer [1824–1906], [Wolf]
> Shestapol [1832–72]. I grew ever more absorbed in these unique compositions that
> were suffused with the perennially distinctive quality of Jewish life. But the more
> deeply I delved into these compositions, the more there grew in me the longing to be
> like them, the generations of cantors that piously and conveying fear of heaven sang
> out the tears and hidden longings of their people.[18]

Alongside his generational cohort of performers and critics in the Yiddish-speaking
intelligentsia, Kwartin valorized nineteenth-century Jewish music figures. Cantors
like Nissi Belzer were presented as an Eastern European counterpart to Sulzer and
other Central European "Westernizing" composers. These cantors were not drawn
from a mythological past but had been intimately familiar to the generation of
"gramophone" cantors, a number of whom had trained as Belzer's choir singers.

The Jewish community in the United States entered what has been referred to
as a "cantor craze" beginning in the 1880s, roughly coinciding with the period of
Jewish mass immigration from Eastern Europe (ca. 1880–1924).[19] In a mirroring
of the urban "choir synagogues" in the European capitals, Eastern European Jews
built synagogues on a grand scale and hired star cantors imported from Europe
to fill them. Cantors played a prominent role in the life of the community, ubiquitous in the Yiddish press and performing not only in synagogues but in major
concert halls. The well-known Russian-born socialist activist and author Chaim
Zhitlowsky (1865–1943) included cantorial music in a list of Jewish communal

matters that "reveals the ideals of the people's culture."[20] The conception of canto-rial music as a distillation of Jewish historical experiences, especially those related to persecution and displacement, is frequently cited in the writings of Eastern European cantors working in the United States.[21]

In response to the intimate connections between cantors and new technologies, identities, and popular culture, a discourse of chastisement arose around cantors, focusing on their gramophone recordings. The lead voice in the antigramophone ideology was Pinchas Minkovsky (1859–1924), the cantor of the prestigious Broder Synagogue in Odessa. Minkvosky was not connected to emerging conservative Orthodox ideologies, and in fact was associated with the adoption of modern cho-ral music into the Russian synagogue. He had been a student of Salomon Sulzer as a young man and, according to some accounts, had left his home of Berdichev under duress, having fallen afoul of the Hasidic community for his modernizing dress and musical innovations. In Odessa, Minkovsky had advocated for the inclu-sion of women in cantorial choirs in response to the norms of Western art music, and he later adopted the use of an organ, a key point of controversy in synagogues. Despite his ongoing struggles with rabbinic authorities and his adoption of musi-cal innovations across his lifetime, Minkovsky was outspoken in his role as a can-torial "elder," castigating the younger generation for their immoral expansion of the reach of cantorial performance into the new electric media, resulting in "a mix of impure and pure, of holiness and whoredom."[22]

Minkovsky makes an unfavorable comparison between the innovations of his cantorial generation, which sought to elevate the Jewish people through appeals to prestigious and rarified styles of music, and the populist gramophone. Rather than a controlled appropriation of high-prestige elements of "non-Jewish" culture, records would facilitate anarchic eruptions of Jewish sound and feeling. Minkovsky suggests that gramophone cantorial records yoke Jews to unsavory elements of the non-Jewish world, degrading the sacred by making religious music available in the "secular" spaces of Jewish life.

In his 1910 book-length diatribe against cantorial gramophone recording, *Moderne liturgiye in unzere sinogogn in rusland* (Modern liturgy in our syna-gogues in Russia), Minkovsky deplores the effects that modern technologies have on sacred Jewish music. He asserts that cantorial records are a sign of the immoral times. By divorcing sacred music from the space of the synagogue, the affective power of the music inevitably will be abused for erotic or illicit purposes that are degrading to the cantorial profession in particular and the public reputation of the Jews in general. Minkovsky savages the gramophone with a litany of disjointed juxtapositions of the sacred and the profane. In one passage he quotes a conversa-tion with a young man who claims to have listened to records of Gershon Sirota while visiting a brothel in Warsaw.[23]

In Minkovsky's estimation, this hyperbolic and travestying verbal combat was necessary in order to muster the cantorial community against the allures of the corrupting culture industry. Minkovsky was far from alone in reviling the gramophone and concert stage as twin vices challenging the dignity of the cantorial profession.[24] Publicizing the sacred sounds of the community outside the synagogue will have the effect of corrupting tradition, degrading the achievements of his generation of cantors who painstakingly built a conception of cantors as high-status artists within the community. Minkovsky frames his antigramophone rhetoric as a form of pastoral care, seeking to protect Jewish listeners who were being ensnared by the sensuality of cantors who refused to contain their outpourings of feeling in the appropriate container of culturally intimate Jewish spaces. As anthropologist Michael Herzfeld notes, artefacts that express intimately recognizable aspects of communal identity can be transformed into sources of embarrassing or degrading stereotypes when exposed as performance for the "outside" world.[25] Yet for those within the community, these signifiers of identity can be read differently as desired representations of an intimately recognizable portrait of the community.

In the aftermath of World War I and the destruction of Jewish small-town life, the theme of memorializing the Jewish folkloric past was heightened and expanded—notably, in the influential records made by Kwartin in New York in the 1920s. Cantorial vocal practices specific to the synagogue, which were understood by Jewish audiences to represent a folkloric style, were synthesized with elements of opera, which was undergoing its own popularization on record. The primary sound of cantorial music found on the interwar period records is commonly referred to as "nonmetered" setting of prayer texts, usually featuring a broad melodic range that emotively spotlights the powerful tenor upper register favored by cantors and their listeners. Cantors repurposed the term *recitative*, borrowed from opera, to refer to their compositions in a heavily ornamented vocal style.[26] The style of cantorial prayer leading in the synagogue associated with star cantors was characterized by extended soloist compositions utilizing an idiomatic vocabulary of vocal techniques, including coloratura, ornamentation, and vocal gestures such as the *krekhts*, or sob, which thematize emotion through noises suggestive of the sound of shedding tears.[27] Often, cantors were themselves composers or skilled improvisers.

The sense that cantors functioned as a "key to the Jewish soul,"[28] who spoke for the community was important in explaining the popularity of the music and the breadth of its reach beyond ritual contexts. Critics noted that khazones united socialists and Orthodox Jews in its fan base. Yossele Rosenblatt (1882–1933), the star cantor of the golden age most associated in contemporary memory with traditional religiosity, was a featured performer on benefit concerts organized by leftist labor organizations. Rosenblatt joked that "it would seem now that Yossele Rosenblatt takes the place of Karl Marx," foreshadowing John Lennon's quip about the Beatles being bigger than Jesus.[29]

An oft-repeated anecdote about Rosenblatt locates him at the center of the controversy between secular and religious sites of performance. Rosenblatt famously refused a contract to sing at the Chicago Grand Opera Company in 1918, apparently at the insistence of the synagogue where he was employed at the time. Although this incident has been interpreted as a triumph of traditional piety over the corrupting influence of popular culture and assimilation, Rosenblatt was active in an even more populist arena of performance: the vaudeville circuit. Rosenblatt also took a star turn in *The Jazz Singer*, the first sound film made in 1927. Yiddish scholar and cultural critic Jeffrey Shandler notes that Rosenblatt was able to maintain a public persona as a representative of religious tradition through an assertive public relations strategy that was constructed in part through his visual presentation as a Hasidic Jew.[30] His "lapses" from the traditional space of cantorial performance in the synagogue, however, did not go uncriticized. Rosenblatt's peer, the famed cantor Berele Chagy (1892–1954), wrote a scathing article in which he leveled a thinly veiled attack on Rosenblatt:

> Our concerts have been turned into actual vaudeville: twenty cantors on one concert for fifteen cents a ticket, which makes a cent and a half a cantor. Cantorial beards in the vaudeville houses. Where earlier there appeared dogs on bicycles, naked lady dancers dancing the well-known shimmy, and for the finale the "main attraction," a cantor with a beard and a yarmulke with a *siddur* [Hebrew, prayer book].[31]

While the association of cantors with popular culture was a source of controversy, performance venues outside the synagogue created opportunities for singers with nonconforming identities to become performers of sacred music. As Judah Cohen has argued, the establishment of a professional cantorate in the nineteenth century had the impact of excluding women prayer leaders from the emergent "modern" synagogue.[32] Radio, gramophone records, and the Yiddish theater stage offered new venues to women cantors, who were often referred to by the Yiddish term *khazente*. Singers such as Sophie Kurtzer (1896–1974) and Perele Feig (1910–87) sang repertoires associated with male cantors, creating a sense of gender ambiguity in their presentation of sacred music that was complimented by their performance attire in cantorial robe, *tallis* (Hebrew, prayer shawl) and mitre.[33]

Male cantors, perhaps responding to the absence of female voices in the public prayer space, appropriated elements of sonic "femininity." Cantors cultivated a repertoire of emotive vocal "noises" imitative of the sounds of crying, defying Western gender binaries that associate masculinity with control over emotional expressiveness. Star cantors, notably Chagy and Rosenblatt, were celebrated for their falsetto work. At pivotal emotive moments in their recorded compositions, they would erupt into virtuosic passages in a stylized vocal range that blurred normative distinctions between male and female voices.

In the years after World War II, the prevalence of cantors in popular culture went into decline. Major record labels jettisoned their "ethnic" record departments, and Yiddish-language print media contracted. The cantorate shifted its emphasis from the cultivation of star careers and idiosyncratic soloists serving the immigrant community, to the establishment of a unionized and seminary-trained work force that was prepared to serve in the proliferation of suburban synagogues serving acculturated second- and third-generation Jewish Americans. But the decline narrative that dominates in contemporary discussions of the cantorial golden age misses the continued popularity into the mid-twentieth century of cantors who continued to perform in the khazones idiom and record on smaller record labels marketed and distributed within the Jewish community.

The Malavsky Family Choir is a notable example of khazones continuity into the post-Holocaust period in the United States. Helmed by Samuel Malavsky (1894–1983), a protégé of Rosenblatt, and featuring his daughter Goldie Malavsky (1923–95) as lead soloist, the Malavsky's cultivated a sound inspired by the *meshoyrer* (Yiddish, cantorial choir singer) sound reminiscent of cantors in the Russian Pale of Settlement in which Samuel was born and got his professional start. The Malavsky's popular recordings also drew on sounds of jazz and pop music in their distinctive arrangements. The Malavskys were out of step with the conservative norms of the American synagogue, particularly with regard to their flexible approach to gender in sacred music. To avoid the regulation of Jewish religious institutions, they produced their own services and concerts outside the synagogues in theaters and Jewish resorts.

Although Malavsky and his generational peers, including Moishe Oysher (1906–58), Moshe Koussevitzky (1899–1965), and Moshe Ganchoff (1904–97), continued to present khazones on record, in concert and in prayer-leading services into the second half of the twentieth century, the footprint of their style was greatly diminished in American Jewish life. The gramophone-era style, characterized by an ideal of dramatic intensity, emotive noisiness, and stylized Jewish vocal techniques, may have been a victim of its own success in representing the cultural preferences of the immigrant Jewish milieu. Targeted as anachronistic by the seminary-trained professional cantorate, and simply unfamiliar to second-generation American Jews who were acculturated into the norms of popular culture, khazones took a subordinate role in the development of Jewish American liturgical music.[34]

New forms of comportment during ritual in the emerging American synagogues of the post-World War II period promoted an ideal of decorum and bodily restraint during services, distinct from the noisiness of immigrant synagogues.[35] New embodied attitudes in American synagogue social life perhaps had an effect in diminishing the social basis of cantorial performance. Consumers of khazones in synagogue engaged in forms of participatory listening that we have only scant information about. In field recordings of mid-twentieth century prayer services led by elder cantors and in the rare present-day Orthodox services where a cantor presides and performance is intentionally foregrounded, we can perceive that the congregants, despite the concert-like presentational form of the service, participate in the creation of the service. Congregant participation in cantorial prayer leading was far from silent. Congregants made themselves audible through sound-generating movement and gesture, and knowledge of Hebrew prayer texts that participants recited aloud, sometimes in a heterophonic fog of unsteady unison with the cantor.[36] The shared knowledge of prayer performance seems to have played a role in shaping the phenomenon of star cantorial performance in the synagogue, bridging the space between performer and listener and creating a sense of shared experience rather than a dynamic of power being hoarded by the cantor in the expression of prayer.

Although new recordings of khazones slowed after the Holocaust, in the late 1950s Jewish record labels began to reissue compilation LPs of classic recordings that had originally been released as 78rpm singles. Labels operating in Brooklyn starting in the 1960s, such as the Greater Recording Company and the Collectors Guild, released anthologies on LP and cassette of cantorial 78rpm records from the pre-World War II era. These records were distributed primarily by Judaica book-shop retailers. Reissue anthologies have insured that the sounds of classic cantorial recordings have never completely disappeared. Reissue anthologies have also sta-bilized a standard repertoire focused on a few dozen performers who have come to be looked on as the masters, largely because of their commercial success and the preservation of their voices on recordings. Not surprisingly, female voices were excluded from the representation of the cantor's voice on the key anthologies that have shaped present-day conceptions of cantorial artistry and achievement.

CANTORS AND HASIDISM IN HISTORICAL CONTEXT

The innovations and controversies of the gramophone era extended and height-ened tensions around cantors that were long-standing throughout the Jewish world, including in the Hasidic community. In parallel to debates between elite cantors and critics writing in the secular Yiddish press, the profile of cantors as nonconformist figures with a blurry ethical profile was also prominent in Hasidic discourse about music and prayer. These debates did not keep Hasidic leaders from calling on cantors to represent the community at times, expediently leveraging the popularity of artists to heighten the charismatic draw of the Hasidic rabbinic elite.

As in its approach to religious practices and rituals, an attitude of traditional-ism adheres in the Hasidic musical sphere. In practice, however, Hasidic music is characterized by a tendency to borrow from non-Jewish musical sources, a cus-tom that has accrued its own theological explanations. Complex and, at times, contradictory attitudes toward music in the contemporary Hasidic community are traceable to tensions in the theological discourses of foundational rabbinic figures. The potential for music to serve as an invigorating aspect of sacred experience was universally acknowledged by the disciples of the Baal Shem Tov and their ante-cedents, who employed music as a form of outreach to new followers.[37] Hasidic conceptions about what forms of music could be acceptable for the multiple needs of the community are not consistent. Two contrasting views of music asserted themselves that are relevant to the Hasidic cantorial scene.

On the one hand, Hasidic rabbis argued that music from aesthetically desirable non-Jewish repertoires was a legitimate source for worship music. They justified this attitude, which is seemingly at odds with the Hasidic rejection of the non-Jewish world, through recourse to the kabbalistic doctrine of divine sparks trapped inside unholy husks.[38] The metaphor of returning holy sparks to their source is frequently cited to describe the process of appropriating melodies into the Jewish sound world. In a famous story told about the rebbe of Koliv, Isaac Taube (1751–1821), the revered Hasidic leader payed a non-Jewish shepherd to teach him a melody that he believed to have been derived from the song of the ancient Levites. In the process of this purchase, the shepherd lost his ability to sing the song, thus "proving" that the song had been thoroughly imbibed into its new Jewish sacred context.[39] Melodies were described allegorically as existing in a state of exile, like the Jewish people themselves. The intrinsic holiness of a melody can be accessed by restoring the melody to its imagined source through performance in Jewish ritual or a devotional context. This doctrine stresses the sacred potentials of appropriation and aesthetics over the perceived ethical valences of the provenance of a piece of music. The positive valuation of aesthetics as the basis for spiritual practices would seem to work in the favor of cantors, who have long been accused of aesthetic excess.

Other Hasidic rabbinic authorities opposed integration of music that was perceived as excessively aesthetic, especially when that excess is derived from explicitly non-Jewish sources. Along these lines of reasoning, cantors have been reproached for similar kinds of cultural borrowing that Hasidic rabbis were celebrated for. The Levitical theme of idolatry imported into the Jewish worship space has haunted cantors for centuries, in part because their work was so often a staging ground for borrowing elements from the surrounding non-Jewish culture.[40] Hasidic discussions of the ethical import of music continued these musical debates and anxieties. Rabbi Nachman of Bratslav (1772–1810), a great-grandson of the Baal Shem Tov, developed a doctrine of positive and negative aspects of the divine that he applied to discussions of music. His theological innovations stress the power of music to influence internal spiritual processes that have mystical potentials to resonate beyond the human realm.[41] Nachman's writings on music are primarily associated with a mainstream Hasidic celebratory approach to music's spiritual powers, yet these mystical interpretations set the stakes high in the discussion of musical powers—music can achieve either spiritual repair or corruption, rendering close speculation of music and musicians a necessity for protecting the community and its spiritual integrity. These ethical concerns map onto negotiations over control of the experience of prayer and the locus of power in the intimate space of the synagogue.

The musical form most thoroughly associated with Hasidism, both among non-Hasidic Jews and Hasidim themselves, is the *nigun* (plural, *nigunim*).[42] Nigun is a Hebrew/Yiddish word that means melody, but in the Hasidic context it is used to describe a genre of devotional melodies, frequently sung without words. Nigunim are typically sung in group unison as part of paraliturgical gatherings, such as the *rebbes tish* (Yiddish, the Rabbi's table), a gathering at which a Hasidic leader gathers together with his disciples in gender segregated all-male spaces. As Ellen Koskoff has argued in her study of the Brooklyn Hasidic Lubavitch sect, singing nigunim offers Hasidic Jews an opportunity to perform their identities as members of the group, strengthening their ties to their spiritual leader and to other Hasidim.[43]

In contrast to the positive associations with communal melodies and nonprofessionalized paraliturgical music performance, khazones has held a more ambivalent place in the Hasidic world, both historically and today. The issues at stake in defining the appropriate music for prayer leading are both musical and social. Since at least the medieval period, cantors, as a professionalized class of musicians, have been routinely suspected of aesthetic innovations that are unsuitable to the Jewish experience of prayer.[44] A denigrating attitude toward cantors is far from unique to Hasidic authorities but it has a distinct cast in the Hasidic context inflected by their antimodernizing separatist doctrine.

Hasidic hierarchies of power are specifically built around the rebbe and his lineage. Investing musicians with spiritual authority was seen by some rebbes as a challenge to both spiritual purity and the retention of dynastic power. Writing in 1864, Hayim Halberstam, the rebbe of Zana, condemned in no uncertain terms the hiring of a cantor by one of the communities he had influence over, admonishing a synagogue leader to "let the fear of God be awakened in your heart to smite the crown of the wicked and to drive out from the house of the Lord the hazzan and his helpers."[45] Halberstam stressed that the theatrical music of a cantor could never compare to the spiritual purity of a tsadik's prayer. This imperative to reserve the right to lead prayer for the rebbe himself is reflected today in some Brooklyn Hasidic communities.

Hayim Halberstam's unambiguous condemnation was on the far end of the spectrum of attitudes about cantorial prayer music. Other Hasidic rabbis held a more practical approach to cantors, employing them in their courts or patronizing traveling cantors to cultivate an atmosphere of musically heightened experience that would symbiotically add to their charisma. Examples of rabbis who patronized cantors include the Baal Shem Tov himself; he was purported to have inspired a disciple to embrace a career as a cantor who was henceforth closely associated with the great leader.[46] In the mid-nineteenth century, as the grand court system of Hasidic leaders was ascendant, some rebbes derived benefit from the talents of their personal cantors whose musical skill represented the holiness of the spiritual leader they served. In the politics of cantorial hiring in the heavily Hasidic milieu of the Ukraine in the late nineteenth century, support of a cantor sometimes acted as a proxy for allegiance to the Hasidic rebbe the cantor was associated with.[47]

For some Hasidic leaders, developing a profile as a patron of cantorial music was key to the success of their charismatic outreach. The influential Rabbi David of

Tolnoe (1808–82) worked closely with a cantor named Yossele Tolner, who served both as a prayer leader and a composer of popular nigunim. Yossele's melodies were cited as an important tool in Rabbi David's successful campaigns to recruit Hasidim to his court. Yet Rabbi David was not limited to his personal court bal tefile in working with musicians to create a richly expressive atmosphere in his home base of Tolnoe. He was also a patron of Nissi Belzer, a figure who is often cited as the most popular and broadly influential cantor of late-nineteenth-century Russia. According to Pinchas Minkovsky, who began his career as a choir-boy with Nissi Belzer, Rabbi David's patronage of the famed cantor was not unique; he also claimed that all of the most prominent cantors had Hasidic patrons who vouched for the sacred legitimacy of their music.[48] Another example of musical life in an elite Hasidic court was Tchortkov under the leadership of Rabbi David Moshe (1828–1904). His court was able to attract Mannish Khazn, a renowned cantor who had trained in a German "choral synagogue." The Hasidic community of Tchortkov boasted a choir that, in addition to singing pieces by famed cantors such as Yeruchom Hakoton and Belzer, also performed works by Handel, Schubert, Mozart and other European art music composers.[49]

The support of rebbes were foundational to the careers of cantors such as Zeidel Rovner (1856–1943) and Yossele Rosenblatt, two key figures of early twentieth-century cantorial music who developed international careers. Rovner was first encouraged to become a cantor at the urging of Rabbi Yaakov Yitschok Twersky, the Makarover rebbe, in 1881. In turn, the Makarover rebbe cultivated a relationship with Rovner, a popular artist whose work came to be seen as infused with the holiness of the rabbinic court, adding to the prestige of his spiritual sponsor.[50] Rosenblatt, the best-known figure of the gramophone era, obtained his first cantorial appointment by merit of the endorsement of the Sadigurer rebbe in 1900.[51] In their support of cantors, these Hasidic rebbes were not acting in a uniquely Hasidic manner; rather, they resembled the rest of the Jewish world. Jewish institutions of a variety of cultural and religious standpoints drew on the popularity of cantors to attract energy to synagogues and to fundraise for communal undertakings.

A clear line of demarcation between khazones and Hasidic Judaism is difficult to draw. This is in part because many of the best-known figures of the modern cantorial golden age, whose dossiers included theater performance, opera, and mass media, were born into Hasidic families. Peering into the biographies of famous cantors can cause a degree of confusion between supposedly stable categories of traditionalism and modernization that these two spheres of Jewish life are often presumed to occupy. Some of the star cantors continued to identify as Hasidic later in their careers as they assumed identities as modern, assimilated artists who ceased to adhere to the lifeways and sartorial conformity associated with Hasidism. For example, Ben Zion Kapov Kagan (1899–1953), a gramophone star with a public image as a modern Jew who served a controversial term as president of the *khazonim farbund* (cantorial union), during which he advocated for cantors to join the American Federation of Labor, was also an adherent of Rabbi Isaac Heschel, the Mezbyzher rebbe. This association between cantor and rebbe began in Odessa but was maintained in New York after Kapov Kagan's immigration and subsequent high-profile recording career.[52]

In their recordings and performances in the United States, cantors took on the role of champions of old world Jewish memory, an area of concern that was shared with Hasidic leaders. Figures in the popularization of cantorial music in the United States, such as Pierre Pinchik (1900–1971) and Leib Glantz (1898–1964), were praised by fans as representatives of a Hasidic musical approach, indicating an assessment based on a generalized sense of their heartfelt emotion and regarding the specifics of their musical approach, such as the inclusion of nigun-like motifs.[53] These artists were distinctly not Hasidic in their personal and professional lives: Pinchik worked as a state-sponsored folk singer in the early Soviet era in Russia; after immigration to the United States, he was notorious for his nonconformity to religious conventions. Glantz, while maintaining religious orthodoxy in his personal life, was an ardent socialist and Zionist political activist.[54] Yet these "modern" cantorial stars were not completely cast out from the musical life of Hasidic Jews. A few of their most famous pieces are maintained in Hasidic public memory through cover versions by mainstream Hasidic musicians. In particular, Pinchik's classic 1928 recording of "Rozo D'Shabbos" has a special salience in the Hasidic community and has been performed and recorded by numerous Hasidic singers and bal tefiles.[55] This is in part because the text for the piece is drawn from the *nusakh sefard* variant of the prayer book used by Hasidic Jews. Comparing the approach to timbre, breath control, and ornament in Pinchik's original to the approach of contemporary Hasidic bal tefiles who sing his composition is illustrative of the stylistic differences in these two different approaches to prayer leading, even as the bal tefile and cantorial forms of prayer leading overlap in their repertoires.

The blurry line between khazones and American Hasidic musical life is illustrated by the career of Cantor Moshe Teleshevsky (1927–2012). Teleshevsky was born in Russia into a cantorial family with ties to Chabad Hasidism. After immigrating to the United States, he continued to work as a cantor, serving the Modern Orthodox congregation Agudath Sholom in the Flatbush neighborhood in Brooklyn, while at the same time he maintained his ties to Chabad. His two cantorial albums, released on small independent labels and with no date listed on their packaging but apparently from the late 1960s, are in a khazones style. The liner notes of both albums state explicitly, "The cantorial renditions are in the style of the great Cantor Pinchik." Teleshevsky also sings on the 1965 album *Chabad Nigunim Vol. 5*, where he is featured as an expert representing the communal musical repertoires of Chabad Hasidim. In these recording efforts, Teleshevsky is heard code-switching between two distinct vocal affects: the cantorial vocal style characterized by a bel canto timbral approach, virtuosic coloratura singing, and a wide vocal range; and the Hasidic bal tefile style, characterized by a smaller melodic ambitus, a rough-hewn approach to breath control, and a less controlled approach to ornamentation.[56]

The Lubavitcher rebbe, Rabbi Menachem Mendel Schneerson (1902–94), voiced a critical attitude toward khazones, comparing the artistry of cantors unfavorably to the putative spiritual purity of nonprofessional prayer leaders: "A ba'al t'fillah for the most part brings out the best in worshipers, whereas a hazzan for the most part causes them to sin."[57] "Chabad houses," community centers established by the Lubavitch community in almost every corner of the world where Jews live, offer services usually led by the local rabbi and generally do not employ cantors. Some cantors hold the view that Chabad houses have undermined the cantorial profession and the aesthetics of prayer. Yet Teleshevsky worked at times within the community as a purveyor of classic cantorial repertoire, at the request of the rebbe himself. Teleshevsky was frequently called on to sing Israel Schorr's popular piece "Yehi Rotzon Sheyibone Beis-Hamikdosh" (recorded in 1927) at mass meetings presided over by Schneerson. This piece was a favorite because of its messianically oriented text, which accorded with Schneerson's mission to usher in the era of redemption.[58]

Despite a dearth of communal support for professional cantorial performance, in the late twentieth century several prominent cantors emerged from the Hasidic world, including Benzion Miller (born 1945) and Yitzchak Helfgot (born 1969). Notably, both Miller and Helfgot were born outside the United States, Miller in a displaced persons camp in Germany in the aftermath of the Holocaust, and Helfgot in Israel. Miller and Helfgot are singers with exceptional vocal talents who became international stars working in prestigious orchestral concert contexts, often in Europe and Israel. In particular, Helfgot's collaboration with Itzhak Perlman on the major record label release *Eternal Echoes* (2012) seems to have played a role in broadening the sense of cantorial performance as an attractive form of performance with possibilities for popular reception among young Hasidic singers. The careers of Miller and Helfgot were perceived as outliers by fans of cantorial music, who were at first unaccustomed to cantors with publicly visible Hasidic identities.[59]

The story of cantors and their reception in the Hasidic world is characterized by contingency. Hasidic rabbis have called on cantors and their music to raise the profile of their charismatic courts when it has suited the specific needs of the moment. In other cases, Hasidic leaders have chastised and opposed cantors. What emerges from this discussion of cantors and rebbes is a picture of artists with an unclear status and a potential to receive approbation from a leadership class invested in maintaining the ethical and political stability of the community. Unlike singers of communally sanctioned repertoires whose music is made and received primarily within the Hasidic world, cantors are more vulnerable because of the association of their music with non-Hasidic and, at times, non-Jewish communities. Historical precedents for the rejection of cantors by the Hasidic community reach into the lives of contemporary Hasidic cantorial revivalists, sowing instability in their attempts to establish themselves as prayer leaders and popular artists.

Hasidic cantorial revivalists today reject the ideology that castigates golden age cantors as spiritually corrupted by excessive commercialism or as degraded by their association with mass media and (non-Jewish) popular culture. They look to the gramophone era for reliable testimony about the sounds of the Jewish past and as a genre of art music on which to base their creative pursuits. Cantorial revival bears a utopian stamp—it is a musical pursuit that seeks an answer to musical needs in the present through sounds of the past, bypassing concerns with legibility to contemporary audiences or the possibilities of commercial success. Like other kinds of artist who are antinormative in their aesthetic commitments, Hasidic cantorial revivalists gesture toward a future that cannot yet be imagined. At the moment, these possibilities are realized primarily in the space of music-making communities outside the mainstream, focused on individuals and their artistry, not yet legible to a broad listening public. Their art practice is preparatory toward a future in which artists with outsider identities can elevate and expand the possibilities of Jewish ritual as a transformative social and aesthetic experience.

ANIMATING THE ARCHIVE, CREATING THE FUTURE

Hasidic cantorial revivalists encounter cantorial records in two primary settings: in the context of listening as part of a homosocial environment shared with other cognoscenti, and as learners delving into the material, usually with specific goals of mastering new pieces. Cantor Yanky Lemmer described listening to the cantorial radio show Thursday nights on WSNR hosted by Charlie Bernhaut every week with his father as a child.[60] This weekly session of listening was treated as "the Holy of Holies" by his father, who demanded total silence while listening. Yoel Kohn describes listening to cantorial records as part of a homosocial experience with male members of his family across generations, with loud conversations comparing the virtues of different cantorial voices cutting across the music playing on the stereo. On occasions when I listened to records with Yoel, he offered a continuous commentary on the music while we listened. Zevi Steiger offered a similar portrait of social listening to records with his dorm roommates at yeshivah, who, by good fortune, included a few other cantorial fans. Steiger recalls the desire to impress his friends as being a motivator to expand his knowledge of cantorial music.

In the context of the highly structured and conformist Hasidic community, the impassioned cantorial subculture might appear to have some of the trappings of a rebellion against institutional authority. My ethnography suggests that rebellion against Hasidic identity is not a primary motivation for the work of cantorial revival. Rather than playing a role in establishing a "secular" identity outside the community, immersing themselves in the archive of cantorial records allows Hasidic cantorial revivalists to explore the boundaries of prescribed behaviors for

Orthodox Jewish men. Their music creates a space in which potentially subversive aesthetic pursuits are integrated into a set of practices that are at their core deeply concerned with cultural preservation and a theology of dialogue with the divine. Even Yoel Kohn, the only participant in this project with an outspokenly antiauthoritarian and antireligious public identity, is an intense traditionalist when it comes to cantorial music. He frames cantorial performance as deriving the signature aesthetic friction that he venerates from the urgency of cantorial dialogue with the divine, even if he no longer believes in the God he addresses in prayer. In Yoel's words, "it's the screaming that matters, not who you're screaming at."

In contrast to the boisterous scenes of musical sociality recounted by Steiger and Kohn, listening as an act of learning typically takes place in solitary concentration and has a devotional quality. In a video that Yoel Kohn shared with me, Yoel is revealed in a private moment studying Yossele Rosenblatt's classic recording "Ribono Shel Olam," originally recorded in 1927 at the Victor Records studio in Camden, New Jersey. The video is an intrusion into the mystique of the virtuoso performer, revealing the patient relationship he bears to his source material. In the practice video, Yoel closely follows the vocal line on the original record, singing along, sometimes anticipating Rosenblatt, sometimes tightly following the original recording. As Yoel jokes in a mix of Yiddish and English to his friend, who is off camera holding a cellphone and filming him, "*Gibst oys di soydes fin khayder* [You're giving away mystical secrets], it's a terrible thing. Obviously *der malakh Gavril iz mir nit gekimen lernen keyn Yosseles in mitn di nakht* [the angel Gabriel doesn't come and teach me Yossele's (pieces) in the middle of the night]."

The video shows Yoel polishing his performance, learning the small details of Rosenblatt's vocal nuances and ornamentations. These types of details give vibrancy to Yoel's performance and help him hone a sound that adheres to the intonation of the classic cantorial records. The video also demonstrates the learning trajectory that led up to the moment being filmed. Yoel's vocal musculature is already remarkably homed in on what is heard on the recording. Rosenblatt's performance offers a template for how to perform a cantorial coloratura that Yoel has spent a great deal of time learning to replicate with a remarkable degree of verisimilitude. Yoel actually begins almost every phrase of *Ribono Shel Olam* by singing the phrase *before* Rosenblatt begins singing on the record. Yoel has already nearly mastered the piece but desires a degree of precision before he will begin to feel comfortable taking liberties with the piece in the context of performance. The record is so familiar to Yoel that he betrays a hint of impatience with the record. He seems to be eagerly seeking the moments in the recording where he has not yet fully mastered Rosenblatt's phrasing.

In the practice video, we can see a variety of forms of embodied response to the music. Yoel evinces an ebb and flow of physical tension, expressed through his mannerisms of holding his face, stroking his beard, and knitting his brow. These gestures are more pronounced during the moments of intense concentration when Yoel is pushing himself to hear new details in the already familiar recording. His relaxation when he allows himself to "simply" listen is visible in the stillness of his bodily comportment.

Although Yoel's mastery of classic recorded material has reached an elevated level of sophistication, internal debate persists for him about how best to implement his knowledge. For Yoel and his generational cohort of cantorial revivalists, questions abound about how to develop their own creative voices. Performing "covers" of classic records is a standard practice for Hasidic cantorial revivalists but it is fraught—both because of fears of being compared unfavorably by audiences to the legends of the genre and because of internal anxieties about being inadequately creative as artists. At times, Yoel is filled with self-doubt about his own ability to live up to the creative example of his heroes. These insecurities are keenly felt and they offer a discursive space for aesthetic self-examination. As Yoel told me:

> Like I said, I had a long transition from being a, from thinking, it's almost like davening [Yiddish-English, prayer leading] with ta'amey hamikra [Hebrew, the markings that notate Torah cantillation]. This has to be said this way. This has to be said this way. Work it out [i.e., in advance], have a shtikl [Yiddish, cantorial composition], have a piece. Be prepared. And going to a place where I don't daven the same thing twice. Because I want to enjoy the davening too . . . I started doing that and I started enjoying it. And I realized, holy crap, you can actually enjoy davening. It was a mind-blowing realization for me. I don't think I'm in an improvisational freedom where I want to be. I tend to get stuck in a single mode. That's a problem for me. And I, looking around, I don't want to mention, I don't have to mention names, but looking around I see everyone else is struggling with the same thing. It's very hard for us. (Interview, January 15, 2019)

In this statement Yoel draws a comparison between the work of cantors who are completely dependent on recorded music for their prayer leading to a Torah reader who is compelled by synagogue tradition to rely on trop, the traditional Jewish system of neumatic musical notation for scriptural chanting, in order to chant the text with the correct melodic figuration. Unlike the Torah reader, for whom the legitimacy of ritual performance lies in strict adherence to the prescribed melodic patterns, Yoel suggests that strict adherence to recorded cantorial sources actually undermines the validity of cantorial artistry. The gramophone culture that created the classic cantorial canon demanded that cantors squeeze their creativity into neatly entextualized three-minute-long versions of Jewish prayer sound, sealed off from the liveness and spontaneity of prayer in ritual contexts. Ethnomusicologist Regula Qureshi has suggested that in the case of musical forms that have been mediated by gramophone reproduction, two musical cultures emerge: the recorded form, which is shaped by the contingencies of technological limitation and the demands of marketing and distribution networks, and the live form revealed in performance contexts.[61] Yoel observes of current cantors that the recorded form shapes expectations of the performance of the live, with old records insinuating themselves into moments of prayer performance and influencing musical choices both on the level of stylistic vocal comportment and in terms of repertoire selections.

> You have so many people, every *kvetsch* [Yiddish, whine, here used to mean ornament or stylized vocal break that imitates the sound of crying] they do is a Koussevitzky imitation [Moshe Koussevitzky, 1899–1966]. So, you got a lot of little Koussevitzkys going around. And at some point, it becomes boring. Now Koussevitzky himself had a wider range of building blocks of improvisation than the people who imitate him because he was musical. He wasn't imitating Koussevitzky [*laughs*]. So that seems to be the go-to style. (Yoel Kohn interview, January 15, 2019)

In Yoel's estimation, being a "little Koussevitzky" does an injustice to the art form. He offers his own path toward being able to spontaneously create within the context of cantorial prayer leading as an example of successful appropriation of cantorial identity and artistic function. Yoel is not satisfied with his current level of creative fluidity, a sign of his dedication to his craft and the unfolding, nonlinear nature of the revivalist musician's learning process. As Yoel suggests, there is a jagged relationship between learning cantorial classic pieces from old records and developing the skills of a prayer leader.

In the following chapters I will explore how Hasidic cantorial revivalists take their intimate knowledge of old records into new communities. The personal project of mastery of cantorial repertoire and the resulting artistry of these musicians begs for recognition and requited love from listeners. Attaining this kind of communication with an audience is challenged by the multiple streams of reception that cantors have encountered in the past and the limitations on the life of khazones in the contemporary Jewish world. The skills carefully cultivated by revivalists who can interpret music heard on old records are not necessarily suited to the needs of a synagogue cantor. In their attempts at professionalization and employment, Hasidic cantorial revivalists run into a set of limitations that have challenged all professional cantors for at least the last fifty years. The next chapters will focus on how Hasidic cantorial revivalists transform their knowledge of old cantorial records into the requisite skill set for employment. But at the outset I will offer the first of three Interludes in which we will get a closer look at the lives and music of the cantors. Through a portrait of the Lemmer brothers, Yanky and Shulem, I will paint a picture of the world of music in the Hasidic community and the problematic fit of cantorial performance in Orthodox Jewish American life. The story of the Lemmer brothers echoes both the history of conflict between cantors and the Hasidic community, and the exuberance and aesthetic explorations of the gramophone-era cantors.

Interlude A

The Lemmer Brothers

Music and Genre in Orthodox New York Life

Yanky Lemmer and his brother Shulem Lemmer are two of the most prominent artists in the contemporary New York Hasidic music scene. Born in the Orthodox Jewish enclave of Kensington, Brooklyn, the Lemmers were raised as Belz Hasidim and continue to identify as Hasidic Jews, adhering to the ritual, linguistic, and sartorial norms of the community. In broad outline, their life trajectories have hewed to a path that is conventional in their community: both studied at Hasidic yeshivas in Brooklyn; later, each spent several years in advanced study in Israel. Despite their high-profile work as singers, both men have careers outside music: Yanky, the elder brother, as a special education therapist working with children in Orthodox Jewish schools in Brooklyn, and Shulem, the younger, working in marketing and high-end retail sales. Both men are married and have growing families, and are raising their children speaking in Yiddish, living in Orthodox neighborhoods, and attending similar parochial schools to the ones they attended.

In their unusual vocal talent and their individual choices to pursue paths as artists, however, Yanky and Shulem depart from the norm of their birth community. Yet even within their shared path as musicians, Yanky and Shulem diverge from one another. Although they share a passion for musical self-expression and frequently collaborate with each other, Yanky and Shulem have distinct musical identities: Yanky is a cantor and Shulem is a "singer"—that is, a singer in the style of pop music that constitutes the primary musical style heard in the contemporary Hasidic world. Yanky's choice of genre places limits on his career growth and demands educational pathways that are distinct from Shulem's musical career. In this interlude, I will clarify the differences in the musical genres the Lemmer brothers represent and explore the motivations and meaning behind Yanky's devotion to a more obscure, less commercial, and more formally demanding musical style.

In many ways, Yanky and Shulem's musical lives have overlapped. Both grew up in the same household suffused with their father's love of khazones; both have remarkable vocal talents; and both share an unusual interest in early twentieth-century Eastern European Jewish and immigrant-era Yiddish American music. Both men are artists working in Jewish music whose careers emerged from a Hasidic cultural milieu in Brooklyn and who have expanded to broader audiences. Indeed, the Lemmers are frequently cited as two of the most promising voices in contemporary Jewish music.[1]

Despite the parallels and intertwining of their musical paths, the Lemmer brothers are distinct in their musical identities. Their individual paths are representative of the stylistic line between Orthodox pop music and the niche and underground scene of khazones revival, as well as the blurring that occurs between these two musical terrains. Shulem, a star of the Orthodox pop scene, is able to keep a foot in the world of cantorial performance, appearing annually as a cantor for the High Holidays. His repertoire and cantorial knowledge are heavily shaped by his older brother, Yanky, on the other hand, has cast his lot more deeply into his identity as a cantor, although at times his work engages with the pop music scene in the Hasidic world. The division between these worlds of performance and career opportunity go deeper than a simple matter of musical interests. The choices the Lemmer brothers have each made invoke a set of aesthetic commitments that bear a distinct ethical stamp.

Although cantorial revival might appear to the uninitiated to be a conservative musical choice, within the economy of expressive culture in the Hasidic world, khazones has a distinctive outsider tinge. By contrast, Orthodox pop is almost universally embraced and forms a dominant part in the street soundscape of New York Orthodox life. My description of Orthodox pop as part of "the normal" of Orthodox Jewish life, however, is in contrast to other scholarly appraisals that consider Orthodox pop as a marker of musical rebellion against religious conformity.[2] There are high-profile instances of condemnation of Orthodox pop artists, notably visible in the career of Hasidic pop star Lipa Schmeltzer, who has made controversy a part of his "brand" as an internet-era sensation, and among some rabbis who fulminate against pop music as a means of bolstering their reputation as bulwarks of conservatism. I understand these cases to be exceptional. What emerged from my ethnography was a sense of pop music as unmarked, mostly uncontroversial, and omnipresent in the lived experience of committedly devout Hasidic Jews. Rather than fostering rebellion, Orthodox pop appears to bolster community solidarity through the prevalence of a shared musical vocabulary.

The contemporary Orthodox pop phenomenon emerged in the late 1960s and early 1970s, but its history can be traced back to the emergence of Jewish independent record labels a generation earlier. The gramophone era saw Jewish vocalists, especially cantors and Yiddish theater stars, recorded and promoted by major record labels. Jewish records in the earliest decades of the twentieth century sold in the hundreds of thousands. Starting in the 1930s but accelerating precipitously after the Holocaust, Jewish records lost their mass market appeal. In the 1940s, Jewish music migrated primarily to smaller independent record labels, such as Tikvah and Menorah, which continued to release large numbers of cantorial and Yiddish-language records geared toward an increasingly secular Jewish market. Records in this period frequently embraced a more pronouncedly "American" sound, with cantors such as Moishe Oysher and Samuel Malavsky accompanied by Hollywood-style orchestrations, and Yiddish song-stylists paired with Latin-tinged Jazz rhythm sections.[3]

In the late 1950s, as these Yiddish American secularizing-oriented music plat-forms began to wane in popularity, a handful of record labels helmed by Orthodox Jews were founded, prominent among them the Greater Recording Company and the Collectors Guild. As the name of the latter implies, these labels were originally concerned with the preservation and reissue of old Jewish records, usually canto-rial records that had been out of print for a generation or more. The founders of the Collectors Guild, husband and wife team Benedict and Helen Stambler next turned their eyes toward the resurgent post-World War II Hasidic community.[4] They produced albums of Hasidic singers on albums of *nigunim*, metered devo-tional melodies, which are often characterized by a wordless but vocalized singing style. Many of their Hasidic nigunim albums—notably, the 1960 album *'Nichoach' Chabad Melodies*—were collaborations with musician Velvel Pasternak, a wedding band leader and arranger. Pasternak played a pivotal role in the emergence of a post-World War II American Jewish music that combined Hasidic song with con-temporary wedding band sounds. Landmark record projects such as the multivol-ume series *Songs of the Lubavitcher Chassidim* helped frame a space in the market for new records of Orthodox Jewish music.[5]

As the 1960s wore on, wedding bands in the Orthodox world increasingly drew on sounds of rock drums, guitars, and electronic keyboards. The debut albums of singers Mordechai Ben David in 1973 and Avraham Fried in 1981 solidified the role of disco and mainstream pop as legitimate stylistic trends in the Hasidic com-munity. The mass popularity of Ben David and Fried consolidated the stylistic elements of Orthodox pop: pop drum kit beats, the timbres of rock instruments such as the synthesizer and electric guitar, and an approach to song composition that borrowed from the Vegas stage show and the Broadway musical, with dra-matic orchestrations and instrumental interludes. This orientation toward disco and Broadway-tinged orchestration is prominently on display on landmark hits such as Ben David's 1975 "Soul." Songwriting in Orthodox pop, although stylis-tically drawing from pop music models, features lyrics in Hebrew drawn from the Bible or prayer book, or Yiddish lyrics with pietistic themes.[6] The Orthodox pop phenomenon formed the sound world in which Yanky and Shulem and other young Brooklyn Hasidic singers grew up. Hasidic cantorial revivalists often refer to Orthodox pop as "normal music," implicitly casting their own musical interests as outsider, fringe, and perhaps transgressive.

Yanky and Shulem were somewhat unusual in that they grew up in a home with a father who loved cantorial music. Yanky describes himself as having been a maven of cantorial records at the age of seven, able to recognize and differentiate between the voices of David Roitman (1884–1943), Mordechai Hershman (1888–1940) and other golden age cantors as a small child. He recalls the experience of hearing Moshe Stern (1935–2023), an elder cantor, lead services in a Brooklyn synagogue and being intrigued and amazed by the power of the trained voices of the singers in the choir.

> I remember telling this to my father. I must have been seven years old. *Es iz a* sound *vi a* piano [Yinglish, it sounds like a piano]. Like when the choir gave a chord it just sounded like an organ to me. I couldn't fathom it. That was like, wow! Then I started to like khazones and to understand it a little bit more. You know when I was a little older. So, I've heard khazones in my life. I used to go to Beth El. I used to go shul hopping. [Temple] Emanuel [in Borough Park] was still around . . . And by Hasidim, there's always these one or two guys who have better voices and know how to elaborate a little bit more. (Yanky Lemmer, August 9, 2015)

As Yanky indicates, cantorial prayer leading was something that existed primarily outside the Hasidic community. Live cantorial performance was something he heard at occasional special events, like Moshe Stern's guest prayer-leading services, at synagogues that were not affiliated with Hasidic communities. Experts in liturgical performance in the Hasidic community were anomalies and were heard only sporadically, with prayer leading generally being lay-led and not assigned to musical experts.

Like other Hasidic cantorial revivalists, Yanky highlights the outsider quality of his musical obsessions and the ways in which it distinguished him: he was an intellectual and a sensitive child, and later a young man whose needs for aesthetic stimulation were not fully met by the culture of the Hasidic community. He found his aesthetic outlet in an expressive form that was Jewish but subtly outside the normative. While Yanky's father was a fan of cantorial performance, it was far from an unmarked and "normal" part of Hasidic Brooklyn life.

Khazones is a product of the Jewish Eastern European experience, coming from a context out of which Hasidism also emerged. It is a sacred music genre that sets prayer texts that are intimately familiar to Orthodox Jews from daily repetition in the statutory prayer services. The widespread popularity of cantorial records in the first half of the twentieth century renders khazones legible to contemporary Orthodox Jews, even if its current fan base has waned. On the surface it would seem that an interest in cantorial music would converge neatly with the goals of cultural preservation and Jewish separatism that are of primary importance to contemporary Hasidic communal leaders. This is not the case. Instead, khazones is looked on as a musical form with a questionable ethical valence, in part because it was created by a generation of artists whose focus was on aesthetics and whose form of Jewish observance was lax by contemporary Orthodox standards.[7]

As was noted by Haym Solveitchik in 1994 in his classic essay "Rupture and Reconstruction," a turn toward textual sources, rather than orally preserved life-ways and traditions, has led to the reconstruction of Orthodoxy along lines of greater stricture and less attention to aural cultural sources.[8] This shift is especially salient in regard to women's lives, with areas of women's control over domestic life increasingly litigated by male rabbinic authorities and structured by sacred texts, rather than reliance on oral traditions shared among Orthodox women, as Soloveitchik claims was the case before World War II. Contemporary Orthodoxy was built to withstand contact with secular American society and the mainstream of Jewish assimilation. Paradoxically, this has been achieved in the musical sphere through the creation of an entirely new musical genre that sounds like mainstream pop music but is perceived as representing the separatist values of the Orthodox community. The "orthodoxy" of Orthodox pop is achieved through its lyrical con-tent and the carefully cultivated image of Orthodox pop artists as faithful and sincere members of the identity group. By contrast, the key artists in the cantorial golden age held layered identities, with one foot in the Jewish world and the other embroiled in conceptions of aesthetics indebted to Romanticism and (non-Jewish) European art music.

The conception of khazones as linked to an "irreligious" past can partly be explained through an analogy to the attitude toward pre-World War II Yiddish culture in the Hasidic community. Yiddish popular culture, with its countless love songs and musical parodies of religious life, are viewed by contemporary Hasidic Jews as inappropriate for consumption by religious Jews. Yanky and Shulem's father discouraged them from listening to old Yiddish musicals because of their ostensibly irreligious character.[9]

Yanky developed a repertoire of cantorial pieces he learned from classic records, and later joined the choir of Benzion Miller, one of the only cantors work-ing in the golden age style as a regularly performing prayer leader in Brooklyn, at Temple Beth El in Borough Park. Benzion's performance style was understood as a throwback to an earlier era and was connected to non-Hasidic forms of prayer that foreground aesthetics; Yanky, however, was not the only Hasidic person attracted to the cantorial music subculture at Beth El. The Beth El scene served as a kind of incubator for Hasidic cantorial talent and a small but intense fandom in the com-munity; I will discuss the Beth El devotional music community in interlude B. In addition to Yanky, other well-known Hasidic cantorial revivalists, including Ushi Blumenberg, have served in Benzion's choir.

After an online video of Yanky performing a piece in a concert produced by Miller at Beth El went "viral," Yanky's career as a cantor began to expand. As he told me when we first met, his career grew much faster than his knowledge, and his first years of professional life were characterized by playing catch-up with his new persona as a star cantor. As I will discuss in chapter 2, Yanky had recourse to a variety of forms of learning in order to be able to fulfill the requirements of his prestigious cantorial position at Lincoln Square Synagogue, one of the premiere cantorial jobs in New York. Indeed, it is one of only a handful of cantorial jobs in an Orthodox synagogue in the city with the largest Jewish population in America. It goes without saying for Yanky that he can only seek employment in an Orthodox synagogue; Modern Orthodoxy represents the furthest "left" that is within the realm of possibility for a Hasidic cantorial revivalist to associate with.

Shulem's path in music was also shaped by the experiences of their shared home life but it has led in a different direction from that of his brother. After initially rejecting his father's tastes as out of date and oppressive, Shulem came to appreciate his father's musical interests. He was guided by his brother in studying cantorial music and eventually took over Yanky's High Holiday cantorial job at Congregation Ahavath Torah, a Modern Orthodox Synagogue in Englewood, New Jersey, after Yanky was hired at Lincoln Square. At the same time as he was following in Yanky's cantorial footsteps, Shulem was also pursuing a career in the world of Orthodox choirs. In comparison to the cantorial scene, which is characterized by its marginality to contemporary musical tastes, the Orthodox choir scene is a popular and commercially vibrant musical scene, with ample opportunities for performance and a robust online presence. Shulem's rise to success as a pop singer was initially dependent on his brother's tutelage but it expanded steadily thanks to the varied and rich opportunities offered by the world of Orthodox pop.

> When I was a teenager, fourteen, fifteen, I still had a kid's voice. And Yanky actually knew someone that was recording an album in Borough Park. And he was like, I'm looking for this kid. Hey, you know what, my brother, maybe you can try him out. And we went to the studio that night, and we ended up recording three songs. One thing led to another . . . we did another album. When I was in Israel, I went to study [in a yeshivah] . . . I got my knowledge and professional training in Israel singing in these adult choirs, backing up the greatest singers in the Hasidic world. And then I got back to Brooklyn. I joined the highly acclaimed Shira Choir . . . One thing led to another and I'm the soloist there. And I met my producer Yochi Briskman. And he's like, OK let's go. You've got a full solo career here. Check out the things on YouTube. We covered from cantorial music all the way to today's Hasidic pop music. And we actually released an album, [titled] Shulem . . . And yeah, since then we've been all over the world performing. (Shulem Lemmer, January 31, 2018)

As Shulem explains, the limitations of the Orthodox pop market are also its affordances. Shulem told me:

> At the end of the day when you decide you want to become a singer, you already have twenty, thirty thousand fans right away because it's such a closed community. And this is worldwide within the Hasidic community. So, you have in Israel, and in London and in Brooklyn, obviously. Antwerp. The whole New York State, Muncie.

Shulem's career encompasses cantorial prayer leading, working as a soloist working with Hasidic choirs, recording and performing as a singer in the Orthodox pop scene, and most recently a star turn as a crossover vocal artist signed to Decca Gold, a mainstream major record label. This final career move provoked a great deal of attention in the media. Shulem is the first Hasidic pop singer to be signed to a major label. His 2019 major label debut, *The Perfect Dream*, featured show tunes and light pop songs, mostly in English. Only three of the album tracks bear a specifically Jewish profile, the Max Janowski setting of "Avinu Malkeinu," made famous by Barbara Streisand; the old standby of mid-century Israeli music, "Jerusalem of Gold"; and the Passover song "Chad Gadyo," which was a viral video sensation for Shulem in his Hasidic choir period.

Despite its appeal to a mainstream market, there is no suggestion that the album would push in opposition to expressions of piety and communal ideals that are typical of Orthodox pop. From a musical perspective, the album is similar to his previous recorded output, but with higher production values—for example, a string orchestra is featured, instead of the more typical Orthodox pop synthesizer accompaniment. In fact, one of the show tunes Shulem sings, "Bring Him Home," from *Les Miserables*, is sometimes sung as a contrafact melody for Mi adir, a prayer from the wedding liturgy, in Orthodox weddings.[10] The songs on the album express gentle sentiments of piety, offering nonspecific prayers for peace and harmony that are in accord with the ethical commitments of Orthodox pop.

While the Orthodox pop music industry has room for a talent and a career path such as Shulem's, Yanky's musical identity fits more jaggedly into this world. As Yanky explains

> There's an industry out there, a Jewish music industry. For me, it's not that much. It's very different for me than it is for Shulem. Shulem has a producer. Shulem's doing a lot of new music. His album is almost completely new music. He does weddings, he does a lot of musical stuff. I do a lot of *hazzanut*.[11] But the stuff I do, personally, is mostly either just *davennings* [Yinglish, prayer-leading services]; I lead the services a lot, and I get called around the world mostly to do cultural events . . . For me this is the trajectory. I don't see any huge spikes or anything. I'm just gonna be doing my thing. But I am working. The stuff I'm working on is much more for personal artistic gratification than anything else . . . I think for Shulem the future is a lot more exciting. For me it's exciting that I'm preserving something old and I feel very good about that. And hopefully I can inspire others. For Shulem it's a lot more exciting . . .
> (Yanky Lemmer)

The decisions the Lemmer brothers have made that have led to their distinct career paths involve questions of aesthetics, commerce, the maintenance of reputation, and issues of piety. Yanky believes in the unique aesthetic powers of khazones. He believes that khazones has a unique ability to act on the bodies of listeners to elicit experiences of prayerful feeling. This belief is not abstract; it is based in his own experience of being transported by the sound of hearing elder cantors perform or by listening to old records. Yanky specifically compares the capacities of khazones to act on the body of the listener to the pop sounds of "normal music" in his community, as well as to the musical choices his brother Shulem has made:

> I can almost guarantee you he doesn't get goose bumps from the stuff he sings now. But I can tell you when we work on certain things in concerts, he does. It's the same with me. I also enjoy singing certain things [i.e., pop songs]. I'm moving away from it simply because there comes a point when you have to define what you do. I enjoy singing regular stuff as well. But the stuff that moves me, that really moves me, is khazones. (Yanky Lemmer, July 16, 2019)

From a commercial perspective, Yanky is one of the most successful Hasidic cantorial revivalists. He is one of a few for whom the pursuit of excellence in khazones is profitable. In addition to his prestigious pulpit position, he regularly performs on international concert stages, especially in Poland and Israel, the two largest markets for Jewish music outside the United States. Despite these enviable markers of success, Yanky is keenly aware of the commercial limitations of his career. He has chosen khazones, and despite occasional gestures in the direction of pop music,[12] his lot is cast, a decision that he is proud of but at times expresses melancholy over. He described his feelings:

> You have to be willing to be a martyr. Because you may be successful, you may not be, because the market is so small. Especially I'm talking from an Orthodox perspective only. From the Orthodox perspective there's a tiny market. Not many concerts. Handful a year . . . And it's not easy. Look at my brother Shulem. He kind of tinkered with both. And he's being sucked into this singing thing. Probably rightfully so. It's just economically so much more rewarding. (Yanky Lemmer)

Yanky is an energetic and charismatic performer; yet in moments of reflection on the limitations of his career and his chosen musical field, he strikes a somber note, inflected by a century of cantorial discourse that has steadily prophesied imminent doom. Already in 1924, critics foretold a bleak future for khazones, in part because of what conservative voices in the community considered to be the lack of consistent piety and ethical comportment by cantors.[13] In the decades after World War II the American cantorate remade itself as a unionized workforce with new cantors trained in seminary-based conservatories.[14] Despite unparalleled economic resources, cantors told themselves a story dominated by a decline narrative centered on the changing tastes of Jews and their lack of comprehension of cantorial art.[15] Yanky's sense of scarcity and the commercial limitations of cantorial music is shaped by his own experience but is reinforced by the lachrymose narrative propounded by professional cantors—and it withstands evidence from his own career that suggest broader audiences for his work might in fact exist.

The accusation of improper personal comportment and attacks on the reputations of cantors in the golden age of gramophone record stars continues to resonate in the life of Hasidic cantorial revivalists today. Yanky's remarkable vocal talent has led to opportunities for performance outside the synagogue. These opportunities have been criticized and, in some cases, stymied by conservative voices in his community. Sometimes critiques of the appropriateness of the outlets of his career have stemmed from members of his own family; sometimes they come from Yanky himself.

Opportunities to perform within the Belz Hasidic community are almost non-existent. Yanky has said that he believes the Belz rebbe is aware of his talent and career. He imagines the rebbe's attitude toward him as "a love-hate relationship. He can't approve of what I do. Singing for mixed crowds. That kind of thing." Yanky's performance career is focused outside the community, and it frequently extends to audiences of secular Jews (and sometimes non-Jews) in venues that embrace standard concert practices of mixed gender audiences, as opposed to the gender segregation that is normative at public events in the Hasidic community. Yanky's imagined relationship to the Belz rebbe may in part be based on his actual relationship with his father. From the conservative standpoint of his father, even Yanky's position at the Lincoln Square Synagogue is problematic.

Lincoln Square is a Modern Orthodox congregation, and while its leadership is drawn from elite Orthodox yeshivahs, the synagogue's members are "modern" in their style of Judaism, as represented by their integration into American middle-class lifestyles. The most troubling aspect of the congregation, from a conservative contemporary Hasidic perspective, are the steps the synagogue is taking to achieve gender parity, mostly in the form of all-women prayer groups in which women play a leadership role. Maintaining traditional gender roles and male authority in the area of religious practice is a pressing concern for rabbinic leaders and conservative voices in the Hasidic world. Yanky's performance career in contexts of less stringent approaches to gender separation has led to criticism. Members of the Hasidic community have publicly criticized him in internet chat rooms, exacerbating tensions in his family around issues of appropriate public behavior that have arisen from his career.

In 2018 Yanky received an offer to appear in a major Hollywood film, *The Song of Names*, a Holocaust period drama. In the film Yanky was to make an appearance playing a cantor, singing a song of great importance to the plot that gives the film its title.[16] With this project, Yanky would have an opportunity to reach a mass audience while working on a project memorializing European Jewry, a theme of pivotal importance to his career and musical orientation. Embracing this opportunity would have created a deep challenge for Yanky's identity as a Hasidic Jew. The film was to be the product of the "free-thinking" world, not bounded by the norms of comportment and the limits on behavior and public expression that prevail in the Hasidic community. It even was to include a sex scene, perhaps the most closely guarded boundary to cross into the perceived excesses of the nonreligious world. Ultimately, Yanky rejected the offer, reasoning that "So much can go wrong if I *do* do it. And if I don't do it; OK, it's a missed opportunity. I'm still not 100 percent whole with that decision. But it's the decision."

Yanky's soul searching echoes the issues faced by Yossele Rosenblatt about whether or not to appear on the opera stage and on the silver screen. Yanky faces what is in some ways a more conservative and more powerful Jewish Orthodoxy than Rosenblatt did in the 1920s. For Yanky to step outside the norms of his community could have lasting repercussions for his reputation and his family. In contrast, Shulem seems to have faced no special approbation for his forays into the secular music business. This would appear to stem from a sense that the pop music field that Shulem works in is less problematic than the khazones legacy that Yanky has made his own.

Yanky's personal sense of piety, focused on his connection to khazones and the aesthetics of prayer, is in tension with Hasidic Orthodoxy, which seeks conformity in matters of religious life and public behaviors. Cantorial performance almost inevitably involves communities outside the Hasidic world. Despite (or perhaps because of?) these ruptures of identity boundaries, Yanky imagines khazones as a uniquely powerful means of bridging aesthetic impulses to the experience of Jewish prayer, a music he has referred to as "the most pure form." As a sacrifice toward extending this form of sacred music into the future, he appears to be willing to offer himself as "a martyr." He faces a market characterized by uncertainty and a public that vacillates between indifference, condemnation, and occasional crescendos of accolade. Khazones may fail as a commodity, but its function as an icon of the history of Jewish prayer and as an art form with unique affecting powers is palpable for Yanky and his peers in the scene of Hasidic cantorial revivalists.

2

Learning *Nusakh*

Cultivating Skill and Ideology
in the Cantorial Training Studio

Noah Schall is so old he taught my grandfather. When I visited him in his house in the Five Towns region of Long Island, he regaled me with stories about many generations of cantors, including my grandfather Jacob Konigsberg as a young man. He recalled Konigsberg's vocal talent—"he had some special notes"—words of high praise from a man of strong judgements and decisive musical opinions. He also remembered how my grandfather, a temperamental artist even as a novice cantor, would sometimes yell at *him*, the teacher, for being critical of his singing.

Noah and I would sit together in the small, cramped study in the back of his house, next to an antique upright piano and bookshelves overflowing with Jewish sacred books and cantorial sheet music. Old music manuscripts poured out of carboard boxes. On top of one pile was a handwritten sheet of music from an anonymous cantor in Odessa; the yellowed piece of paper was over one hundred years old. It is in this room where Schall meets with his cantorial students, including several of the participants in my research with Hasidic cantors.

Schall began his career as a cantorial pedagogue when he was still a teenager. He was born in Williamsburg, Brooklyn in 1929, the son of a singer who worked with the legendary Russian-born cantorial composer and choir leader Zeidel Rovner (1856–1943).[1] Rovner's son Elias, also a cantor and composer, taught Schall to read music and was his first music teacher. During his first forays into cantorial pedagogy, Schall would offer his services to up-and-coming cantors who could not read music. His students would bring him sheet music they had bought or otherwise acquired and Schall would teach them how to sing it. At first, he would barter his services for access to unpublished written music by important cantorial

FIGURE 1. Noah Schall. Photo by the author.

composers, copying out pieces by hand and developing the personal library that
was to become an important part of his professional identity.

Over the better part of a century Schall has been training cantors, producing cantorial records, and publishing anthologies of cantorial scores, including
his own prolific output of original compositions.[2] He has taught at all three of

the cantorial training programs associated with the seminaries of the three main branches of American Judaism: Reform, Conservative, and Orthodox. Throughout his career, he has maintained his own private cantorial training studio. He has advised professional cantors, helping some of the best-known artists in the field develop material for concerts and recording, especially Moshe Ganchoff, one of the last European-born "star" cantors working well into the late twentieth century. Rovner and Ganchoff are just two of many legendary figures with whom Schall had deep professional and personal connections.

In his instruction for novice cantors, Schall combines pedagogical knowledge of what a cantor must know in order to function in a professional pulpit position with an aesthetic orientation toward the sound and repertoires of the pre-World-War-II-recorded cantorial legacy. It is this combination of the promise of professionalization and access to the musical world of classic artists and old records that makes Schall an especially appealing teacher for Hasidic singers who aspire to become cantors. Schall offers cantorial revivalists a pedagogy that speaks to their aesthetic; the musical concept he teaches addresses the problems of making the transition between being an interpreter of golden age recorded recitatives and attaining competency in the performance of the full liturgical cycle of synagogue prayer-leading. In this chapter I will explore how the musical ambitions of Hasidic cantorial revivalists intersect with the ideologies of the professional cantorate. Schall's educational offerings help revivalists to negotiate a musical identity for themselves as both artists dedicated to a highly specific aesthetic and cantors who must integrate into a set of professional norms.

THE PROBLEM OF LEARNING

As I discussed in chapter 1, classic cantorial recordings provide the form and substance of the Hasidic cantorial scene, offering aspiring singers a repertoire and a model of idiomatic vocal techniques to be studied and emulated. Being able to sing a recitative learned from a classic record, however, does not involve the same skills as being able to lead a prayer service in cantorial style. To achieve the knowledge required of a pulpit cantor, some manner of formal education is usually required. Each of the cantors I worked with in this study addressed the problem of learning in his own way, putting together a curriculum from a variety of sources, usually including some formal classes, private instruction, and online resources.

Cantorial training involves both a practical issue of how to learn and an ideological question of how to decide which kinds of music are valuable. While the aesthetics of early recordings may be the force behind forming an affective connection to khazones for many Hasidic cantorial revivalists, the need driving cantorial education is synagogue employment. Aspiring cantors need to figure out how to attain skills that will make them appear to synagogue hiring committees as knowledgeable, competent, and worthy of employment. There is a specific body of knowledge that confers professional status on a cantor in the synagogue market-place. The goal of this chapter is to elucidate what constitutes professional cantorial knowledge and to discuss how Hasidic cantorial revivalists go about achieving this knowledge.

The process of attaining professional cantorial knowledge inevitably involves obscuring other musical possibilities. Professional cantorial knowledge has been regulated by cantorial unions and educational institutions since the mid-twentieth century. The goal of these institutions was to streamline the heterogenous body of multiple Ashkenazi liturgical traditions into a consistent body of music. The resultant set of professional musical practices has had the effect of foreshortening the internal diversity of Jewish liturgical sound in favor of musical expression characterized by consistency, coherence, and regulation by institutionally authorized texts. For Hasidic Jews who were enculturated in a ritual practice not led by the professional cantorate and who have immersed themselves in early twentieth-century cantorial styles, attaining professional cantorial knowledge is a special problem. For these singers, professionalization may involve disenchantment from the fantasy of reinhabiting "star" cantorial identities and aesthetic achievements.

The twentieth century saw a shift in the education of Eastern European Ashkenazi cantors from an apprenticeship model to training in accreditation-granting seminary conservatories in the post-World-War-II period.[3] In the biographies of early twentieth-century cantors and other Jewish musicians (especially Yiddish theater performers), a picture emerges of an apprenticeship system for learning to be a cantor. Young boys, often from impoverished economic backgrounds, would be farmed out as live-in choral accompanists to cantors at a young age, becoming a *meshoyrer* (Yiddish, cantorial choir singer; plural *meshoyrerim*). Meshoyrerim would learn the cantorial repertoire over a period of years while serving in a professional capacity, a classic example of what education theorist Jean Lave calls legitimate peripheral participation, or learning through labor.[4] Some practices reminiscent of the meshoyrer system were found in the United States in the early decades of the twentieth century and choir singing continues to play a small role in cantorial culture. However, the apprenticeship model of learning mostly disappeared in the aftermath of World War I. The reproduction of cantorial culture was radically disrupted by the dismantling of rural and small-town Jewish life that occurred after the establishment of the Soviet Union, and later the destruction of Jewish European life in the Holocaust.[5]

In the early decades of the twentieth century, most cantors working in the United States were European-born and had learned their trade through the meshoyrer system or from elder relatives.[6] In the years after the immigration restriction of 1924, the cantorial market had more room for American-born singers, creating a demand for new educational models. Cantorial training studios run by individual pedagogues seem to have emerged as an important style of cantorial education starting in the 1920s. Noah Schall was one such teacher, an exception in that he was born in the United States. Other cantorial pedagogues included Louis Lipitz and Shimon Raisen, men who were born in the late nineteenth century in Russia and who had worked as cantors in Europe and the United States.[7] Their pedagogy consisted in part of writing the entire liturgical cycle, adapted to the particular vocal strengths of their voices, for each of their students by hand.

Dyadic lessons created a context in which a teacher could work with a student one-on-one to help them master subtleties of timbre, ornament, and expression that would allow an American-born singer to develop a convincingly "cantorial" vocal approach, from the perspective of an Eastern European-born cantor. Given the centrality of written music for cantors who had not trained as choir singers, gradually being enculturated in the norms of cantorial performance, learning to interpret scores with the appropriate forms of phrasing and ornament took on a special importance. American-born cantors who were trained in this style include Leibele Waldman, Charles Bloch, Sydney Shicoff, and my grandfather, Jacob Konigsberg.[8]

The crisis of continuity posed by the horrors of the Holocaust brought into sharp focus what had long been a goal of the cantorial community: the establishment of a seminary-based conservatory training. In the decade after World War II, the three main denominations of Judaism in America launched cantorial schools at their flagship institutions: the School of Sacred Music at the Reform Hebrew Union College-Jewish Institute of Religion in 1948 (now the Debbie Friedman School of Sacred Music), the Cantors Institute at the Conservative Jewish Theological Seminary in 1951 (now the H. L. Miller Cantorial School), and the Cantorial Training Institute at the Orthodox Yeshiva University in 1954 (now the Belz School of Jewish Music). These three schools are still in operation today, although JTS has only five cantors enrolled in its 2022 cantorial class.[9] When it was first established, the School of Sacred Music at HUC-JIR was intended to be a training program for Jews from Reform, Conservative, and Orthodox communities. Its primary prayer music curriculum is an anthology of prayer melodies composed by Cantor Adolph Katchko that is broadly praised for its beauty and rich idiomatic reflection of cantorial traditions. The Katchko anthology has had an outsized impact on the sound of American synagogue prayer music in the second half of the twentieth century.[10]

Despite the prestigious pedigree within the cantorial community of some of its founders and principal teachers, it would be deeply taboo for a Hasidic man to study at the Reform seminary or at JTS. Some of the Hasidic cantorial revivalists I spoke to were aware of the cantorial school at HUC, spoke admiringly of their curriculum, and are fans of Cantor Jackie Mendelson, one of the senior educators there. The preservation of older forms of cantorial music is a central theme in Mendelson's public persona both as a teacher and as a stage and screen performer. Yet none of the aspiring Hasidic cantors would consider enrolling there. This leaves the Belz School of Jewish Music at YU as the only option for institutional cantorial training open to Hasidic singers. At the time of this writing in 2022, there are no institutions for the study of liturgical music in the Hasidic community.

YU serves as an institution where Hasidic cantorial revivalists can study professional cantorial repertoires, but the school itself represents a form of Orthodox Judaism that is distinct from the norms and lifeways of the Hasidic community. Modern Orthodoxy seeks to adhere to traditional conceptions of Jewish ritual practice based in *halakhah* (Hebrew, religious law) while simultaneously making room for Jewish people to interact with the "modern" non-Jewish world in their professional lives and some aspects of their social experience. For Hasidic Jews, Modern Orthodox Judaism acts as a middle ground that allows them to interact with aspects of the non-Jewish world. For some areas of study related to professional life, Hasidic Jews may find it expedient to study in institutions such as YU. It is worth emphasizing here that khazones is among the "worldly" areas of learning that Hasidic Jews must look outside their birth community to access.

The Belz School of Jewish Music at YU offers a similar form of pedagogy to HUC and JTS, emphasizing a version of prayer melodies that was standardized in the mid-twentieth century and that positions knowledge of this musical tradition as definitive for cantorial competence.[11] However, the Belz School is not aligned with a cantorial union that offers employment assistance to its members, as do its Conservative and Reform counterparts. Studying cantorial arts at the Belz School does not function as a conduit to employment. This is because few Orthodox synagogues today employ a professional cantor. In part because the school does not hold out a goal of professionalization for its students, the training offered at the Belz School is far less comprehensive than what is offered at the liberal movement cantorial seminaries. The Hasidic cantorial revivalists I spoke to who had taken classes at YU appreciated the experience, but they were aware of the limitations of the program, seeing it as one of a number of avenues to pursue rather than a final destination in their training. Aryeh Leib Hurwitz, a cantor who was born and raised in the Crown Heights Lubavitch community, described the Belz School as offering basic musical training in piano and music theory, which he valued highly, but its classes on prayer leading were "more like a *farbrengen* [Yiddish, social gathering] about khazones. It was more talking about it, discussing it." To attain his desired level of cantorial competency Hurwitz sought training from a variety of sources:

> I started off with some basic recordings of different cantors that just recorded the basic *nusakh* [i.e., commercially released instructional CDs of prayer melodies]. There's one by Dovid Horowitz, Eli Lipsker, and Yossel Weinberg, and Mottel Berkowitz. Those are the four I learnt, and I kind of used a mix of all of them. Eventually I got a little more complex listening to Moshe Ganchoff [1905–97]. There's also, Yankel [Jacob] Koussevitzky [1903–59]. So, he has live davenings [i.e., bootleg recordings of actual prayer services] which are very educational because his davenings, they're not so cantorial, he's more of a bal tefile, but they're beautiful and they're simple and they're *nusakh*. And it's easy to follow. It just gives you good ideas . . . I was the khazn for this program named Destinations [a Chabad outreach program], that was the

name of the program. By them everything is in Ashkenaz [meaning "mainstream" non-Hasidic prayer texts, not the variant used by Hasidic Jews]. So, I had to learn Ashkenaz as well. For that I used Rabbi Lichtenstein, his stuff online. Sometimes it gets confusing because I'm used to one way and now you have to do something different ... I'm glad I did, because now my repertoire is much broader. (Aryeh Leib Hurwitz, interview June 27, 2018)

In this statement describing his education, Aryeh Leib Hurwitz uses the word *nusakh*, a shortened version of the phrase *nusakh hatefilah* (Hebrew, the manner of prayer), to refer to the musical performance of prayer texts. *Nusakh* is used as a term in cantorial discourse to describe the body of melodies and modalities for the chanting of prayers. Online sources were the most prominent part of Hurwitz's training in nusakh. His learning ecology included Hasidic and other Orthodox Jewish prayer leaders who have made instructional albums to teach prayer melodies, as well as bootlegs of golden age cantors recorded during actual prayer services as opposed to commercial records of performance pieces decontextualized from ritual. He also makes mention of the differences in prayer texts between Hasidic and non-Hasidic Ashkenazi Jews, an important piece of liturgical code-switching that must be studied in order to move fluidly between different Orthodox Jewish communities. Finally, Hurwitz references how he put these resources to use in a modest cantorial job that served as a practicum where he could test his knowledge and develop his skill in the context of labor, the ultimate goal of his self-directed curriculum.

CULTURAL MEMORY
AND THE IDEOLOGY OF NUSAKH

In an oft-repeated cantorial truism, it is said that a knowledgeable Jew should be able to walk into a synagogue and know the time of day (morning, afternoon, or night), the time of week (whether it be Sabbath or weekday), and the season of the year (according to the seasonal festival being observed) simply from the melodies being sung. An association of time with sound, represented by a set repertoire of melodies and modalities for the different prayer services, is a cornerstone of cantorial professional knowledge. Training in the melodic forms for the different services is one of the key concerns of cantorial pedagogy.

Cantors place great stock in the conception of there being a *correct* nusakh for each element of the liturgy. How the ideology of nusakh functions, and how Hasidic cantorial revivalists interact with this ideology, are the subjects of this section. The conception of nusakh currently adhered to by seminary-trained cantors emerged in the mid-twentieth century and was constructed by an American cantorate concerned with standardizing professional knowledge and institutionalizing the trade. The professional cantorial nusakh is a distinctive body of music, characterized by its privileging of textual sources over aurality as the basis for defining correct performance. Cantorial nusakh is stylistically distinct from the forms of prayer sound heard on old liturgical records, as well as from the prayer music of the Hasidic community.

For Hasidic singers who are interested in gramophone-era cantorial music and who were enculturated in localized Hasidic prayer practices, learning the body of professional cantorial prayer-leading melodies is a challenge. Learning cantorial nusakh is a required step on the path from being an interpreter of old recorded cantorial recitatives to a musical expert with the requisite knowledge to qualify for synagogue employment outside the Hasidic community. Working outside their birth community is the only option for Hasidic cantorial revivalists seeking to professionalize because Hasidic synagogues as a rule do not hire professional cantors.

The term *nusakh* has a textual origin. Before being adopted to describe synagogue music, the word "nusakh" was used in the context of discussions of liturgy to connote variations in texts used for the statutory prayer services, usually based in community affiliation and geographic origin. Within the world of Eastern Europe Jews, *nusakh Ashkenaz* and *nusakh Sefard* commonly refer to the division between the "standard" prayer text used by European Jews that was mostly fixed by the seventeenth century, called the Ashkenaz liturgy, and the variant embraced by Hasidic Jews in the eighteenth century, influenced by the Kabbalistic rabbis of Safed, in Palestine. In a confusing terminological palimpsest, although the Hasidic liturgy is called *Sefard*, in reference to Sephardic Kabbalists, this liturgical variant is distinct from the version of the prayer book that is used by Sephardic Jews (i.e., the Jews with roots in the Iberian Peninsula, exiled during the Inquisition in the fifteenth century, and later taking up residence across the Mediterranean world and in other international diasporic locations).

Beginning in the nineteenth century, the cantorate entered a period of modernization, with cantors who worked in urban metropolises creating new repertoires of synagogue music that would reflect the changing political status of Jews on the cusp of emancipation and the aspirations of Jews to participate in the social and economic life of their non-Jewish neighbors. The new synagogue music, epitomized by the work of Viennese cantor and composer Salomon Sulzer (1804–90), was characterized by a Romantic choral style that reflected the musical trends of Western art music and church hymns. To reflect the difference between new and old repertoires, a variety of terms came into use to describe the musical traditions used for chanting prayers that predated the new compositional styles. Yiddish terms such as *skarbove* (sacred), *gust* (mode), and *ur alte* (ancient) circulated in essays written by cantors and as instructions on the pages of cantorial music anthologies to describe what was understood to be an older Jewish music of prayer.[12]

The nineteenth century saw an explosion of cantorial publication, embracing both new compositions of synagogue music and transcriptions of older prayer melodies, often in the same volume of the personal repertoire of a specific cantor. In 1859, Hirsch Weintraub (1811–1881) published *Schire beth Adonai*, a three-volume anthology of his music.[13] The first two volumes contained his personal compositions in the contemporary choral style, while the third volume was devoted to the music of his father Solomon Weintraub (1781–1829), a legendary figure in Polish-Jewish music.[14] The transcriptions of this older body of music document a highly florid, nonmetered melismatic vocal style that foreshadows the sound of gramophone-era cantors. It is stylistically distinct from the "rational" art music approach to choral cantorial composition of the period. One of the best-known cantorial anthologies, Abraham Baer's *Baal t'fillah oder Der practische Vorbeter*, published in Gothenburg in 1877, is notable for including multiple musical variants for the same element of the prayer texts, labeling some melodies as stemming from Polish or German traditions. Baer's pioneering work indicates an awareness that musical traditions of Jewish prayer were multiple and contingent upon regional stylistic variations.[15] These are just a few of the better-known examples that established the field of published Jewish liturgical music and laid the foundation for the standardization and professionalization of cantorial practice that was achieved in a more consistent form in the twentieth century.

In the context of the mass immigration of Eastern European Jews to the United States (ca. 1880–1924), some cantors were able to establish themselves as star performers, mirroring developments in the major metropolises of Europe. Cantors created identities as popular performers in concert, on record, and sometimes in films. The stylistic trappings of star performance were also heard in the synagogue. Cantors leveraged the format of the lengthy Sabbath morning and holiday services as sacred concerts that would feature a potpourri of styles and approaches, including nineteenth-century choral repertoire, as well as the partly improvised virtuoso recitative, an emotional focal point of prayer leading that was valued for its ability to elicit tears from the listening congregation.[16] Having a unique and affecting repertoire for prayer leading was a requirement for cantors who were in competition for a limited number of positions. A culture of competition and athletic vocal talent was ascendant in the American cantorial scene of the 1920s, the period of the cantorate most represented on commercial records.[17] Despite their innovative musical approaches and public profiles as composers, cantors seem to have been valued in part because they were understood to represent a connection to the Jewish past. To an extent, cantors seem to have shared a commonly held body of prayer melodies for key elements of the liturgy, albeit in variants reflecting regionalisms and creative license.[18]

The term *nusakh* was used by cantors writing in Yiddish to connote musical traditions at least as early as the 1930s but was brought into its current prevalent use as a musical term by cantors in the mid-twentieth century.[19] The term is associated with the work of Abraham Binder (1895–1966), a key Jewish musical ideologue and one of the founders of the School of Sacred Music at HUC. The frequent use of the term *nusakh* in publications and in pedagogical materials for cantors helped establish the sense of an intellectual lineage that would cement the connection of brand-new repertoires and institutions to the European heritage and the "timelessness" of Jewish prayer music. At the same time, the music of Binder and other mid-twentieth-century Jewish synagogue composers sought to establish boundaries of taste and decorum that would map onto the aspirations for dignity and middle-class identity that were key elements in the developing Jewish community.[20]

Working in opposition to the heterogeneity and flamboyance of the star cantors and their focus on individualistic approaches to prayer leading, the cantorial training programs founded after World War II focused on training singers who would be knowledgeable in a uniform body of prayer music. Professional cantors were to be responsible for upholding a recognizable musical tradition. Their prayers would be expected to adhere to an ideal of decorum in the synagogue.[21] Pulpit cantors would perform a body of prayer music that fit with the emerging status of Jews as middle-class participants in American life. The cantorial training programs were helmed by cantors such as Binder and Israel Goldfarb who sought to establish an approach to prayer music that would meet the needs of the changing Ashkenazi Jewish populace that was increasingly confident in its "American" identity and less attracted to or familiar with the sounds and language of their European-born parents' generation.

The founders of the Cantors Assembly (CA), established in 1947 as a union for cantors in the Conservative movement, rejected the figure of the star cantor and the dramatic virtuoso style of the immigrant era.[22] In exchange for the instability of the charisma-based approach of the cantorial market in its early period, the CA successfully advocated to institutionalize salary norms and job placement for cantors in the growth market of suburban synagogues. The golden age cantorial style, while still extolled for its beauty and authenticity, was castigated as a relic of the past, even as key figures in the style were still living and enjoying successful careers. Instead of the stylistic heterogeneity of cantors in the immigrant era, nusakh was presented as a body of musical knowledge that would represent the Jewish past in a purified form.

At a 1951 Cantors Assembly convention in New York, Cantor Merrill Fisher offered an opinion that was perhaps representative of professional cantorial discourse: "It behooves us to offer the most noble and inspiring music in our services. We cannot condone the usage of secular tunes and shades of operatic arias in our services. Let us sing only the tunes that are indigenous to our people, i.e. the nusach."[23] Fisher was one voice in the movement to frame nusakh as a system that could be distilled into a singular body of musical knowledge. This rational approach to prayer music was well-suited as the foundation for curriculum, standardized knowledge that could be assessed, and the basis for a professional labor force.

The first generation of cantors trained in the cantorial seminary schools were the children of the immigrant generation; their aesthetics resonated with the styles of European cantors and their competence was usually expected to include idiomatic vocal approaches consistent with the practices of the gramophone era style. In the second generation, a shift was in progress toward musical scores as the paradigmatic source of prayer knowledge. Musicologist Boaz Tarsi has described the Katchko anthology, used as a standard curricular material at HUC, as constituting a "nusakh America" because of the prevalence of its melodies in synagogue practice. Mark Slobin's fieldwork with cantors in the 1980s shows consistency in the nusakh "improvisations" of cantors, revealing the stamp of conservatory training in creating a uniform approach to prayer chant. In his ethnography conducted at the School of Sacred Music at HUC in the early 2000s, Judah Cohen found slippage back into the textual meaning of the term *nusakh*, with some students identifying the term completely with mid-century cantorial anthologies they learned from.[24]

Noah Schall teaches his own unique conception of nusakh that encompasses a body of melodies and a motivic approach to improvisation. His style represents an ornate and sophisticated variant of the music taught in cantorial conservatories and adhered to by most professional cantors. In its attention to detail, variation, and differentiation of the melodic structure for each of the different prayer services, Schall's approach is exemplary of the ideology of nusakh—it is an arcane body of knowledge that requires professional skill to execute. The work he has produced is recognized and revered by a broad range of cantors and is held up as a marker of authenticity. Schall himself is often invoked by his students as a totem to prove their connection to tradition.[25]

Schall's work is one node in a lineage of cantors seeking to establish and stabilize a *cultural memory* of Jewish music. Cultural memory, a term associated with historians Jan and Aleida Assman, refers to the ways in which publicly held knowledge is structured through texts, monuments, and institutionalized practices. Canons and traditions are established by authorities, conferring validity on hierarchical social structures that control access to central texts and their interpretation.[26] Like Maurice Halbwachs's "collective memory," or Erving Goffman's "frames" for the analysis of behavior, the concept of cultural memory suggests a method for exploring the ways in which knowledge is structured by texts and social norms. Cultural memory offers a framework for attending to the ways in which tradition is shaped by authority.[27] The successful establishment of a cultural memory simultaneously preserves and destroys. It codifies elements of tradition, and it excludes others, in the process conferring authority on experts in the realms of officially legitimated fields of knowledge.

In post-World War II United States, the cantorate organized to control memory by creating textbook anthologies for the training of cantors in seminary conservatories. Learning the codified form of Jewish sacred music taught in cantorial schools and graduating as an accredited cantor was a mandatory step for employment in the expanding market of Conservative and Reform synagogues, further consolidating the legitimating power of institutions. Foundational figures in the establishment of the American postwar cantorate, such as Goldfarb and Binder, worked to shape the cultural memory of Jewish Americans. Their vision of Jewish liturgical music largely bypassed the efflorescence of cantorial creativity during the period of mediatization and popularization of cantors in the first half of the century.

The postwar cantorate focused on honing a consistent standard of competence in leading prayer services (rather than developing the flamboyant, virtuoso soloist approach), cultivating new liturgical song traditions (with an emphasis on metered melodies that could be sung by congregation members in unison), and commissioning new music for the synagogue (typically in prestigious classical music styles but sometimes embracing jazz sounds, an area of innovation that had a long-term impact of opening the synagogue to the influence of American popular music).[28] These priorities reflected assumptions on the part of rabbis and cantorial institutional leaders about acculturated congregation members who were imagined to be less knowledgeable about Jewish religious traditions and uninterested in the immigrant culture of Yiddish-speaking Jews.[29]

Noah Schall fits jaggedly into the postwar scene of cantorial pedagogy because his work is committed to two closely related but fundamentally different legacies: the golden age of khazones and the ideology of nusakh. He is the product of a cantorial family and a community-based music scene that privileged competition, creativity, and a rarified aesthetic concept in cantorial soloist prayer leading. Like other cantors of his generation, Schall seeks to represent a truth about the Jewish collective, filtered through the imagined ethnographic reportage of his own creativity. However, unlike in the realm of cantorial records and star performance careers that were based in the creativity of individual stylists, the ideology of nusakh is predicated on ideals of anonymity and fidelity—a conception of cultural memory that is validated by texts and regulated by institutions. In its post-Holocaust iteration, cantorial knowledge is not supposed to be created; instead, it is figured as a form of preservation and its ethical valence is based in claims to tradition. In discussions of nusakh, cantors use terms like *real, authentic,* and *correct* to describe their knowledge rather than foregrounding their agentic creativity.

My purpose in this discussion is not to question the authenticity of the nusakh taught in cantorial seminaries, or the highly personal version of nusakh that Schall teaches his students. Rather, I am seeking to draw attention to the constructed category of authenticity in regard to Jewish prayer sound. Two centuries of cantorial anthologies, commercial recordings of cantors, and newly released field recordings of prayer leaders made in the Pale of Settlement in 1912–14[30] all attest to the heterogeneity of prayer sounds and melodic forms employed across the realm of Ashkenazi sacred music.[31] Whether the nusakh taught by post-World War II cantors is "real" or "invented" is an emotionally fraught question; the categories of *real* and *invented* have an ethical import related to the cantorial imperative toward memory. Cantors are deeply invested in the idea that contemporary understandings of nusakh are a form of fidelity to the lifeways of pre-Holocaust European Jews. Critical analysis of the sources of nusakh seems to be in tension with the faith and investment in the reality of nusakh that is demanded of cantors by their educational processes.

In multiple discussions with cantors across a variety of generational cohorts and professional communities, I have been consistently surprised by the lack of knowledge about the provenance of their musical corpus. Anecdotally, cantors seem to be broadly accepting of the idea that the prayer music they call nusakh is a musical tradition with a lineage stretching into the anonymous folkloric past. With a few significant exceptions, published works that offer a theoretical analysis of synagogue "prayer modes" in general take cantorial anthologies at face value as a neutral source of traditional knowledge, rather than critically engaging their contexts and ideologies.[32] The work of analyzing how and why mid-century cantors made the decisions they did in constructing the body of professional nusakh has been indefinitely deferred. The reticence to train a critical lens on the concept of nusakh seems to stem in part from the sedimented norms of cantorial culture and its claims to authentically access a singular truth. The idea of a singular "correct" nusakh for prayer recitation is clearly ahistorical. Yet this conception has a staying power because of its usefulness as the source of both a coherent musical language and a professional identity.

Schall follows the trend in American cantorial pedagogy and effaces his role as composer in his presentation of nusakh to his students. In an inversion of the Romantic conception of heroic creativity as a source of spiritual and aesthetic authority, for cantorial educators, impartiality as a conduit of tradition is upheld as an ideal. The erudite cantorial expert, in this post-Holocaust paradigm, is a kind of empty vessel, transmitting a sacred knowledge that has its basis in the anonymous past or in the achievements of the legendary cantors of Eastern Europe. This personified anonymity, in which the creative individual subsumes their identity into a folkloric anonymity, is perhaps influenced by rabbinic tendencies toward pseudopigraphy. In numerous classic rabbinic texts, authorial voice is ventriloquized through the figure of a revered figure in the past; in some cases, innovative religious thought is ascribed to hidden traditions that are revealed through the intercession of an angel or spirit.[33] In cantorial education, appeals to cultural memory, rather than individual artistry, are a technique for creating a sense of continuity.

For Hasidic singers who are interested in becoming cantors, accessing the professional knowledge of cantorial nusakh is a pressing concern. Learning the professional cantorial nusakh can present additional challenges for Hasidic Jews because the cantorial version of the prayer melodies is distinct from what is sung in most Hasidic synagogues. Many of the basic musical structures are different from what would be heard sung by a bal tefile in Hasidic contexts. Finding resources to learn the melodies is an initial challenge; figuring out how to integrate cantorial nusakh with the sounds of khazones learned from old records poses an additional problem that is unique to a revivalist musical orientation. Toward this goal of professionalization *and* integration of stylistic elements of the gramophone-era cantors into prayer leading, some Hasidic cantorial revivalists turn to Noah Schall.

THE CANTORIAL TRAINING STUDIO AND THE LEARNING ECOLOGY OF HASIDIC CANTORIAL REVIVALISTS

Noah Schall provides a powerful resource for unlocking the professional and aesthetic goals of Hasidic cantorial revivalists. Schall is a maverick figure who works with Jewish liturgical musicians across denominational lines—while he himself identifies as Orthodox, his students are drawn from multiple communities. His long career and his vaunted musical gifts help him transcend denominationalism to achieve a near universal status as a revered teacher of nusakh.

Schall's tutelage aligns with the goals of Hasidic aspiring cantors along three primary lines:

1. Schall is a universally acknowledged expert in nusakh; the pedigree of being his student, while not bearing the practical significance of a seminary diploma, holds a certain prestige and mystique. What he teaches is recognizable as an authentic representation of tradition to synagogue cantor-hiring committees, which tend to be made up of members of a given community with the most conservative conception of "correct nusakh."
2. Schall teaches a version of nusakh that resonates stylistically with the sounds of golden age cantorial records. His pedagogy embraces a conception of nusakh that is linked to improvisation, creativity, and sensitivity to the multiple forms of Ashkenazi Jewish liturgical music tradition stemming from different geographic, historic, and social conditions. His music emphasizes vocal coloratura and ornament, signatory aspects of phonograph-era khazones that characterize the historically informed performance practices of Hasidic cantorial revivalists.
3. Beyond musical skill, Schall offers his students a socialization in the culture of cantorial music and the role of cantors in synagogue social life. Schall provides this aspect of cantorial education through storytelling, an element of his pedagogic approach that his students have noted to me and that I experienced in my lessons with him as well. Through anecdotes, scandalous gossip, and bracing analysis of the personalities of legendary figures in the music, Schall gives his students a window into how cantors related to their communities.

In what might appear a surprise to outside observers, the education Hasidic cantorial revivalists acquire from Schall in order to prepare for synagogue employment is strikingly similar to elements of the training of their peers at HUC-JIR, the

Reform seminary. Schall worked for many years at HUC and, in conversation with me, cited the Katchko anthologies as being a premiere source for nusakh. As is highlighted in Judah Cohen's ethnography of Reform cantorial training, storytelling and cantorial anecdotes are also key ingredients of the socialization of cantors in liberal movement training programs.[34]

What sets the training of Hasidic cantorial revivalists apart from their Reform peers is its fragmentary and intermittent nature and reduced reliance on the skills of music reading. Hasidic cantorial revivalists typically do not read music, although many acquire a partial ability to read in the course of their burgeoning professional lives. Hasidic cantorial revivalists also differ from Reform cantorial students in a variety of cultural elements, some obvious and others more subtle, including their bilingualism in Yiddish, Orthodox yeshivah education, their enculturation into Hasidic prayer music, and, crucially, their focus on gramophone records as a primary focus of their creative lives and source for their conception of cantorial sound. While both Hasidic and Reform cantors train in the professional cantorial nusakh, the focus of Hasidic cantorial revivalists on listening to old records leads them to develop a set of cantorial vocal techniques rooted in the sound of early twentieth-century performance that distinguish them from cantors of their age cohort, even when they are singing the same musical material.

Noah Schall's private cantorial training studio has been a key element in the education of three of the participants in this study (Yanky Lemmer, Zevi Steiger, and David Babinet); two others studied with Schall indirectly by learning from his students (Shulem Lemmer was trained in part by his brother Yanky, and Aryeh Leib Hurwitz studied voice with David Babinet); and another cantor studied with Schall in preparation for a special service he led as a guest cantor at a prestigious synagogue (Zev Muller).

Toward the goal of elucidating the process of learning for Schall's Hasidic students, in this section I will offer a sketch of the *learning ecology* of two of his students, Yanky Lemmer and Zevi Steiger. The concept of the learning ecology takes into account multiple experiences that complement each other, analyzing education as a process that takes place in a variety of sites and social contexts that are not restricted to formal learning settings.[35] For Hasidic cantorial revivalists, the learning ecology must take into account family enculturation, the sonic world of Hasidic prayer houses, Orthodox pop, and cantorial records, among other sources. The self-consciously educational experiences of online learning resources, seminary classrooms, and private lessons are pivotal points of musical education, but they are informed by the entirety of the ecology of sound, music, language, and religious education that have occurred over the course of the learner's life.

Yanky Lemmer's biographical outline is already familiar to the reader from interlude A: he began his cantorial soloist career with a concert performance in 2007 at Young Israel Beth El, a synagogue in Borough Park, Brooklyn, where he was a singer in the choir of Cantor Benzion Miller. Lemmer points to a YouTube video he posted of him singing at this concert as the starting point in building a star reputation that resulted in invitations to sing in concerts and lead services at prestigious synagogues.

> I sang one piece, it went up on YouTube and all of a sudden, I get these requests, gigs here, gigs there and I was so not ready for it. So, I keep saying this, my career grew much faster than my education . . . It's good and bad at the same time.

Lemmer took classes at the Belz School and was directed by instructors there to the cantorial training studio of Noah Schall.

> I called Noyakh [Yiddish, Noah] Schall. I want to learn some nusakh. [*Imitating Noah's voice*] *What do you need it for?* 'Cause I want to learn some khazones. *It's dead!* [*Chuckles.*] That's Noyakh, you know. But I was persistent. I said, it might be dead, but I want to go hang out with the dead. Fine [*laughs*].

Lemmer described his classes as lengthy experiences, heavy on conversation.

> It was a lot of *schmoozing* [Yinglish, chatting]. I won't sugar coat that in any way, but that's part of the learning process in my opinion. It's like he had seven hundred anecdotes of every khazn that you have to know before you know the piece. And he would tell you about all of these quirks of the khazanim of the golden age. And it was very interesting. But then he would say, "OK here's a sheet. Let me write out the Dorian mode for you. OK practice that."

Lemmer's training was cushioned in the sociality of conversations about cantors, delivered in Schall's characteristic unsanctimonious style. He came to Schall with a bifurcated profile as a musician, lacking many basic musical skills, but extremely advanced in his knowledge of cantorial performance repertoire and vocal techniques he had learnt from old records. Conversation functioned, perhaps, as an enticement, offering a view into the world that the fledgling cantor could access through the more laborious aspects of learning, like scale singing.

Listening to Lemmer's prayer leading in synagogue, I could recognize characteristics of Schall's style. One significant example is the use of preparatory motifs in what cantors refer to as "*freygish,*" a Yiddish variant on the musical term Phrygian, used to describe a major-sounding pitch group with a characteristic augmented second interval. Schall emphasizes a style of florid mode mixing in the area of the fifth below the tonic, an area of motivic variation heard in some of the best-known cantorial records, such as the opening of Yossele Rosenblatt's *Hinenee heone* (1926) or Israel Schorr's *Yehi Rotzon Sheyibone Beis-Hamikdosh* (1927). I have heard Lemmer and other Schall students use this type of phrase as the basis for brilliant vocal effects in their prayer leading. Emphasizing exquisite, detailed motifs that ornament and punctuate the prayer melodies allows Schall's students to engage their special cantorial techniques of coloratura, ornament, and distinctive timbre sequence. Schall's personal vocabulary of musical elements offer Hasidic cantorial revivalists ideas about how to interpolate riffs and ideas they already have at the ready from their study of old records into their performance of the professional nusakh.

Zevi Steiger, another of Schall's students, was born and raised in the Hasidic community of Antwerp. Although his family was Lubavitch, because of the small and tight-knit nature of the Hasidic community there, he grew up familiar with the prayer customs of numerous Hasidic sects. He and his father also occasionally visited the Great Synagogue, where Cantor Benjamin Muller presided over services. Steiger briefly took lessons with Cantor Muller to learn a cantorial recitative, Yossele Rosenblatt's *Tal* (1923), as a performance piece to sing at his older brother's bar mitzvah. As a teenager, Steiger became a devotee of classic cantorial records. He spent numerous years studying and later working in international Lubavitch yeshivahs, including periods in England, France, and South Africa, before settling in Crown Heights, Brooklyn, the center of the Lubavitch world. Throughout his yeshivah years, Steiger found small cohorts of friends who shared his interest in khazones with whom he would listen and who he would perform for in an informal manner. Steiger and a friend began visiting Schall together after hearing about him from an older Lubavitch cantor, Levi Kaplan. Steiger found Schall at first to be discouraging.

> I would look a lot for approval from him. I would want him to say, you have a great voice, you should go into this. But he was very pessimistic about khazones. In general, he wasn't a guy who was into compliments . . . He was like, you want to get better this is what you do. He didn't take me as serious at first. He was like, what do you need me for? Go to Moshe Teleshevsky [*laughs*]. He said that to me . . .

As noted in chapter 1, Moshe Teleshevsky (1927–2012) was perhaps the best-known cantor in the Brooklyn Lubavitch community; Schall was denigrating him as a representative of the putatively simpler approach to prayer music.[36] Schall seems to have been trying to discourage Steiger by suggesting to him that he stay within the musical parameters of his community rather than trying to master the more technically challenging and, from Schall's perspective, more aesthetically advanced style of khazones.

Schall demanded that Steiger abandon the melodies he learned in prayer contexts throughout his life and build a new musical basis for prayer leading.

> Then you can learn how to improvise, but if you don't have a base . . . this was like two years into my studies with him [*laughs*]. *You don't have a base. You don't even know nusakh.* He kind of thought, which is kind of true, I'm just parroting, I'm just copying what I heard as a child, and I didn't really understand it [cantorial nusakh].

Ultimately, Schall did teach Steiger skills relating to ornamentation and variation.

> He asked me to say *Shokhein ad* [the beginning of the *Shakhris* Sabbath morning service], so I did a *Shokhein ad*, I did the whole thing. And he basically went through an

entire *Shakhris*. It sounded basic, but it's not basic. And then we learned to embellish a little bit. My basis is on that, pretty much every week.

Throughout the years when Steiger was studying with Schall, he was employed as a cantor at the Southampton Jewish Center, a Chabad house in an affluent area on Long Island. Through connections in his community, Steiger met a rabbi with an affinity for cantorial music who hired him as a regular cantor to lead services every Shabbos. This is an unusual arrangement for a Chabad house and it provided Steiger with a practicum enabling to put his lessons with Schall into practice in the context of labor. Such situations are an element of education that are of great value to novice cantors but are extremely difficult to find. In his prayer leading at Southampton, Steiger employs melodic variations, ornamentation, and coloratura in his execution of the nusakh melodies, in a manner that is characteristic of Schall's style.

STORYTELLING AS CULTURAL PEDAGOGY

Noah Schall's stories communicate intangible cultural knowledge about what it is like to be a cantor, or what it was like in previous generations. His stories frequently focus on the eccentricities of cantors and how their outsider behaviors emerged in moments of friction with the broader Jewish community, often with a comic or satiric intent that ridiculed the sanctimony of Jewish community leaders, or the outrageous "star" personas of the cantors, or both. A sampling of anecdotes from my conversations with him included:

1. A story about the sexual profligacy of Mordechai Hershman (1888–1940), a cantor with an international performance career and one of the key recording stars of the gramophone era. Once, when Hershman was interviewing for a cantorial position, he went to visit the community's rabbi in his bedroom. The rabbi was ill at the time and was lying in bed. Hershman introduced himself with one name, assuming the rabbi would know all about him. The rabbi did indeed know about him but was focused on his reputation as an irreverent rule-breaker rather than his music. "Oh, it's Hershman, we can't have him." The punch line of the story is Hershman saying, "It's the first time anyone ever said 'no' to me in bed."
2. An anecdote about a visit Schall payed to the famed Samuel Malavsky (1894–1983), in his later years. Malavsky was a protégé of Yossele Rosenblatt and the leader of a family choir that became one of the most popular acts in Jewish American music in the 1950s. In his later years, Malavsky became alienated from Judaism because of his anger over the disrespect that had been directed at his daughters, especially Goldie Malavsky, a brilliant cantor whom he had groomed as his successor but who could not gain employment

as a cantor because of the gender rules of the synagogue. Malavsky would no longer go to pray in a synagogue. Schall asked Malavsky, "But how do you say *Kadish* [the mourner's prayer]?" Malavsky pointed to a small pond near his house and answered, "I say Kadish with the ducks."

3. A story about Leib Glantz (1898–1964), a major recording star and an ideologue who wrote extensively about Jewish music, leading a service at a synagogue on the Lower East Side of Manhattan. A packed synagogue awaited the star cantor. Glantz preceded the service with a lecture on Jewish music, in which he made claims about the pentatonic scale being the basis for all Jewish music. After this unexpected start, Glantz launched into a version of the service that was so strange, so astringently modernist to the ears of the assembled Jews, who had clear expectations about what a cantorial prayer service would sound like, that the synagogue began to empty out. The punchline of the story is, "By the end of the service, they barely had a *minyan*" (the required minimum of ten needed to conduct a prayer service).

These stories share in common a perspective that accentuates cantors' sensuality, outsider perspectives on spiritual life, and eccentric artistic behaviors. They humanize legendary figures whose records Schall's students have spent countless hours poring over. With his anecdotes about the stars, Schall intimates to his students something about how cantors fit into their communities, or how they subverted communal norms. Cantors served as an emotional vector in the prayer life of the Jews, offering a desired experience that was of value in attracting people to the experience of prayer. As famous artists, some cantors were allowed a degree of nonconformity, in exchange, as it were, for the emotional labor they caried out on behalf of the community through the affecting powers of their music.

In addition to their beautiful singing, cantors brought some of the energy and enticement of art and performance into the synagogue, allowing Jews to experience their own parallel to the world of the concert hall or the opera. Cantors were entertainers, who brought qualities of excitement to the communities they served. Watching Yanky Lemmer at his job at Lincoln Square, I could see how he embodied some of these qualities of cantorial performance in his interactions with congregants. I noticed that when he was not leading the service, he could deftly switch from prayer leader to charming jokester. I observed Lemmer entertaining his boosters in the community with a light informality as they chatted in the hallways of the services during the parts of the service when he was "on break" (such as the Torah service when scripture is chanted by a member of the community other than the cantor).

During one gossipy conversation with congregants, Lemmer heard some voices in the sanctuary singing "Siman tov umazel tov," a song performed at celebratory life cycle events, apparently in honor of a congregant. Lemmer immediately turned away from his interlocutors and rushed in to sing along and lend his prominent voice so that all would hear the cantor elevating the celebration. One of the men in the chat circle that had formed around the cantor remarked, "He switched characters." Lemmer pedals between his social role as a down-to-earth, charmingly antisanctimonious comrade to his fans in the shul and his official capacity as the ritual functionary who drives the emotional experience of prayer. Yanky's good humored style of behavior with his congregants points to the ways in which the "rule bending" of sanctimony may actually be a needed form of synagogue behavior that is part of the cantor's social role. Social knowledge about how a cantor is supposed to act relates to the worldview of cantorial culture that Schall's cantorial training studio imparts, connecting musical practice with a conception of what kind of a person a cantor can be in the social life of a synagogue.

. . .

Schall's attitude toward his talented young Hasidic students who are interested in khazones bears a degree of ambiguity. Over the course of his lifetime, Schall has watched interest and support for cantorial music wane in material ways that are unmistakable. His overarching sense about the genre is that it is a music without a future. The dedication of a subset of singers to khazones draws into question the single variable equation of the decline narrative shared by Schall and many elder cantors. If there are young performers who are dedicated to the craft, then the music will continue to resound in the present and beyond, even if it is unclear how the musical culture will transform in the absence of synagogue institutions to support it. Schall noted, with perhaps a degree of condescension, that a "Hasid has more chance of sounding like a cantor than an American boy," seeming to draw into question the reality of Hasidic Jews as members of Jewish America, and the relevance of their work with khazones to American Jewish life. In conversations where I asked him about his Hasidic students, he did not seem to me to have reflected more deeply on what needs the music fulfills for them or what possibilities their work might open in the future.

Schall's tutelage provides his students with skills they need to professionalize and gain employment. His version of nusakh adheres to the normative ideology promoted by the cantorial seminaries and is considered valuable by cantorial hiring committees in Modern Orthodox synagogues. His approach to nusakh provides a musical bridge to the sounds and repertoires of the golden age style while simultaneously providing immersion in the professional skill of cantorial nusakh. For Hasidic cantorial revivalists whose primary connection to cantorial music is through gramophone-era recordings, Schall's pedagogy is especially suited to fostering a creative approach to prayer leading that mimics aspects of the concert-like prayer-leading style of cantors in the early to mid-twentieth century.

The stories Schall tells as part of his curriculum about the revered cantorial stars encourage his students to imagine themselves as connected to the social life of the music and to develop habits of synagogue sociality. As artists, a cantor's persona has a quality of doubleness. Cantors are expected, perhaps, to be able to code-switch between registers of piety and play in their bearing with congregants. Schall has successfully trained a handful of Hasidic students to be able to fulfill social and musical roles as pulpit cantors. The question remains as to whether or not there is room in the world of the contemporary American synagogue for the musical skill set these young cantors possess. As I will discuss in the next chapter, the opportunity to perform the role of cantor in the synagogue is rare; it requires cantorial revivalists to make a variety of aesthetic and personal compromises.

3

Cantors at the Pulpit

The Limits of Revivalist Aesthetics

When I first reached out to Yanky Lemmer about visiting Lincoln Square Synagogue, the prestigious Modern Orthodox synagogue where he has held the cantorial pulpit position since 2013, Lemmer warned me that the service would be "light on khazones."

The first time I heard Lemmer at Lincoln Square on a Shabbos morning in 2015, I was struck immediately by the fineness of his tenor voice and the confidence of his coloratura singing. As Lemmer launched into *V'chulam mekablim*, his vocal mannerisms recalled the idiomatic phrasing of gramophone-era cantors. I felt as though I was privileged to hear Mordechai Hershman singing in 1927. The sound of his prayer leading was an uncanny and deeply affecting experience for me. I got choked up listening to him, moved by the powerful timbre of his voice, the wealth of associations conjured by his musical references to classic recordings, and by the vivid sense that his voice offered a musical translation of the Hebrew prayer texts.

I wondered if the other bodies in the room resonated to his voice in the same way that mine did. This question, about the generalizability of my own experience of listening and the emotional response to the prayer leading of cantorial revivalists, is one that troubles me and that I have no evidence from my research to offer certain testimony about. What I have been able to ascertain is that Lemmer does not stay within the musical domain of his khazones expertise during prayer leading, but rather embraces a variety of musical styles over the course of a service. According to Lemmer and other cantors I have spoken to, musical choices they make during prayer leading reflect the reality that their chosen musical genre is not loved or understood and must be limited and substituted with sounds drawn from other styles of music.

As Lemmer reached the *Kedusha*, usually one of the musically marked elements of a cantorial prayer leading service, he launched into a melody that surprised me. The melody he used was a contrafact, a commonly used technique in Jewish liturgical contexts in which a melody from one song is used for a different lyric text. In Jewish prayer leading, contrafacta serve as an opportunity to engage with popular or aesthetically desirable genres in the context of the service. The melody Lemmer used for the Kedusha prayer was taken from Josh Groban's 2003 hit "You Raise Me Up," a song that has remained popular in the adult contemporary category of light radio friendly fare for close to two decades. Rather than being an outlier for an Orthodox cantor to sing this sentimental mainstream pop song, the melody is in fact a popular choice in Orthodox communities and is often sung at weddings, frequently as a contrafact for the prayer text Mi Adir from the marriage ceremony liturgy.[1]

Lemmer's performance of the pop song was impactful and activated his clear and strong upper register. The kinds of ornamentation he used in the song were far removed from cantorial coloratura, showing that he possesses other forms of musical skill. His approach sounded stylistically idiomatic to the source recording, recalling the vocal quality of Groban or pop R&B singers such as Michael Bolton. The stylistic chasm between this rendition of the Kedusha and the V'chulam Mekablim he had sung just minutes earlier outlined the multiple worlds of sound that Lemmer is expected to be able to traverse in his pulpit position. Both "You Raise Me Up" and his finely detailed nusakh, which he had learned from Noah Schall, are showcases for musical skill and register as emotional labor, offering two different conceptions of the kinds of aesthetic that are required of a cantor.

Nusakh-based chant intimates a sense of the cantor as a musical expert who can effectively reference sounds of the Jewish communal past. Improvisatory play with nusakh melodies invokes Jewish heritage through reference to old records of the cantorial golden age and makes room for creativity, within a tightly bounded set of parameters. The contrafact Lemmer sang for the Kedusha sent a different kind of message about the cantor and congregation. Singing pop melodies also presents Lemmer as a musical expert, but one whose domain of knowledge includes contemporary commercial music with no explicit connection to Jewish culture, other than that it is enjoyed by Jewish people. Lemmer's job requires that he be able to channel the musical desires of his congregants and fulfill their urge to participate in the musical life of bourgeois America, even in the particularistic Jewish space of the synagogue. While Yanky's mastery of older forms of Jewish prayer music are considered to be a prerequisite for employment as a cantor, it may in fact be his willingness to embrace pop genres that is key to his success as a pulpit cantor.

The multiple musical competencies demanded of a cantor and a perceived diminished compatibility of nusakh with the musical interests of American Jews have been noted by ethnographers of the American synagogue music for the past four decades. Mark Slobin's research with cantors in the 1980s, focused on

Conservative cantors but with all denominations of American Judaism represented, demonstrated that a generational shift was in progress. The cantors Slobin studied had received a style of training in which nusakh was presented as a complete system for prayer leading. The focus on nusakh in cantorial education was still in the foreground when Judah Cohen undertook his ethnography on the training of Reform cantors in the early 2000s. The cantors in both Slobin and Cohen's research cohorts expressed the sentiment that nusakh was less well understood and appreciated by their congregants than by the cantors themselves. Today, cantors are increasingly focused on song leading in styles of Jewish devotional music that sideline soloist performance. Lay-led prayer leading has become a new norm in many synagogues that previously employed professional cantors.[2] These long-standing trends in the American synagogue are reflected in the musical lives of Hasidic cantorial revivalists and have broad implications for their paths to professionalization and experiences in the synagogue.

In this chapter I offer a series of ethnographic sketches that show how the aspirations and musical individualism of Hasidic cantorial revivalists become entangled with the professional cantorial culture of the United States. The specific parameters of musical and liturgical authority that have emerged in the American cantorate over the course of the twentieth century shape the ways in which the expressiveness of cantorial revivalists can be given presence and voice in the synagogue. Hasidic cantorial revivalists look to the gramophone-era style as an aesthetic with radical possibilities for self-exploration and experimentation. Khazones as a musical genre emerged from the synagogue, but its place in contemporary Jewish institutional life is contested, to say the least. Rather than being a signal point of unleashing of fantasy, talent and education, the synagogue is a place where cantorial revivalist dreams of self-actualization as an artist must be tempered and given new shape. For Hasidic cantorial revivalists, this dynamic is often perceived through the lens of the decline narrative that is prevalent in professional cantorial circles.

Cantor Zevi Muller is the pulpit cantor at the West Side Institutional Synagogue in Manhattan. Muller was born into a non-Hasidic Haredi family in Antwerp. While his family history diverges in some important ways from the other singers profiled in this book, his yeshivah background, self-directed musical education, and personal aesthetic orientation toward the early twentieth-century cantorial style closely mirror the Hasidic cantorial revivalist scene. Muller described the relationship of his congregants to cantorial prayer thus:

> We need to recognize at least for the Modern Orthodox community I would say they don't have that same connection to the nusakh the way I have, I think. It's sad. I want them to have it because it will make them richer. But many of them don't . . . So, the Modern Orthodox, many are walking on a thin line . . . They need a khazn . . . If they would have someone who doesn't know nusakh it would sound strange to them . . . They understand what nusakh is. They know that it's the right

way. They're Orthodox, they're still kind of conservative. They don't want to change those things. But you know when young people come to my shul, they don't know much about nusakh. They know that their khazn needs to know nusakh because it's the proper way, but they don't connect to it emotionally the way I connect to it . . . So, they listen to modern music, you know, rock and roll, or R&B, or reggae, or I don't know what. They have their styles. So, you need to be able to connect. So, pop Jewish music provides some of that connection. Because we live in a world of minor, major songs, simple type of structure.[3]

In my conversations with cantors about their pulpit positions, alienation from synagogue musical norms and the need to negotiate with local tastes were consistent themes. After having spent considerable time and effort developing skills and performance repertoire based in the gramophone-era cantorial style, cantors who are talented, disciplined, and fortunate enough to achieve employment in a synagogue must then learn to access a new set of prayer-leading skills related to the musical conventions of their communities of employment. In this chapter I will discuss the trajectory of musical knowledge cantors must master in their pulpit jobs and the normative synagogue musical styles the cantors encounter when they enter the job market. In the negotiations of musical style and meaning between cantors and the communities they serve, it is the cantors' conception of aesthetics that must compromise and transform.

The learning path of Hasidic cantorial revivalists involves a series of replacements of musical knowledge. Orthodox pop music, the "normal" music of their birth community, is replaced by a passionate interest in old cantorial records, a style considered anachronistic in most sites of contemporary Jewish life. "Hasidic nusakh," the sounds and styles associated with prayer in the Hasidic community, is replaced by the more prestigious "cantorial nusakh," which is considered essential professional knowledge for a cantor seeking synagogue employment. In their careers at the pulpit another stratum is added to the mix, as cantors learn to fulfill the musical desires of their congregants, often by returning to pop music sounds that they rejected at the onset of their musical journey as musically unsophisticated and unsatisfying. These processes of replacement are not unilateral and permanent, but rather form a palimpsest of musical knowledge, in which different periods of a life spent in Jewish music inform each other and inflect manners of performance and habits of musical expression. Even as cantors reject some forms of musical style in favor of others, these musical decisions are not permanent and unalterable.

Not all of the cantors who participated in my research aspired to professional work in synagogues. For some Hasidic cantorial revivalists, studying old records is the end goal of their interest in singing, and recital-type performance, often in informal settings, fulfills their artistic ambitions. For others, a professional pathway in the synagogue is strongly desired. For those bent on professionalization, the primary channel to employment is in Modern Orthodox synagogues. In this chapter, I focus on the work of the small number of Hasidic cantors who are employed to perform regularly in synagogues, and especially at their Sabbath services, which are the bread and butter of a pulpit cantor's work life.

Regular employment for a cantor is extremely rare in the Orthodox world. Many synagogues only hire part-time cantors for the High Holidays, the liturgical apex of the Jewish calendrical cycle with its own specialized liturgy demanding expert musical knowledge that lay members of a synagogue usually are not capable of performing adequately. Paradoxically, the High Holidays, which have the most complex liturgy and which most resemble a theatrical frontal performance, are the job most available to novice cantors. The High Holidays liturgy is usually the facet of liturgy that is studied first, specifically in preparation for a job.

The Orthodox synagogues that do employ a year-round pulpit cantor in the United States are, almost without exception, Modern Orthodox synagogues, not Hasidic or other Haredi synagogues. As Yoel Kohn has described it, "Somehow the Hasidic community has been producing most of them [cantors] nowadays. But the Hasidic community itself does not consume it. It's an exporter of cantors." For some Modern Orthodox synagogues, hiring a cantor is a mark of prestige and is considered an important element of communal life. A cantor from a Hasidic background adds to the self-conception of the community as elite and preservationist of tradition. Modern Orthodoxy has a profile as the most "moderate" branch of contemporary Orthodoxy. Its members generally wear clothing typical of the American bourgeoisie, undertake secondary education in secular universities, and are similar to their non-Jewish peers in terms of consuming "mainstream" popular culture. Yanky Lemmer has suggested to me that this sense of difference between Modern Orthodox and Hasidic Jews leads to Hasidim being perceived as a source of greater Jewish "authenticity."

> Even if we don't sync up 100 percent, like, we're both Jews, we're both Orthodox, we both keep Shabbos, we both keep kosher. Yeah, we're different culturally and frankly they find it fascinating. Like when we have people over for Shabbos dinner sometimes, they're fascinated. *Oh my gosh you had an arranged marriage. What!? You met for forty-five minutes?! We can't believe it.* That kind of thing. But in terms of davening, it's just the opposite, it's actually a plus. Because the nusakh coming from the *khasidishe velt* [Yiddish, Hasidic world] is, and they know this, *is* the nusakh. It's the real deal. In most senses, in most ways.[4]

"Ultra-Orthodox" Jews are often looked to by Jews in more liberal communities to provide religious services, such as kosher certification, scribal skill for writing Torah scrolls, and rulings on matters of *halacha* (Jewish ritual law). In general, these matters of "traditional" expertise are dominated by the religious service providers—communal norms demand that communities accept the rulings of rabbinic experts. In the area of liturgy however, this dynamic is upended. In cantorial performance in the synagogue, it is the "experts" who must become the students of local musical knowledge and liturgical practices.

THE ARCHIVE AND THE REPERTOIRE
OF HASIDIC CANTORS

Performance studies scholar Diana Taylor has described a division between forms of knowledge she refers to as the archive and the repertoire. In this rubric, the repertoire represents forms of knowledge embedded in family and communal life, elements of experience that generate "embodied memory: performances, gestures, orality, movement, dance, singing—in short all those acts usually thought of as ephemeral, nonreproducible knowledge."[5] In contrast, the archive is supported by institutions and encoded in texts that are afforded official forms of respect by power holders. The archive, says Taylor, "works across distance, over time and space . . . What changes over time is the value, relevance, or meaning of the archive, how the items it contains get interpreted, even embodied."[6]

In the context of the musical lives of Hasidic cantorial revivalists, the repertoire can be understood as representing the sounds of Hasidic prayer. The archive in this paradigm would represent the forms of professional cantorial knowledge— both the old commercial records the cantors love and seek to reanimate, and the professional cantorial nusakh that they must master as fledgling professionals. In the process of achieving professionalization, the archive is ascendant over the repertoire of Hasidic prayer knowledge.

The Hasidic *shtibl* is a sonic environment characterized by heterophony and noise. In this site of public prayer, all male participants (men and women are segregated by gender; indeed, public prayer is in general a male undertaking) are expected to recite the entire liturgy of the service being performed. Each praying body is a prayer leader of sorts, generating their own sonic experience. Services in Hasidic synagogues are usually led by nonprofessional singers. Professional bal tefiles are a relatively small group of singers in comparison to the enormous number of prayer houses—usually prayer services are led by nonexperts. In general, bal tefiles have a markedly different vocal sound than that which is usually achieved by the trained voices of professional cantors. Yanky Lemmer refers to the sound of the bal tefiles he heard growing up as "more organic." As a rule, prayer is carried out very quickly in the Hasidic context, in part because of stringent rules that require the recitation of lengthy prayers, encompassing thousands of words of printed Hebrew text, on a daily basis. The requirements of fulfilling the *mitzvah* (Hebrew, commandment) of prayer demands that the texts be chanted quickly. Regularity and repetition engender an intimacy with the prayer book. A complete memorization of the prayer book is common among Hasidic Jews; this gives Hasidic singers a great advantage as they study liturgical music based on these texts.

"Hasidic nusakh," the melodies used in Hasidic prayer, offer a degree of heterogeneity based on sect and sometimes individual family traditions. Different Hasidic groups have localized customs that distinguish them from other groups; in general, the melodies of prayer used by Hasidic Jews differ in multiple ways

FIGURE 2. Yanky Lemmer, "Hasidic Mariv."

from the music that has been propagated by professional cantors in the twentieth century. As Yanky Lemmer notes, "a lot of the *nusakhos* [Hebrew, plural of nusakh] that I grew up with are not exactly the nusakhos that the world has accepted." In this statement, "the world" is a shorthand for non-Hasidic Jews in general, and Modern Orthodox synagogues, such as his place of employment, in particular. As I highlighted in chapter 2, "correcting" Hasidic prayer musical habits and adopting the professional cantorial ideology of a professionalized nusakh as the standard is one of the goals of cantorial training for Hasidic singers.

For reasons that are unclear, one of the most musically distinct elements of the liturgy that differentiates Hasidic nusakh from "the world" is the set of melodies used for the Friday evening prayer at the beginning of the Sabbath. There are two distinct versions of the Friday *Mariv* (Hebrew, evening) service that are commonly sung in the Brooklyn Hasidic community today. Cantorial pedagogue Noah Schall refers to these nusakhos as "Hasidic minor" and "Hasidic major." The Friday night Mariv Hasidic minor was sung for me by Yanky Lemmer at an interview we conducted at one of our first meetings.

The Hasidic major nusakh for Friday night Mariv is distinct from this minor melody and shares a sense of melodic outline with the major modality typically associated with the chanting of Kabbalos Shabbos, the suite of Psalms and mystical texts that initiates the Sabbath. The following transcription is from a performance

FIGURE 3. Yoel Kohn, Friday night Mariv "Hasidic major."

of Yoel Kohn at an unusual cantorial concert in the form of a prayer-leading service called *Nachalah* (Hebrew, inheritance) held at Hebrew Union College (HUC) and organized by veteran cantor, teacher, and advocate for cantorial music Jacob Mendelson. Nachalah was envisioned by Mendelson as a showcase for cantorial tradition and was presided over by himself and his students. I introduced Kohn to Mendelson in 2018 in the hopes that his traditionalist approach would be appreciated by the cohort of young cantors at HUC, leading to multiple invitations to present at Nachalah. In the concert notes that were produced for a service performance Kohn participated in, his version of the *Barchu* from the Mariv service was

u' ma vir yom - u mey vi - lay la

sings without words

FIGURE 4. Yanky Lemmer, "Cantorial" Friday night Mariv.

labeled "Hasidic nusakh," unambiguously commenting on the difference of his style from the mainstream approach taught at HUC and heard in liberal movement synagogues.[7]

While these two styles (Hasidic major and minor) seem to be prevalent among Brooklyn Hasidic Jews, they are not necessarily both well-known across communal boundaries within the Hasidic world. For example, when I sang Kohn the Hasidic minor nusakh I had heard from Yanky Lemmer, he did not recognize it. Both these melodic forms are distinct from the "cantorial nusakh," which is considered the mainstream by professional cantors and which Lemmer performs in his pulpit position. This rendition of the cantorial version of the same text was sung for me by Lemmer moments after he demonstrated the version he grew up with.

This version of the Mariv service is included in cantorial training anthologies and is the standard in American synagogues. However, at the time of the founding of the cantorial training institutes, both major and minor variants of this melody were in circulation. Adolf Katchko, whose anthology is used as a standard work at the HUC Debbie Friedman School of Sacred Music, included both major and minor variants in its first edition.[8] The Friday night nusakh is one of the most radical point of difference between Hasidic and non-Hasidic prayer practices and was cited by almost all the participants in this research as an example of friction between the different forms of prayer music. Many of the participants in this study cited the Friday night service as a liturgical moment when they became keenly aware of the differences between their musical upbringing and the norms of "the world." This musical shift makes the replacement of Hasidic "repertoire" by professional cantorial "archive" unambiguously audible.

Hasidic cantorial revivalists are valued for their perceived access to tradition, their performance of classic cantorial compositions, and their mastery of professional cantorial skills. As I have shown in previous chapters, Hasidic cantorial revivalists take great pains to develop their knowledge of khazones and cantorial nusakh. In practice, however, these markers of cantorial excellence are subordinated to yet another domain of liturgical skill. Contemporary styles of synagogue music, such as the contrafact pop melody I described at the beginning of this chapter, play a major role in cantorial performance and are a dominant force in sculpting the soundscape of the synagogue.

CHARISMA TO DECORUM, PRESENTATION TO PARTICIPATION: MUSICAL AND SOCIAL CHANGE IN THE AMERICAN SYNAGOGUE

Something happened to cantorial music in the years between World War II, when cantorial music constituted a vibrant element of Jewish popular culture in synagogues and media, and the 1980s, by which point khazones had had taken up a seemingly permanent fringe position in the life of the American Jewish community. Identifying the causes of this shift involves sifting through memory, myth, and sedimented layers of nostalgia and prejudice. For lovers of khazones and some professional cantors, the shifts in the sounds of American Jewish life have taken on a semi-official status as a narrative of decline and loss.[9]

In this section I will briefly outline some of the shifting cultural forces that contributed to the lachrymose narrative of cantorial culture. This narrative of loss is not only a retrospective melancholy theory of Jewish music; it is also descriptive of material circumstances. Most American synagogues no longer employ cantors or have shifted musical practices toward new musical styles that do not adhere to the conception of tradition (the ideology of nusakh I discuss in chapter 2) that is taught by cantorial training institutions and harbored by many cantors. For Hasidic cantors, the history of social change in the synagogue and how it has shaped the sounds of prayer are formative of their professional working environment and the kinds of music they can make at the pulpit.

Listening, as Peter Szendy has argued, is regulated by "regimes" that reflect ideologies and political contexts. In any musical experience, the listener coconstructs meaning and authorizes—or, conversely, denies agency to musicians.[10] Jacque Ranciére has suggested that the senses and their uses in aesthetic experience reflect political contexts that regulate who can speak and what can be understood.[11] As historian Sophia Rosenfeld has noted, "basic auditory perception, as well as the kind of hearing we call active listening, is historically variable; it depends on incidental and deliberate changes in technology, the environment, aesthetics, and social relations and is also generative of those changes."[12]

The changing perceptions and practices of cantorial music in the American Jewish community not only reflect a shift in musical tastes; these changes speak to emergent identities and political contexts that mirror the constitution of the identity category of "American Jews." In each chapter of this book, I have gestured toward describing shifts in the sociality of listening that have attended the historical development of Jewish liturgical music in the United States. Jewish American habits of listening define and delimit the aesthetic context in which Hasidic cantorial revivalists work. The reflections on shifts in music and listening in this section are by necessity partial and provisional but will hopefully be helpful in illuminating some of the problems of listening that Hasidic cantorial revivalists face in their synagogue employment.

Writing in 1948 in the Yiddish newspaper *Der morgn-zhurnal*, cantor and journalist Pinchas Jassinowsky described the prayer leading of recording star Cantor Samuel Vigoda in a New York synagogue:

> It wasn't long before the group of people were cradled in prayer and were transformed from indifferent listeners to devoted *daveners* [Yiddish, ones who pray]. The commonplace feeling disappeared from every Jewish face and the people were as if wrapped in a *talis* [Hebrew, prayer shawl] of holiness . . . Gathered together were religious and secular; young and old; women and men bearing deep emotion on their faces and in their longing countenances shone the spirit of their grandfathers and grandmothers, from long disappeared generations, who still live in their gazing into the old sacred place.[13]

Jassinowsky's prose reads to us today as stylized and romanticized. But the phenomenon he describes, according to which listening to cantors constituted a popular form of sacred experience, is broadly represented in the Yiddish press and literary descriptions of cantors in Jewish literature.

The memory of this kind of communal consumption of cantorial prayer leading, and the vestiges of long-form cantorial improvisations in ritual contexts still practiced by a handful of elder cantors, haunts cantorial revivalists. This kind of cantorial musical production offers a tantalizing concept of artistry and reception that Hasidic cantors romanticize and that some seek to reproduce.

The sounds of these kinds of concert-like prayer-leading services are preserved in bootleg recordings of cantors in synagogues, recorded surreptitiously starting in the 1950s and 1960s, as tape recorders arrived on the consumer market. Field recordings, referred to as "live davenings" by fans, represent a more intimate and raw depiction of cantorial sound than what is heard on commercial recordings. Whereas commercial records featured entextualized versions of cantorial performance, rendered as aria-like renditions of music of prayer tailored to the time constraints of 78rpm records, live davenings capture the art of cantors *in situ*, as a form of ritual.

Live davenings capture some of the great artists of the cantorial golden age in their later period. They document a broadly diverse set of approaches to prayer leading that foregrounded expressiveness and individual stylistic approaches. Listening to live davenings of gramophone-era stars like Pierre Pinchik or Moishe Oysher reveals a heterogeneity of musical material, encompassing a variety of musical sources and an approach that seem to be heavily improvised. The sound of prayer leading on live davening recordings disturbs the sense of nusakh as a unitary source of melodic material. Long-form cantorial prayer leading heard on these recordings emphasizes the role of charisma, creativity, and individual style in constituting the cantorial approach to prayer leading.[14]

These recordings document a variety of compositions and improvisations in the renditions of prayers sung by cantors. The noise and activity of the bodies at prayer in the synagogue can also be heard. The public that listened to creative cantorial prayer leading in synagogue was far from passive and silent. The congregation sings along at moments in unsteady heterophony, but it can also be heard in a variety of other forms of sound making, including bodily movements and the flowing monotonal individual chanting of the prayer service. Live davenings bear the imprint of a sociality of listening that involved forms of sound-making expressiveness on the part of the listeners.

For the listening participants in cantorial prayer services, the aesthetic labor of the cantor was a focal point of the musical experience but was not the only source of sound. How cantors responded to the "noise" of the synagogue was perhaps not uniform; Pinchik was said to have shushed his congregation from the pulpit at times, dramatically demanding silence so he could exercise the full dynamic range of his voice. But the polyvocal environment of the synagogue was a marker of a synergistic relationship between cantors and their congregation. The Jewish public seems to have understood cantorial performance as contributing to a legitimate and desired form of Jewish prayer.

These recordings are crucial evidence for contemporary singers who endeavor to learn how to lead services in the creative style of the masters of the idiom. Hasidic cantorial revivalists cite live davenings as a keen source of inspiration and aspiration. Discussing the aesthetic compromises he makes in his prayer leading, Yanky Lemmer comments:

> If I was completely in charge, well, I know I'd have no audience. I would try to daven like Ben Zion Miller, or like Moshe Stern back in the day. You hear their live davenings and I get goose bumps fifteen times throughout *Shakhris* [the morning service].[15]

The reception of live davenings is significant both for its value as a pedagogic and aesthetic source but also as a form of antinormative community building. Live davenings constitute what media studies scholar Blake Atwood has called an "underground distribution network," a social mechanism that surreptitiously shares forms of media that are either illegal or otherwise marginal to the economic and cultural mainstream. In the days before the internet, fans would swap recordings of revered cantors that they had made themselves. Today, the internet has democratized access, but some fans continue to hoard their live davenings, only agreeing to share with other collectors who can exchange similarly rarified sonic treasures.[16]

Live davenings document and repurpose an experience that is intended to remain ephemeral. They are a trespass against the typical norms of synagogue life. In order to record a cantor leading Sabbath or holiday services, fans would surreptitiously sneak recording devices into synagogue spaces where the use of electricity was formally forbidden on these occasions by normative interpretations of *halacha*. For deep lovers of khazones, the aesthetic value of these recordings transcends the halachic prohibitions that attended their creation. The sense of controversy around these objects is barely acknowledged by the Hasidic musicians I have spoken to. The existence of live davenings is generally celebrated and the recordings are considered to be at least as important a source of cantorial knowledge as the commercial recordings that constitute the "standard repertoire" of young cantors.

As I have shown in previous chapters, the post-World War II American synagogue shifted away from the cantorial paradigm of creative davening, supported by the sociality of a polyvocal synagogue sound environment. The reasons for this shift are beyond the scope of this study, but they seem to relate to the process of suburbanization, the generational shift from immigrant to native-born American cohorts as the dominant communal force, the move toward an assimilatory identity as middle-class Americans employed in the professions and educated in public schools, and the adoption of an orientation toward Zionism as a cultural focal point for the community.

This latter development had a distinct aural impact on prayer. In the 1950s, American synagogues began to adopt a version of the "modern" Hebrew Israeli phonology for the performance of prayer. This change had a powerful impact on Jewish vocal music traditions based in the Yiddish-accented pronunciation of prayer. The sounds of Yiddish phonology play a distinctive role in cantorial vocal production.[17] The move away from this marker of the European immigrant heritage had a radically disrupting impact on the sonic-memory qualities of prayer, as noted by Cantor Moshe Ganchoff (1905–97). Ganchoff quoted one of his mentors, Pierre Pinchik, as saying, "What's that word, *a-TA* [Hebrew, you, pronounced with the stress on the second syllable]? The right word is *A-to* [with the accent on the first syllable]. *Dos is idish. Ata is nisht idish* [Yiddish, That is Jewish. *Ata* is not Jewish]."[18] For Pinchik, the use of the modern Hebrew phonology evacuates the prayer texts of their signification of Jewish identity. Even the word *ato*, the masculine singular second person pronoun used constantly in prayer to address God, becomes foreign-sounding when it is changed to meet a set of political conventions that are external to the social and spiritual logic of Yiddish expressive culture.

Shifts in the listening habits of Jewish Americans, generally toward embracing popular culture, occurred simultaneously to the establishment of a new kind of cantorate. In the period after World War II, cantors were trained in seminary conservatories in a style of prayer music that was text based and discouraging of the kinds of populist exuberance that characterized some of the stars of the phonograph era. Rather than having to rely exclusively on performance charisma as the basis for employment, the cantorate was transformed into a unionized workforce that provided a service for synagogues as prayer leaders and educators.

The perceived alienation of acculturated American-born Jews from the offerings of their synagogues was noted with some frustration by members of the Cantor Assembly, the union of Conservative cantors, in their professional journal. In a representative screed in the *Journal of Synagogue Music* from 1967, Samuel Rosenbaum dubbed prayer "the lost art," accusing his congregants of being "uncomfortably well dressed, faces, fixed, eyes shallow, focused on things far away . . . And the prayer, the prayer we so desperately need, it lies buried in the untouched recesses of the heart."[19] Rosenbaum's negative assessment of American Jews accords with Riv Ellen Prell's description of the mid-century American synagogue as being preoccupied with "decorum" at the expense of cultural intimacy and popular engagement with the experience of prayer.[20]

In response to the acknowledged problem of communicating with their congregations, some pulpit cantors introduced new musical styles. Commissioning new pieces of music by classical composers had been a staple of the musical life of elite synagogues since the nineteenth century. Picking up the pace of embracing new styles in the 1960s and 1970s, some cantors commissioned pieces that incorporated elements of jazz and pop music in an effort to regain relevance to the musical lives of their congregants.

In the same period when these cantor-driven commissioned projects were being composed and performed (and sometimes recorded), another stream of populist liturgical music began to enter the synagogue.[21] Guitar-strumming Jewish singer-songwriters were composing new songs on liturgical texts, influenced by the sounds of the folk revival and the 1960s counterculture. The two most prominent examples of this phenomenon were Shlomo Carlebach and Debbie Friedman, who were associated with the Orthodox and Reform movements, respectively.[22] These musicians produced new music on liturgical texts that have been embraced as a new liturgy geared toward enhanced participation in worship through group singing.

While the music of Carlebach and Friedman is iconic of a new era in liturgy, American Jews have a longer history of calling on group singing of metered melodies to perform "American" identities. Extending back to the nineteenth century, hymn singing in English played a major role in synagogue worship.[23] Recording star cantors helped establish solo vocal styles of prayer leading as normative in American synagogues in the era of mass immigration from Eastern Europe (ca. 1880–1924) but pushback against the "foreignness" of khazones was not long in coming. Already in the 1920s, some rabbis and cantors were appealing to American-born children of Eastern European Jewish immigrants with an approach to prayer that promoted group singing of newly composed metered songs.

The "Young Israel" movement, initiated by Rabbi Mordechai Kaplan, featured congregational melodies as the primary style in its services. Musicians such as Israel Goldfarb, the composer of the ubiquitous "Sholom Aleichem" melody, and Jacob Beimel were two early twentieth-century proponents of participatory music as a form of religious outreach to less "traditional" Jews.[24] The popular melodies of Goldfarb and Beimel provided participatory songs that filtered out into mainstream synagogues, including non-Hasidic Orthodox synagogues, that are still sung today and understood to be "traditional." New liturgical songs, like Goldfarb's "Sholom Aleichem" or Beimel's "Mi Khamokha," were marked by simple melodies and symmetrical phrasing that facilitated ease of performance for nonprofessional singers.

In an echo of these earlier approaches to participatory frames of synagogue comportment, Jewish liturgical songwriters emerging in the 1960s wrote music geared toward communal singing. Their compositions employ metered melodies and conform to the melodic norms and major or minor scalar conventions of Euro-American pop and folk music. For American Jews, the songs of Carlebach or Friedman are easy to sing along with, thereby providing a quality that makes their music palatable and attractive. These musical changes marked a move from a performance framework to a participatory model of worship music-making. In this model it is presumed to be a positive value for as many of the people present as possible to take part in the music-making, usually through unison singing.[25] This shift in the ontology of prayer music from a performance framework to a model focused on the experience of group music-making is not unique to the liberal movements and appears to be normative in many Orthodox contexts as well, especially in Modern Orthodox synagogues.[26] The musical norms of participatory music are adjusted to local ritual practice, the most notable difference being the exclusion of women's voices as prayer leaders in Orthodox synagogues.[27]

In an echo of the reform of cantorial music in the nineteenth century, when Sulzer and other cantors imported sounds of German Romantic choral music into Jewish liturgy, the music of Carlebach, Friedman, and their generation of songwriters "rationalized" Jewish liturgy through the techniques of regular rhythm (in contrast to the "nonmetered" or flowing rhythm of Jewish prayer chant), melodic simplicity (in contrast to the highly ornamented style of Eastern European cantors), and "standard practice" triadic harmony (as opposed to the mode mixture that characterizes khazones and nusakh and that bears an uneasy relationship with conventions of harmonization). But unlike the music of Sulzer, whose reforms were implemented as part of a strategy of professionalizing the cantorate and centering cantorial musical authority, the Jewish liturgical folk song movement was part of a general sensibility of recentering authority.

The binary of "participation and presentation" offers little explanatory power for the experience of aesthetics and listening. From the perspective of Hasidic cantorial revivalists, the dialogue of cantor-artist and their "noisy" congregation engaged in ritual forms of participatory listening speaks to the particularism of Jewish memory and prayer practices. Hasidic cantors who embrace khazones adopt a stance of rejecting the participatory model. The participation-presentation binary is inadequately attuned to the aesthetics of prayer that at one time were deeply entwined with conceptions of Jewish community, mutual aid, and creativity. Lost from this narrative are questions of communal identification with the Yiddish-speaking immigrant heritage and the sacred listening experience of khazones.

In the absence of a Jewish public that embraces the cantorial revivalists' conception of the aesthetics of prayer and affirms the power of their voices to focus and refine prayer experience, the aspirations of cantorial revival are indefinitely deferred. In the career of Hasidic cantorial revivalists, a musical progression is evident from the repertoire of their birth community to the archive of old records and professional cantorial knowledge. In the context of professional life, however, cantors must reorient their musical practices once again to make room for the folk-pop liturgy that makes up a major component of their prayer leading. In the following subsection, I will offer a few vignettes that illustrate how cantors construct a prayer service in their Modern Orthodox pulpit jobs and the multiple musical styles they negotiate in their attempt to fulfill their professional ambitions to work as cantors.

SCENES FROM THE PULPIT:
NEGOTIATING THE CANTOR'S VOICE

Yisroel Lesches is the assistant cantor at Lincoln Square Synagogue, where he has worked since 2016, first as a cantorial intern. Lesches took an entrepreneurial approach to his cantorial career. He offered his services for free to Lincoln Square on the Sabbaths when Yanky Lemmer, the senior cantor, had off. He gradually worked his way up to the position of assistant cantor. Along the way toward more formal employment, he made adaptations in his style of prayer leading, to "correct" the nusakh he learned growing up to conform to the cantorial nusakh used at Lincoln Square.

Lesches was born in 1986 in Sydney, Australia in the small Hasidic community of that city. Like many young Lubavitch men he eventually moved to New York, the center of the international Chabad Lubavitch movement. Although he described himself as more aligned personally with Modern Orthodoxy than Hasidism at the point in his life when we were talking, he recognizes his upbringing as having been a key factor in choosing khazones as his musical path.

> Today, when I walk into a real Chabad shul, like 770 [refers to the building number on Eastern Parkway where the headquarters of Chabad is located], I feel uncomfortable. I feel I don't belong here. I belong in a Modern Orthodox shul. Australian Chabad is more like Modern Orthodox . . . But it's funny, because if I'd grown up Modern Orthodox, I don't think I'd be a khazn. Right? Because it's Hasidic communities that are keeping khazones.

Lesches keeps a spreadsheet with a running list of the pieces he uses for the various liturgical elements of the Shabbos morning service each week. Cantorial nusakh plays a role in his prayer leading, but he rejects the model of sophisticated improvisation, mode mixture, and allusion to cantorial records—a style he associates with Noah Schall and his students—as the basis of his prayer leading.

For example, I love Yanky, but . . . The changes that he'll do are like little modulations in *Shakhris* [the morning service], he'll modulate to minor back to *freygish*. You'll notice, and I'll notice, and nobody else will notice . . . What I feel that a khazn should do is, if I were to split up Shakhris for example, I have till *Kel Adon* [a hymn in the Shakhris service traditionally sung with the congregation]. Kel Adon is its own thing obviously; then from Kel Adon to *Shemoneh Esrey* [the central prayer of the service]. And then *Kedusha* [a musically marked text within the Shemoneh Esrey] till the end. So that's four sections. In every section I'd try to gather six variations. By *variation* I don't mean going to freygish and back because nobody notices that. I mean melodies, actual melodies that are different, very noticeable, but critically, are not longer than it would take to just daven the nusakh. Because once you start to stretch you drive everybody crazy.[28]

The musically marked elements of his prayer leading are drawn from popular sources such as Shlomo Carlebach, or Orthodox pop music icons like Mordechai Ben David, Avraham Fried, and the like. Lesches is self-consciously trying to develop a brand as a cantor whose music is accessible and populist. Yet, despite his efforts to differentiate himself from "serious" cantors, Lesches's prayer leading is not worlds apart from the approach taken by Lemmer.

Some major elements of the Shabbos Shakhris in a cantorial prayer leading service, as observed at Lincoln Square Synagogue:

1. Shokhyen Ad—a series of short prayer texts. This prayer marks the opening of the cantorial performance; the section preceding *Shokheyn Ad* is sung by a lay member of the community. This section is typically sung using cantorial nusakh, with varying degrees of emphasis through improvisation and variation.
2. Kel Adon—a metered poem sung as a call and response between cantor and congregation, or as a unison metered melody. Typically sung to a melody, either from a Shlomo Carlebach song, a Hasidic nigun, or an Orthodox pop source.
3. Shemoneh Esrey—a series of prayer texts said by the congregation to themselves silently or quietly in a rapid chant; these same texts are then repeated and sung by the cantor. The first paragraph of the Shemoneh Esrey ("Avos") has a melody that is sung (with some variants) by most cantors in the Ashkenazi diaspora. The prayer text paragraphs that follow are often treated as "modal" passages suited to improvisation or composed variation on generic themes.
4. Kedushah—a prayer text within the repetition of the Shemoneh Esrey, containing quotations from the prophet Isaiah that describes the prayers of the angels. This section is typically treated in a musically more emphasized or ornate fashion that sees the most variety of approaches; cantors gravitate toward employing contrafacta melodies, often from popular music sources.

5. Torah Service (part 1)—The scriptural reading is typically performed by someone other than the cantor. This part of the service constitutes a break for the cantor.

6. Torah Service (part 2)—*Mishebeirach* and *Rosh Chodesh Bentshn*. At the end of the Torah reading there are a variety of prayer texts, some of which it is customary for cantors to emphasize musically, especially in the supplicatory *Mishebeirach* (May the One Who Blessed) section. This is where the *Avinu Shebashamayim* (Our Father Who Is in Heaven) prayer for the State of Israel is said in some congregations. The Avinu Shebashamayim setting by Paul Zim is frequently performed by cantors in this section of the service. Zim's piece is in a style reminiscent of Broadway or film music genres. On the Sabbath before the new month, the *Rosh Chodesh Bentshn*, the blessing of the new month, is said, often in a musically elaborate setting that calls upon sounds of cantorial recitative.

Lemmer has developed a sophisticated approach to creating variation and musical interest within his prayer leading using tools from his study of old records and Schall's nusakh, but the moments of the service where he utilizes his sophisticated cantorial techniques are an exception in the overall service. The pieces that are given the most time and emphasis are metered songs for congregational singing. Kel Adon, the hymn mentioned by Lesches, is almost always sung by Lemmer employing Carlebach melodies that are well-known to congregants and that encourage group participation through singing. This liturgical element is given ample space within the service. In comparison to the amount of time devoted to unison melodies sung by the congregation, the khazones elements are intentionally condensed.

On one occasion when I was at Lincoln Square, Lemmer put together an impromptu choir made up of some of his fans in the congregation, men who were interested in music or who had some experience in choir singing. Lemmer asked me to join in as well. During the Torah service, which the cantor is often not actively involved in leading, Lemmer convened a quick rehearsal in the Rabbi's office. The piece we were preparing was a rendition of Sol Zim's Avinu Shebashamayim (Our Father in the Heavens), a prayer text composed in 1948 in tribute to the newly founded State of Israel that has since come to be included in the Torah service as part of the supplicatory prayers for healing. Zim's piece was composed in 1988 and was popularized by the chief cantor of the Israeli Defense Forces, Shai Abramson, as a tribute to fallen Israeli soldiers. Avinu Shebashamayim has the stylistic feel of musical theater; it is highly sentimental and divided into sections that build in dramatic tension. The melodically memorable opening section is metered and does not feature ornamentation typical of cantorial recitative. Zim's piece does share with classic cantorial compositions an unabashed dramatic quality. It makes a naked appeal to the emotions—in part through its nationalistic Zionist content.

The piece is popular among cantors who view it as a crowd-pleaser; I have heard it performed during services by Yanky Lemmer, Zevy Steiger, and Zev Muller. While the piece has little to do musically with classic cantorial performance, having more of an affinity with Broadway and film score music, it is an impressive showcase for a vocal soloist. As such, the piece has been adopted by many cantors as an appropriate opportunity to demonstrate their affecting powers in the context of ritual leadership. It is notable that Zim's Avinu Shebashamayim is the "exception" to the general rule of thumb that most cantors with pulpit positions have mentioned: full-length soloist compositions are not permissible in synagogue prayer leading because of the reduced interest among congregants in hearing extended cantorial recitatives during services.

The musical norms at Lincoln Square reflect both broader currents in Modern Orthodox liturgy, as well as the history of the specific institution. The local musical culture was shaped by Sherwood Goffin (1942–2019), the founding cantor at the synagogue who served there for fifty years. During the years when I was conducting research, Goffin, then the cantor emeritus, was always present at services and, as Lesches and Lemmer attested, gave the younger cantors feedback and helped enforce the norms he had established. Goffin emerged in the 1960s as a Jewish folk singer and songwriter, using his prominent pulpit as a position from which to experiment with new populist approaches to participatory music. His album *Neshama* (1972) features songs in a pop style and arrangements played by A-list studio musicians of the day. While Goffin reinvented himself in later years as a cantorial traditionalist and an advocate for "correct" nusakh in his public lectures, his lasting legacy has been his contribution to the growth of the participatory pop-oriented liturgy in the Orthodox world.[29]

As Yanky has mentioned to me, he feels that he must walk a line between showing his talents in the best possible light and being "excessive":

> You have to give them a high note here and there, because they have to know, oh he's got a voice. You have to give them a *dreydl* [Yiddish, vocal ornament] here and there—oh wow, he's a khazn. [I've] kind of got all these tools in my box that are almost wasted, but not. You know what I mean? . . . I learned to like it . . . I'm a pretty good psychologist. I read people and I read crowds pretty well.[30]

In a prayer service led by Yanky and his brother Shulem, Shulem demonstrated how virtuosic performative moments could be interpolated into participatory music, both in a cantorial vein and by using the "tools" of pop vocal music. In this service for Friday night, the Lemmer brothers leaned heavily on the melodies of Shlomo Carlebach during the Kabbalos Shabbos (welcoming of the Sabbath) service, as is typical of their prayer leading. Among the pieces they sang were Carlebach's popular setting of *Mizmor L'Dovid* (Psalm 29) and a contrafacta for the final verse of the hymn Lecha Dodi (Come my beloved) using the melody of Leonard Cohen's "Hallelujah."[31] Cohen is a popular choice for cantors seeking a "mainstream" pop culture item that is perceived to be well-suited to Jewish ritual contexts, both because of the songwriter's religious background and the themes explored in his lyrics. Cohen's songs are increasingly used in liturgical contexts across the Jewish denominations both as contrafacta for Hebrew prayers and sometimes with their original lyrics.

To both the Carlebach piece and the Cohen song, Shulem added improvisatory codas that showcased his impressive upper vocal range and command of coloratura singing. The two improvisatory "solos" referenced different stylistic traits. The Carlebach song, which employs a *freygish* augmented second modality, was appended with a nonmetered coda (see figure 4). In this section, Shulem improvised a passage that made reference to a classic cantorial cadential riff (line 3 in the transcription), heard on many golden age records—like Mordechai Hershman's *Av Horachamim Hu Y'rachem* (1921), for instance. The Leonard Cohen song was also leveraged as the site for an ornamented improvisatory section, but here the musical genre referenced was contemporary pop singing, with a distinct R&B element (see figure 5). Shulem's phrasing, with its persistent syncopation and "jazzy" growl and swooping effects, bore a sonic similarity to pop R&B singers such as Michael Jackson or Justin Timberlake. Shulem cites Jackson as an influence in the promotional text on his website.[32] Of all the cantors who participated in this project, Shulem's involvement with secular pop music is the most thick. Shulem is currently signed to a major label, Decca Gold, and is exploring a career as a crossover artist in the adult contemporary pop genre. While Shulem's career as a pop singer makes him unusually effective in performing sonic code-switching between cantorial and pop sound, the stylistic reference points he touches on are far from unusual. Figures from pop culture such as Leonard Cohen and Michael Jackson are decidedly *not* out of bounds as points of cultural literacy in the musical worlds that Hasidic cantorial revivalists inhabit.

In another example of a Hasidic cantorial revivalist interacting with a community with its own conceptions of synagogue experience, Zevi Steiger leads services at the Southampton Jewish Center, a Chabad house that serves the needs of a community of mostly older, affluent Long Island Jews who for the most part do not identify as Orthodox. Chabad houses are community centers that have been established in countless towns and cities around the world as part of the Chabad program of *kiruv*, or religious outreach to non-Orthodox Jews.[33] The rabbi who has run the synagogue for over twenty-five years makes decisions about the liturgical composition of the service based in part on his perception of the needs of the congregation. This results in a pastiche of Orthodox liturgy with elements borrowed from the liberal movements, such as English-language readings, which are unusual in most Orthodox contexts. The rabbi seems to be following the kiruv philosophy of meeting people where they are in order to draw them closer to the Chabad conception of tradition.[34]

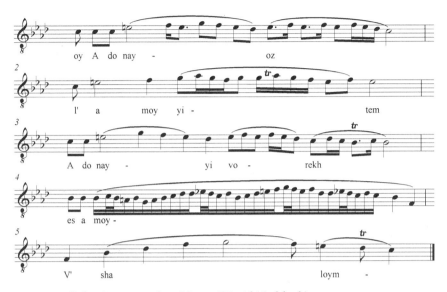

FIGURE 5. Shulem Lemmer, coda to Mizmor L'Dovid (Carlebach).

FIGURE 6. Shulem Lemmer, L'cha Dodi/Hallelujah improvisation.

Steiger's approach to prayer leading comports with the kiruv philosophy as well but is refracted through the lens of a specific style of cantorial traditionalism he has gleaned from his training with Noah Schall. His performance of the prayer service invokes Schall's ornamented and detailed nusakh, interspersed with congregational melodies. Prominent in the mix are American synagogue "standards," melodies such as the well-known Mi Khamokha melody by Jacob Beimel composed in the 1920s.[35] Tunes by Beimel and his contemporary Israel Goldfarb are familiar to the members of the Southampton Jewish Center. Less well-known were the Carlebach songs that Zevi also included, tunes that some-times resulted in Steiger and the rabbi being the only people singing during the "sing along" songs.

In an unusual dynamic that reflects the generational cohort of the congrega-tion, it may be Steiger's khazones, and not his expertise in liturgical folk pop styles, that is most appreciated by the congregants. After the end of a service I attended, the elder members surrounded Steiger, praising his singing and offering comparisons to star cantors from the middle of the last century. Richard Tucker (1913–75), the cantor who was best known for his crossover career as an opera singer, was offered as a point of flattering comparison. I heard an elderly lady say that the service reminded her of going to hear cantors with her grandparents as a little girl. It struck me how even for this elderly person recourse was needed to the grandparents' generation to conjure a vivid memory of cantorial prayer leading.

In discussing his prayer leading, Steiger stressed that aesthetics could not be the only gauge of success and that the experiences of his congregants were key to the decision he made about composing the service. For the older people who come to the synagogue, his singing of melodies that are familiar to them are central to their feeling of belonging and engagement. Mutuality and compro-mise need not only be sources of discontent for cantors. Compromise can also register as a form of pastoral care.

> What I try to do is always get stuff, at least some stuff, that people are familiar with. So, I'm not gonna change the tunes, for example, for the Kedusha so much, because many of the people aren't traditional. That's their only connection to *yiddishkayt* [Yiddish, Jewishness], in general to religion. So, when they come to shul, I want them to see something they're familiar with.[36]

For Steiger, the musical requirements of his job are compatible with his self-conception as a religious Jew, even if they are in tension with his aspirations as an artist.

The social negotiations of the synagogue place limits on the self-expression that Hasidic cantorial revivalists have sought out through their appeal to the genre of khazones and their investment in the idea that it can serve them as a cre-ative artistic field. In their pulpit positions, the cantorial skill set they have pains-takingly acquired can only be partially activated. Instead of developing more deeply in their chosen musical style, Hasidic cantorial revivalists must cultivate new musical skills as prayer leaders. The musical requirements of pulpit positions draw into question the viability of synagogues as an appropriate destination for the skill and talent of Hasidic cantorial revivalists. Khazones revival is driven by a passionate interest in the sounds of the Jewish past, as articulated by artisti-cally minded young singers. These singers hold an outsider perspective on the role of what prayer music can express, how it can function as an art experience, and what possibilities khazones can open up in the life of an aspiring musician.

Their aesthetics and desires put them at odds with contemporary Jewish institutions. Employment as a cantor cannot fully address the needs and musical obsessions of these musicians. Instead, Hasidic cantorial revivalists look outside of the synagogue to find different stages of performance, where, paradoxically, they are better able to fulfill their conception of cantorial prayer music as an art practice and a form of sacred listening.

Interlude B

Fragments of Continuity

Two Case Studies of Fathers and Sons in the Changing Landscape of American Orthodox Jewish Liturgy

In this book I have foregrounded a narrative about young artists working in contexts where they lack communal support for their interests and endeavors. I have used the image of *revival* to describe the relationship of musicians to an art form that falls outside the structures of biological family and community. Revival in this context has to do with the materiality of old records, the experience of listening, and the countercultural and subversive qualities of becoming an artist in a little-known genre.

Some of the singers in the Hasidic cantorial revival scene have self-conscious agendas focused on the revitalization of an old style they feel drawn to. They are doggedly committed to forging careers as cantors, going against the grain of what their social worlds apparently can allow. Several of the artists had never heard of khazones when they first stumbled on the genre through old records when they were already adolescents, and they have created identities for themselves as cantors whole cloth from mediated sources. As I have argued in previous chapters, for these singers, recordings are the central evidence of the cantorial style. Records serve both as pedagogy and object of desire, shaping the path of contemporary singers through practices of deep listening focused on an archive of classic sources.

Two of the key figures in the Hasidic cantorial scene, Yoel Kohn and Shimmy Miller, are members of intergenerational cantorial families; by definition their stories complicate a revival narrative. Instead, their musical lives can be read on a surface level as stories of linear transmission. Both singers are recipients of their fathers' prayer-leading musical knowledge and aesthetic. Although both Yoel and Shimmy stress that their fathers never directly trained them, the aural evidence from the performances of both singers attest to the influence of their families. In this interlude, I will discuss the lineages that produced the cantorial sensibility of these two artists, and I will explore the ways in which these two very different cantorial families reveal narratives of change in the world of Jewish sacred music. Their stories outline shifts in aesthetics and the social structure of prayer within the Hasidic community and in the broader world of the American synagogue. Changes in liturgical practices have had deeply felt personal repercussions on the level of family and individual career paths for both Yoel and Shimmy.

"WE DON'T HAVE OUR NEW ORLEANS":
YOEL KOHN AND MAYER BORUCH KOHN

Yoel Kohn once remarked about young Jewish singers seeking to master the cantorial idiom, "We don't have our New Orleans." His sharp quip about the sense of loss that hovers over Ashkenazi Jewish music creates an analogy between cantorial performance and Black American vernacular music, a comparison that many cantors make in conversation. The analogy to jazz and blues suggests that khazones is an improvisatory art form that is dependent on a body of traditional motifs, timbres, and modalities; that it is an oral culture intertwined with the life of a community. Furthermore, Yoel seems to draw a comparison between Jewish and Black Americans as marked off from the "mainstream" and dependent on a geographically and perhaps temporally distinct "homeland" from which these groups derive knowledge of self and culturally intimate forms of expression. Yoel seems to imply that unlike New Orleans, which offers jazz people a continued source of knowledge, access to Jewish musical knowledge is tainted and obscured by the discontinuities of migration and, especially, the trauma of the Holocaust and the literal destruction of the Jewish bodies that bore the oral knowledge of the musical idiom.

While this frame of post-Holocaust retrospective melancholy is completely reasonable, Yoel's conception of discontinuity is challenged by the fact that his own family has maintained a direct line of transmission of cantorial performance knowledge. As I will discuss in this section, cantorial melancholy retrospection is focused not only on musical artifacts and the lives of artists that were destroyed, but embraces a broadly defined deficit in the culture of listening and communal reception of cantorial performance. As a recipient of a cantorial lineage, Yoel, through his perspective on the prospects of revitalization and creativity in the cantorial scene, is shaped by his perception of a decline narrative he inherited from his father. Yoel, more than almost any other of the young Hasidic cantors, is in a position to access a kind of living culture of liturgical music, a khazones "New Orleans," if you will, alive and well in his very home. Nevertheless, his view of cantorial history and future hews to a narrative of uprootedness, loss, and failure.

The Satmar Hasidic community that Yoel was born and raised in presents itself as a bastion of continuity with the Eastern European past. In regard to the maintenance of the Yiddish language as a spoken vernacular, and sartorial and ritual customs, this would appear to be a justifiable claim, although less monolithic than might be assumed on closer inspection. However, in the realm of musical culture, a more complicated picture emerges. The Hasidic and Orthodox pop musics that have arisen in the past half century have superseded older musical cultural productivity as the norm of the communal soundscape. Within the Satmar community, a Hasidic group with an extreme Right public profile, Orthodox pop music is considered somewhat suspect. While pop singers and songs are rejected at times by conservative voices in the community, pop aesthetics, styles of arrangement, and instrumentation have influenced the way older forms of devotional music, such as nigunim, are recorded and presented in public settings, such as weddings. These aesthetic shifts are pervasive even in the most conservative corners of the Hasidic community and seem to go unremarked as part of the expected norm of the community soundscape.

Despite these changes in musical aesthetics, khazones may perhaps have a more robust representation in the Satmar community than among other Hasidic groups. As David Reich mentioned to me, "In the Satmar community's annual event to mark the Satmar Rebbe's escape from Auschwitz, the only performance allowed was the performance by a cantor who would typically choose a piece by [Yossele] Rosenblatt, [Zawel] Kwartin, or [Yehoshua] Wieder." Contemporary performers of khazones have a recognized function at important community events, including an annual mass celebration of Chanukah presided over by the rebbe and other communal leaders. Yoel Kohn's cousin, Yoel Pollack, a cantor and a composer of nigunim, is one such artist who has been invited to perform at the rebbe's Chanukah celebration on several occasions.

Mayer Boruch Kohn, Yoel's father, is among the "purists" within the community who reject the pop music innovations of Jewish music as being corrupted by non-Jewish culture. Mayer Boruch, born in 1962 in London, is a revered bal tefile within the Satmar community. He was born into a family with a cantorial legacy, in a home where cantorial records played "day and night." His father was also a bal tefile, although both Mayer Boruch and Yoel describe him as having had very limited vocal range and control. A more salient influence on Mayer Boruch was the internationally known Cantor Yehoshua Wieder (1906–64), and the multigenerational Wieder cantorial family. Mayer Boruch's father was a meshoyrer for Asher Wieder, Yehoshua Wieder's father, in Hungary before the Holocaust. As a result of this connection, the Kohns have "inherited" a repertoire of unique melodies from the Wieder family that apparently they alone have preserved.

Mayer Boruch also learned from Shloyme Rosen (d. 1990), a bal tefile in the Hasidic community in London from whom no known recordings have been preserved. According to Mayer Boruch, "this Shloyme Rosen was unique." Mayer Boruch claims that his nusakh is a direct transmission from Shloyme Rosen, which he learned from years of listening to his prayer leading. Although he never had any lessons and has no recordings, Mayer Boruch was able to retain what he heard from Rosen. Yoel emphasized that because both he and Mayer Boruch grew up in homes where they listened to no other music aside from cantorial records, they had no distractions to keep them from retaining musical information. Whatever they heard "rattled around like in an empty barrel."

Mayer Boruch praised his teacher, saying, "Shloyme Rosen had a good line and everything he sang was a *khidush*" (Hebrew/Yiddish, an innovation). According to Mayer Boruch, the correct expression of nusakh demands constant variation within a set of melodic conventions. Yoel explains his father's style as having two primary rules that dictate his musical choices: a bal tefile must use a different pitch for every syllable of every word (i.e., not using a recitation tone), and he must use different variants on the traditional motif, never repeating the exact same idea. This approach demands that a bal tefile create a flow of improvised variations and that he be intimately familiar with the prayer texts and consistently sensitive to the meaning of the words he is saying, rather than falling into a mechanical recitation. Yoel and Mayer Boruch offered mocking imitations of typical Hasidic bal tefiles who rely on recitation tones and repeat the same melody over and over again for every phrase in a given prayer text, creating boring, unmusical phrasing.

In the Satmar community, prayer leading is looked on as a social privilege more than as a specialized musical skill. In Hasidic Brooklyn, most prestigious prayer-leading opportunities are given to the *rebishe layt*, the class of people drawn from elite rabbinic lineages. According to Mayer Boruch, this has led to a great diminishing of knowledge and musicality about *nusakh hatefilah* (Hebrew, prayer melodic forms) in the Hasidic community. Prayer-leading privileges are conferred on the basis of genealogy, not musical talent or even knowledge of the appropriate melodies for the different prayer services.

When Mayer Boruch was growing up, the London Hasidic community was extremely small, and there was room for a skilled-but-otherwise-humble-in-origins-musician like Rosen to have a pulpit position. Today in London the Hasidic community has expanded. New Hasidic rabbinic courts have been established and taken over most prayer-leading opportunities. According to the Kohns, it is unlikely today that a musical expert from a nonrabbinic elite background could get the kind of prayer-leading position that Rosen had in London in the 1970s, when he led Shabbos services every week. Mayer Boruch's current position as the High Holidays prayer leader at the Tartikov shul in Borough Park relies on a reputation he built up after years singing in a *shtibl* (Yiddish, small Hasidic prayer house). In his previous position at the Dushinsky shul in Williamsburg, Mayer Boruch benefitted from the patronage of a *rov* (Yiddish, communal leader, in this case the head of the synagogue) who had an unusual love of cantorial music and who gave him a platform to lead services.

Yoel's practice of khazones approaches the music as a form of historically informed music-making and a creative practice. The two main outlets for khazones are concert formats (including mediated performances in the form of internet-based videos) and prayer leading. The most important source for his khazones style is his father and the family repertoire he learned from him, with lineages that connect to the Wieders and Shloyme Rosen. The other source of Yoel's musical practice is recorded cantorial music, primarily pre-Holocaust gramophone-era cantors who recorded in New York or Europe in the first decades of the twentieth century.

Homosocial practices of debate, analysis, and imitation were part of the culture of listening in Yoel's home. Already as a young boy, Yoel was developing his repertoire of cantorial recitatives under the influence of his father's musical aesthetic and the watchful eye of his conception of cultural and spiritual purity. When Yoel began to perform professionally as a young adult in his twenties, his options were largely shaped by his father's career. Yoel was viewed as a protégé of his father who could lead prayer services in the unique style of Mayer Boruch, and he was hired for the High Holidays in Kiryas Joel and other Satmar enclaves in the suburbs of New York City. He would also occasionally lead Shabbos services closer to home, in Brooklyn. In addition to leading services, Yoel was sometimes hired to sing at wedding engagement parties and other events in the community.

While his prayer leading hewed closely to his father's style, Yoel's interpretations of classic cantorial records marked him as stylistically distinct from his father. Yoel was cultivating his voice and developing a markedly more "cantorial" sound, influenced by the bel canto vocal tradition preferred by gramophone era cantors, rather than the earthier timbre characteristic of Hasidic bal tefiles. In Hasidic music, an earthy, more rough-hewn timbre is associated with spirituality and seems to be preferred by many Hasidic connoisseurs of prayer music. Mayer Boruch's vocal approach reflects this aesthetic norm of his community. He epitomizes a style of a Hasidic bal tefile who is knowledgeable, formally complex, but still holds fast to communal norms of expressiveness through a "noisy" vocal quality. Yanky Lemmer, commenting on the difference between his style and that of Mayer Boruch, foregrounded the ineffable, spiritual qualities of his performance, in contrast to the presumed aesthetic orientation of his own work. "His [Yoel's] father is extremely holy," Yanky said. "He is meant to be. I'm there because of talent, not because of anything else."

Yoel can code switch into a "Hasidic" vocal quality but has spent years developing a different kind of sound from his father, shaped by the aesthetics of golden age cantors. Kwartin, Rosenblatt, and the other old masters were operatic singers in terms of their vocal training. Yoel's evinces a particularly aggressive approach to coloratura singing, shaped by the sound of old records but stylized into a markedly muscular sensibility. On classic records, cantors are heard singing lengthy melismatic passages, with dozens of notes slurred together in complex melodic patterns that frequently surpass an octave in range. This physically demanding and viscerally engaging kind of display of virtuosity inflicts a stunning effect on the listener and is one of the prized qualities of cantorial performance. Yoel has made a unique approach to coloratura one of the trademarks of his performances. There is a kind of "hyped up" quality to his melismatic passages and trills, with complex figuration used in an even greater abundance in his reinterpretation of old records than on the original performances.

Yoel developed a reputation as a rising star of the Hasidic cantorial scene. However, his ability to capitalize on this reputation has been limited by several factors. He initially received invitations to perform at cantorial concerts. These concerts involved singing at events in Modern Orthodox, non-Hasidic synagogues. Concerts in the Modern Orthodox community typically have mixed audiences, with men and women in attendance, and often seated together. Yoel was aware that this kind of performance setting would be difficult for his father to accept. Mayer Boruch, like many men in his community, holds a stringent view on issues relating to gender. He will only sing at events that enforce a complete separation between the sexes; he will only sing for men, except in a synagogue where women sit in a separate section. Yoel sought and received a dispensation to sing at the cantorial concert from a Satmar authority.

It is a fairly common practice for Hasidic rabbis to issue "leniencies" to members of the community in areas relating to making a living. A cantor singing at a concert is generally seen as a category that should be granted leeway so that he can make money. It is generally understood that Hasidic cantors will be required to sing for communities other than their own in order to work, usually in the Modern Orthodox community. Opportunities for cantors to make money in the Hasidic community are extremely scarce. For Mayer Boruch, a rabbinic ordinance was not enough to assuage his discomfort. He told Yoel that he would prefer for him not to sing in a concert with a mixed audience. Yoel accepted his father's request, reasoning that as a bearer of his father's nusakh, he has an obligation to respect his wishes. Yoel came to be known as a singer who would only work in the Satmar world; invitations to sing at prestigious or well-paying cantorial events dried up.

Concurrent with the development of his musical sensibility, Yoel was moving further away from his identity as a Hasidic Jew. Like most men in his community, Yoel married young and started a family. In his telling of his life story, he had already begun to doubt the strict faith of his Hasidic upbringing as an adolescent. By the time he was married, Yoel says he "believed nothing." Although he had a strong desire to leave the strictures of the Hasidic community, a variety of forces predicated against this goal, perhaps most importantly his young children.

Music also played an important part in the choices he made about the shifting shape of his future. He told me, "Without being a khazn, I would have left much earlier. I didn't want to lose that. That was very important to me." After making a clean break with his community, Yoel's talent as a singer and interpreter of classic cantorial recordings continues to make him attractive as a performer in the small community of serious fans of khazones, both in the Hasidic community and the broader world of Jewish music. His performance venues today include parties and private prayer services on the fringe of the Hasidic community, internet videos, and occasional concerts in "secular" settings, including a major concert in Israel in 2018.

Yoel sees the cantorial world through the lens of a decline narrative, shaped in part by his father's pessimistic view of the prospects of cantorial music. According to Yoel, the current scene of young Hasidic cantorial revivalists does not offer a realistic picture of the historic trajectory of the music and its future. Rather, he sees the cantorial "revival" as an anomalous product of a moment of transition in the Hasidic community during the 1980s and 1990s, when he and the other cantors profiled in this study were adolescents. As Yoel sees it, his generational cohort of singers who became obsessed with golden age cantorial records was a product of a specific pre-internet moment.

> We were pre-internet. We all had very restrictive fathers. We had *isurim* [Hebrew, religious proclamations, sometimes in the form of public posters] on these [streetlight] poles, [putting a] ban on the music of Avraham Fried because they were too pop-y . . . First of all, there's no silence [today]. In general, no one is bored. No one is introspective. No one just sits down for a second and looks at the ceiling and hums a song . . . And that's also part of what made us. We were all sort of artistic. We were deprived. We had no outlets. We had to focus inside. We had to become introspective in order to achieve any sort of artistic or creative outlet, any sort of creative climax. And that doesn't exist anymore. I look at my brothers. Yeah, they're sort of, by right, into khazones because this is the sort of family where you couldn't avoid it if they tried. But they're not in it. They don't have the need for it that we did . . . The interest for khazones was never very strong in the Hasidic community and it's getting even less strong because again the audience needs to not have choice. There's no need for that because you have everything else. (Interview, April 12, 2021)

Yoel is intensely devoted to khazones as an artistic style and a performance practice that connects him to his birth community. Yet his musical desires and expertise seem to be incompatible with a career path that follow norms of economic return and public affirmation. His own experience confirms for Yoel the story his father and many other elder cantors tell about the art form as residing in a state of permanent and irreparable rupture and decay.

THE BETH EL HERITAGE:
SHIMMY MILLER AND BENZION MILLER

Benzion Miller was born in 1946 in a displaced persons camp in Germany in the aftermath of the Holocaust, into a family of Bobov Hasidic Jews with a multigenerational cantorial legacy. Miller is an elder star of the cantorial music world. He has performed internationally on major stages and held some of the most prestigious pulpit positions. His son Shimmy Miller, who was born in Canada but raised in Borough Park, Brooklyn, is one of the key voices among the younger generation of cantors. In his vocal talent and style, Shimmy closely resembles his father. But unlike his father and grandfather, and other family members stretching back generations, Shimmy is consistently underemployed as a cantor.

For the past four decades, Benzion Miller has presided at the pulpit of Young Israel Beth El Synagogue in Borough Park. Constructed in 1902, Beth El is a monumental Moorish-style synagogue designed as an ideal acoustic environment for cantorial vocal performance. From the time of its founding, Beth El has boasted a succession of prestigious "star" cantors, including luminaries of the gramophone-era recording industry like Berele Chagy, Mordechai Hershman, Moshe Koussevitzky, and, somewhat more recently, Moshe Stern.[1] According to cantorial gossip, Hershman paid a $1,000 kickback to Jacob Rappaport, the president of the *khazonim farbund* (Yiddish, cantors union) to finalize his contract at Beth El, so coveted was the pulpit position there.[2] Beth El was built to accommodate a congregation of a thousand, but today it rarely attracts more than a few hundred, and often far fewer worshippers.

In the present day, Beth El is the last synagogue in New York City that boasts a cantor and choir regularly performing in the partly improvised, soloist-focused style associated with gramophone-era cantors. Beth El is able to maintain this musical identity in part because of its position in the religious ecosystem of Borough Park. Beth El is associated with the Young Israel movement, a modernizing strand of Orthodoxy founded around the year 1912 with support from Conservative-aligned leaders such as Mordecai Kaplan but that ultimately declared itself Orthodox.[3] Young Israel is a product of an American Judaism that seeks to integrate Orthodoxy with the cultural norms of American non-Jewish society. The Young Israel movement is distinct from Hasidic sects that in general cultivate a separatist philosophy and encourage adherents to maintain a lifestyle of linguistic, sartorial, and ritual difference from the "mainstream."

Hasidic sects predominate today in Brough Park, and "liberal" Modern Orthodoxy is somewhat fringe. Paradoxically, because Beth El is "modern," meaning not dogmatically separatist in its religious orientation, it is able to maintain a form of musical traditionalism that is not typical of worship in contemporary separatist Orthodox Jewish enclaves. Facilitated by the combination of its prestigious musical history, its unusual "modern" religious profile, and the material presence of the building itself, Beth El has taken on the reputation as a living relic, cited regularly by cantorial aficionados as the last of its kind.

Benzion's monthly Sabbath service, held on *Shabbos Mevarchim* (Hebrew, the Sabbath of blessing; the Sabbath on which the ritual blessing of the new month is observed), is a kind of sacred concert with its own following among Jewish music lovers. Benzion is accompanied by a choir made up of up to a half dozen men. The choir has a rotating cast of regulars; some of the choir singers are Hasidic Jews. The services at Beth El that Benzion leads are completely focused on cantorial creativity, knowledge and artistic authority. Everyone who is present has self-selected to attend based on their investment in the experience of cantorial davening as an art experience and a form of spiritual practice. Borough Park is a largely Hasidic area, but the people in attendance are notably more diverse in their Jewish self-presentation than in the neighborhood in general; many or most of those in attendance are non-Hasidic Jews.

It is notable that a large proportion of the attendees at Benzion's services are women. On any given Shabbos Mevarachim morning at Beth El, the upstairs women's balcony is likely to be fuller than the men's section on the main floor. This is unusual in Borough Park, as in other separatist Orthodox enclaves, where the cultural norm is that women are not expected to attend Sabbath services. Because women are not required to attend the same synagogues as their husbands, especially in the Hasidic community, going to listen to a cantor perform serves as a form of religious self-determination, expressed in aesthetic terms. As Shimmy explained to me:

> You see, the women, they don't have to daven in the shul their husband davens in. And they'd rather come somewhere where they enjoy the davening. So, they love it over there. Their husbands on the other hand, they sit in shul every day . . . They wanna daven with their friends. So, they daven in the *shtibelakh* [small Hasidic synagogues] where they daven, or the shuls they daven in. (Interview July 15, 2019)

Women have been important consumers of cantorial music in the United States throughout the twentieth century, and their fandom of cantors at times was a driver for more inclusive synagogue policies. In the 1950s, female fans of Richard Tucker at the Austro-Galician Congregation synagogue in Chicago demanded their shul adopt mixed gender seating because their ability to hear Cantor Tucker was compromised by sitting in the balcony women's section.[4] It is increasingly understood that women were important performers of cantorial music during the golden age gramophone era, despite normative prohibitions on the female voice in the synagogue based on a strict interpretation of Jewish religious law.[5] The *khazentes*, female cantorial singers usually working as concert performers but not in synagogues, were popular enough to inspire fear in communal power brokers. They were cited by conservative critic B. Shelvin of the Yiddish-language newspaper *Morgn zhurnal* as an existential threat to the "future of cantorial music."[6] Less explored has been the role that women played as taste makers and impresarios of cantorial music. For example, Helen Stambler, the cofounder, with her husband Benedict Stambler, of the Collectors Guild record label, was a key figure in the release of reissue collections of cantorial records of the early twentieth century that helped establish the canon of cantorial classics that continue to shape the conception of the genre.[7]

The focal point of the service at Beth El is the *Rosh Chodesh bentshn* [Hebrew/Yiddish, the blessing of the new moon]. There is a special theatrical shift for this part of the service. Instead of remaining at the lectern at the front by the ark where Benzion begins the service, after the Torah service he moves to the raised *bima* (Hebrew, platform) in the center of the congregation where the Torah had just been read. Many of the men in the synagogue press in a tight circle around the bima. The choir stands on the floor facing toward Benzion, like a ceremonial court of witnesses. Benzion treats the *Yehi Rotzon* (Hebrew, May it be your will; the first words of the special blessing for the new month) prayer as a virtuosic improvisation. While he sings, physical responses are evoked from the listeners. Bodies sway; hands are held out with palms upturned. I once observed a middle-aged Hasidic man standing by Benzion doing a kind of interpretive dance to the recitative, gesticulating with his fists at the end of phrases or when Benzion hit high notes. The man's eyes were shut; then he would open them, turning his face upward and outstretching his arms, waving his hands in a thrice-repeated gesture.

It is remarkable to see a congregation responding to cantorial performance with such a degree of visceral intensity. This kind of adulation of cantorial performance is supposed to no longer exist, according to the oft-repeated hand-wringing of fans of the genre. The community of listeners at Beth El resonates with the history of cantorial performance as a popular art form, deeply loved and understood by the Jewish listening public. The congregation at Beth El responds to the music as an incitement to physically engage with prayer. The bodies of the congregation resonate sympathetically to the voice of the singer, reinforcing the power of the sound and urging Benzion on in his labor. The attention and emotional response of the congregation affirms the power of listening as a sacred act, ratifying the cantor's ritual function by allowing his voice to act on their bodies as a call to prayer.

Having Benzion as a signifier of continuity of a historic cantorial performance style has had a powerful influence on young cantors in New York, in part through the institution of the choir. The Beth El choir is relatively new. It was started by Shimmy. The choir has its origins in the period when Aaron Miller, Benzion's father, took ill and could no longer come to shul. Aaron Miller was known as the "Bobover khazn," because of the family's ties to Bobov Hasidism. Aaron brought a style of cantorial prayer leading with him from Galicia, Poland that he taught to his son and grandsons. In his last years, a group gathered every Shabbos to hold services in the elder cantor's home. There, Shimmy and his brother and cousins got their first opportunity to practice leading services, and their close friends and neighbors were exposed to Aaron Miller's melodies and had their first opportunities to experiment with the music of prayer leading. The group that formed to pray with the elder cantor formed the initial cohort of the choir.

The Beth El choir, conducted first by his son Shimmy Miller and now by his older son Eli Miller, features a rotating cast of singers. The choir is an important point of entry into cantorial performance for young Hasidic cantorial revivalists who are seeking training and opportunity for performance. Shimmy described to me a community of singers from a variety of walks of Jewish New York life, including fans of the music whose religious affiliations differ widely from his own, some of whom are not Hasidic and possibly not even Orthodox. Out of this scene of singers united by a love of cantorial music, a number of important cantorial "stars" have emerged. These include Yanky Lemmer, Ushi Blumenberg, and Berel Zucker, all of whom share Hasidic familial backgrounds. In this scene, we have evidence of the ways in which cantorial music draws together people from across divisions of identity. The choir is grounded in the multigenerational Miller family, whose knowledge shapes the experience of acolytes.

While opposition to khazones as overly worldly in its musical outlook plays a role in current Hasidic critique of cantors, contemporary Hasidic cantorial revivalists suffer far more from indifference than overt opposition. Shimmy Miller has stressed in our conversations that the main problem in the cantorial scene is the lack of audience. Having been brought up in a well-known cantorial family, Shimmy's vision of the potential for cantorial music in the future is subdued by the decline in institutional support that has directly affected his family. There are many individual cantorial fans, even in the Hasidic community, but they do not constitute a reliable fan base or drive the hiring practices of large synagogues. In order to forge a path as a cantor, Hasidic singers must engage in the same kinds of entrepreneurship as pop musicians; they need to promote themselves using the tools of the internet and hustle for performance opportunities. But unlike pop singers, cantors are limited by their style from reaching a mass audience.

In Shimmy Millers's view, the current interest in khazones among young Hasidic singers is not a mark of revival, but rather:

> It's called *gesise* in Aramaic, which is a petering out. Meaning it's the last. You have, unfortunately, when somebody dies, they get a little strength back right before they go. So, this is like it's getting its strength back before it goes. I don't see khazones in five years from now, barring a miracle. (Interview, July 15, 2019)

In response to the uncertainty of the market, Shimmy has expanded his career by focusing on the world of choirs, a prominent subsection of the Orthodox pop music scene. Hasidic choirs emerged as a media phenomenon on records made in the 1960s with renditions of nineteenth-century Eastern European Hasidic nigunim. Choir culture in the Hasidic world is influenced by Orthodox pop but has its own aesthetic norms and repertoires that overlap with pop, older Hasidic devotional music, and, to some extent, khazones.

Hasidic choirs are a transnational phenomenon, with major choirs having emerged in the 1960s and 1970s in Israel, England, and the United States. Today, there is a thriving scene of men's and boys' choirs that are a ubiquitous part of weddings and other Orthodox Jewish celebrations. Ensembles such as Shira Choir and Yedidim Choir have become popular through frequent performance and high-production value videos that are popular on social media. Unlike Orthodox pop music, Hasidic choirs draw prominently on older forms of Eastern

European Jewish sound, especially Hasidic nigunim. Choirs also sometimes perform arrangements of gramophone-era cantorial pieces, often drawing from the most popular figures such as Yossele Rosenblatt or Samuel Malavsky.[8] When the choirs are accompanied by instrumental ensembles, they frequently work with orchestral ensembles, reflecting the status of choirs as markers of prestige for public festive occasions. The overall sonic aesthetic of Hasidic choirs tends to be less focused on sounds appropriated from commercial pop music genres, and more inclusive of older Jewish repertoires. But, like Orthodox pop, it is given a unique sonic stamp by the digital processing that is used on the voices, the use of pop drum beats and synthesizers, and arrangements that favor vocal harmonies heavy on the accessible "prettiness" of parallel thirds.

Several of the Hasidic cantors (especially the Lemmer brothers) who participated in this study have, at one time or another, sung in choirs, either as a cantorial guest soloist, or as members of the choir group itself. The world of Hasidic choirs is a musical scene where Shimmy Miller can utilize his years of experience working as choir director for his father. Shimmy has started his own choir, the *Zingers*. He is now so busy with work at weddings and other *simchas* (Hebrew, festive occasions such as weddings) that he no longer has time to sing with his father at his monthly Shabbos davening.

Despite the important symbolism of Benzion Miller's presence, and the practical significance of the Beth El cantorial choir as a training ground, these phenomena are understood by their primary participants as tenuous and endangered. A sense of decline from the period of the music's heyday is pervasive in the way cantorial performers and fans talk about the music. As any fan of cantorial music will tell you, the main limitation in the current scene is that there is no longer a solid base of supporters who are interested in virtuoso cantorial prayer-leading services. Change in synagogue listening habits is the structural reason invoked by cantors for the move away from a virtuoso soloistic presentational style of synagogue music and the pivot toward participatory music influenced by American pop music.[9] Cantorial revivalists are keenly aware of the shifts in musical tastes among congregants and are aware that their work in synagogues requires compromise and dialogue. This dynamic pushes the best voices in contemporary cantorial music away from the classic style of prayer leading, as represented by Benzion. For Shimmy, the decline of the genre is a given.

REVIVAL TOWARDS WHAT?

Shimmy Miller and Yoel Kohn have the most reason, among their cohort of younger Hasidic cantors, to view the cantorial tradition as a chain of transmission. In their families traditional knowledge has successfully resisted the loss of memory and meaning. Yet their musical lives are characterized by a melancholy retrospection that places cantorial aesthetic achievement firmly in the past. While both singers are uniquely capable of "creative davening," employing improvisation and compositional techniques in the styles they learned from their revered fathers, they are curtailed by the marketplace from being able to perform to the fullest capacity of their knowledge and talents.

Of all the singers who participated in this study, Shimmy and Yoel were the most skeptical about my use of "revival' to describe the activities of young Hasidic cantors. This did not seem to be because of a feeling of enthusiasm for transmission and continuity as the framework for understanding their musical practices, although their musical biographies certainly lend credence to a continuity narrative. Rather, they opposed the term *revival* because it implies a living field of activity. Revival, to their ears, intimates a sense of life returning where once there had been silence and, perhaps, the formation of new communities through the mechanism of heritage reenactment.

From their perspective, cantorial performance is a form of communication. Their conception of meaning-making in khazones resonates with the definition of communication offered by linguist Roman Jakobson. Jakobson asserted that communication is dependent on a complete circuit of sender and receiver in order for a message to be completed. According to Jakobson, the message of communication is dependent on the conative, or receptive, element that provides deciphering knowledge and responsive cultural context in order for language to function as a meaning-making code.[10] Shimmy and Yoel have seen khazones in action as a living language, with the communicative musical gestures of cantors, their fathers, being received and acting on their listeners to create a mutually desired experience of Jewish prayer. By placing the language of khazones in the past tense, Yoel and Shimmy are asserting that the musical communication they have studied and mastered is in fact a dead language and that it no longer can function in its intended manner.

When a message is sent but not received, its meaning is obscured. In the absence of a meaningful social context, the terms of the message, no matter how potentially eloquent, result in what linguist J. L. Austin calls a "misfire," a breach of the rules of language that blunt the possibility of speech acting in in its intended manner.[11] A performance that is illegible to its audience is exposed in its theatricality and its potential for meaning making is blunted, becoming opened to ridicule or rejection. Rather than being a meaningful message, given power by mutual intelligibility to sender and recipient and lent efficacy by the deciphering power of the listener, khazones is blunted by the absence of a comprehending public. In Shimmy's view, the cohort of young Hasidic cantors are a *gesise*, a last gasp, which are misconstrued as a sign of sustainable vitality.

The "truth" about khazones, according to both Yoel and Shimmy, can be read in the historical trajectory of the art form and by the situation in the synagogues where cantors work today. According to this narrative, after a century of aesthetic development, cantors reached their aesthetic and popular peak in the first decades of the twentieth century. Khazones then withered after the Holocaust under the complimentary pressures of assimilation, Zionism, and the retrenchment of new forms of Orthodoxy that were radically altered in their aural culture. Contemporary synagogues offer evidence of the impact of this history. Cantors across denominations uniformly attest that khazones must be limited or purged from prayer leading in synagogues where they are employed (as I discussed in chapter 3).

Shimmy and Yoel describe contemporary performance in terms that resemble what sociologist Erving Goffman called "response cries," the exclamations made in response to stimuli when alone, such as yelling after stubbing one's toe. Goffman describes response cries as "a natural overflowing, a flooding up of previously contained feeling, a bursting of normal restraints."[12] Khazones gives voice to an irrepressible need for young Hasidic men to express themselves, using tools of the ambient Jewish culture. Yet the response cry is intrinsically dysfunctional as a form of meaning-making. It exists in a vacuum and cannot register as a form of social interaction or speech act.

Although Yoel and Shimmy would likely disagree with me, I might offer a different interpretation of the work of "cantorial revivalists." By performing khazones, Hasidic singers are creating a heterotopia, a kind of countercultural space that Foucault describes as offering commentary on and a social alternative to the limitations and disappointments of the normative culture.[13] Through musical training and performance, Hasidic cantorial revivalists create an alternative, imaginative space, employing tools of Jewish heritage toward a set of personal and idiosyncratic ends.

As Yoel highlighted in our conversations, khazones offered an outlet for a sensitive, artistically oriented young person. Most of the Hasidic cantorial revivalists I spoke to reported a similar emotional dynamic. Khazones was a generic form that provided the vocabulary with which to articulate a sense of otherness that could not otherwise be formulated. In the spaces where these young men "stared at the ceiling" while thinking, listening to records, singing, imagining themselves inhabiting the role of the star cantor of the golden age, they developed a sense of themselves through recourse to the sensuality and dramatic sentiment of the music. They frame their work as oppositional to the aesthetic impoverishment of their community, and as celebratory of a world of fantasy associated with old records and experiences of transportive prayer leading by elder cantors. The future of the music is less clear, and perhaps less important, than the uses the music is put to by the small cohort of artists for whom it plays a central role in constituting a world of aesthetics and counterculture. The music's future is created by its life in the moment.

Despite the gloomy prognostications of some of the key artists in the field, as we will see in the next chapter, khazones does in fact have a life in the present day. However, the life of the music may in fact be strongest outside the synagogue, its historic setting and the "natural" environment for Jewish liturgical performance.

4

Concert, Internet, and Kumzits

Stages of Sacred Listening

According to Yanky Lemmer, if a cantor sings too much khazones in synagogue, the prayer leader is at risk of being kicked "outta there." Zev Muller commented similarly that he wishes he had known at the beginning of his career not to sing extended cantorial pieces that congregants "did not care for." At times, cantors take a chastising tone toward the congregants who reject the sacred music genre they revere. David Reich told me:

> Davening has become very routine. There's very little place for creativity. They might get someone to daven for an *omud* (lead prayer at the reader's lectern) . . . But being too creative is frowned upon. Most of the people don't necessarily appreciate khazones. People don't have the patience. It requires you to get in touch with certain things in yourself that some people aren't comfortable with. They'd rather just sing melodies, easy stuff. This is deep.[1]

In the eyes of Hasidic cantorial revivalists, the impulse toward participatory music in the contemporary synagogue is often described as a distraction from the experience of prayer through listening to spiritually and aesthetically elevated music that they revere.

The previous two chapters, which focused on cantorial education and synagogue prayer leading, described arenas in which Hasidic cantorial revivalists engage with and are acted on by the norms and traditions of non-Hasidic American synagogues. These institutions of American Jewish life have their own histories with khazones that have pushed both nusakh and the sounds of gramophone-era cantorial performance to the periphery. In these areas, their musical lives closely resemble the situation for their non-Hasidic cantorial colleagues, who have parallel complaints with regard to the usefulness of their training in nusakh. The musical substance of cantorial revival is ill-suited to the cultural norms of most American synagogues. Instead, Hasidic cantorial revivalists find opportunities to articulate their music identities in performances outside the sacred setting of the synagogue.

This chapter focuses on three "out of context"-sites of cantorial performance—the concert stage, streamed video, and *kumzits* music making parties—that afford Hasidic cantorial revivalists opportunities to pursue their aesthetic aspirations in venues that are not specific to Jewish liturgical music. The recontextualization of the sacred accords with the radical project of cantorial revival, that seeks an experience of prayer through an aesthetic rather than through the rabbinically sanctioned avenues that are readily available to religious Jews. Revivalists offer a revision of the history of cantorial music, framing cantors as figures who spoke to the changing identities of Jews in modernity whose lives encompassed multiple conflicting worlds. In their conception of khazones, music of prayer functions both as a symbolic link to the Jewish past and as a transcendent signifier of the sacred reappropriated into individualistic and electronically mediated urban lifeways. This conception of cantorial music supports their project of creating artistic identities, even as it pushes their sacred art out of the conservative space of the synagogue.

For at least the past two centuries cantors have performed outside the synagogue for a variety of reasons, including seeking economic gain, representing the Jewish collective to non-Jews, or pursuing the opportunity to fulfill musical desires and career ambitions that embrace the aesthetics of music worlds beyond the liturgical. While these motivations are still relevant, present-day Hasidic cantorial revivalists have a more pressing concern about how to function as a cantor in the musical form they consider to be uniquely desirable. Whereas cantors a century ago sang in concerts or on records in a style that was developed within the context of worship, Hasidic cantorial revivalists today have learned and developed cantorial aesthetics largely by listening to old records as a mediating source. Unlike their early twentieth-century predecessors, for many Hasidic cantorial revivalists, "out of context" performances are the primary site for their work. Indeed, for some of the most talented singers, concerts, internet videos, and parties are the *only* forums available for performing in this style.

Through ethnographic observation and the historical analysis of concerts, internet videos of cantorial performances, and private home presentations, this chapter illuminates the ways in which Hasidic cantorial revivalists are able to articulate their musical aesthetics. By developing performance careers in venues outside the institutions of Jewish religious life they are able to hone their musical careers around a form of expressive culture that poses a challenge to the role played by music in the Hasidic community and in other contemporary Orthodox communities. Rather than accentuating the collective through a broadly understood and popular music form, singing khazones affords Hasidic cantorial revivalists an avenue for nonconforming self-expression. "Out of context" performances of cantorial music foreground a conception of cantorial music as an aesthetic experience with its own values distinct from the life of ritual in the synagogue.

PERFORMANCE LINEAGES:
CANTORS AS ARTISTS IN THE TWENTIETH CENTURY

Cantorial performance outside the synagogue has played an important part in the economy of Jewish sacred music since at least the nineteenth century. The Viennese cantor Salomon Sulzer (1804–90), the figure most associated with the modernization of Jewish liturgical music and the professionalization of the cantorate, performed in official state concerts at which he represented the Jewish community, as well as collaborating with the elite of the Viennese classical music scene.[2] In his concert performances Sulzer presented a public face of the Jewish community that highlighted the ease of movement of Jews in non-Jewish spaces and their integration into the life of the modern nation state (although the community did not always approve). Philip Bohlman suggests that cantors were responsible for inventing a modern conception of Jewish music, establishing the cantorate as a professional identity in relationship to a new domain of liturgical music expertise.[3] The cantor performed a paradoxical role, claiming to preserve tradition while simultaneously creating new repertoires that sought to elevate congregants through appeals to the sounds of elite European concert and church music. As cantorial concerts became a feature of Jewish life, they were popularly embraced; however, they also inspired controversies about new cantorial repertoires, spaces of performance, and engagements with technology. The choices cantors made in their concert programming aimed to illustrate that Jewish liturgical music could be compatible with elite concert music while articulating a set of social and political ambitions for themselves and their community, and simultaneously appealing to the broad musical tastes of an increasingly urban and educated Jewish public.

Cantorial performance outside synagogues involved a breaking of ritual boundaries that invited skepticism of cantorial ethics. In order to establish the ethical profile of cantorial concerts, cantors carefully constructed narratives around their performance that established the dignity or seriousness of the sacred artist. These performances of identity were achieved through the selection of venue and through concert programming. The writings and performance career of Elias Zaludkovsky (1888–1943) are illustrative of anxieties about concertizing. Zaludkovsky was a cantor and intellectual who published criticism influenced by Pinchas Minkovsky's antigramophone and concert polemics. Zaludkovsky seems to have coined the term *hefker khazones* (wanton cantorial music) to chastise his contemporaries who engaged in recording and other forms of suspect "popular" culture.[4] Despite his ethical concerns, Zaludkovsky concertized frequently both in synagogues and theaters, programming cantorial pieces between operatic arias and his own art song settings of Yiddish secular poetry. Zaludkovsky's concerts are illustrative of how cantors in the first decades of the twentieth century appealed to the tastes of a broad Jewish listening public that was conversant with the elite and popular musics of the day while maintaining a profile as a sacred artist in the rarified lineage of Sulzer.[5] To the consternation of conservative critics such as Zaludkovsky, star recording cantors in the United States performed in a more heterogenous variety of settings, ranging from elite concert halls like Carnegie Hall to vaudeville houses on bills that included acrobats and jazz singers.[6]

Opera, a popular form of entertainment in the nineteenth and early twentieth centuries, posed a particular conundrum for cantors whose vocal powers were ideal for stage roles. In the Jewish popular imagination, opera was represented as the paradigmatic path of corruption for a cantor. Yet at the same time, Jews were consumers of opera. In the frequently retold and mythologized story of Yoel Duvid Strashunsky (1816–50), a cantor in Vilna, an opera role posed a path toward apostacy and, ultimately, crippling madness for a cantor who failed to resist the temptation of a secular music career.[7] The best-known story about a cantor and the opera, in which Yossele Rosenblatt rejected a lucrative contract, carefully dances around issues of the ethics of public performance. According to his son, Rosenblatt justified his stage performances in part by suggesting that performing cantorial music for non-Jewish audiences created a positive image of Jews for the general population, echoing Sulzer's approach to the cantorate as constitutive of a public face of Jewish humanity, seeking social equality through appeals to aesthetics.[8]

While cantors continued to have popular followings and release records in the 1940s and 1950s, albeit on smaller community-focused record labels, the growth of the American Jewish community in this period was focused outside the urban immigrant milieu that favored the offerings of star cantors. Meanwhile, in the Hasidic community, professional cantorial prayer leading in the golden age style was never the norm. The Hasidic cantorial revival of the twenty-first century draws on a musical knowledge that is pointedly underground.

While some Hasidic cantorial revivalists hold pulpit positions, their self-driven musical educations are aligned more closely with a musical style than with the imperatives of institutions and communal norms. Commenting on his own perception that his chosen musical style is held in disfavor among people in his congregation and the broader public, Yanky Lemmer said:

> I really don't care that much. Because I have to do what I feel is right . . . I just feel that's the right thing for me, it's what I do, and I need to cultivate that . . . there comes a point when you have to define what you do. I enjoy singing regular stuff [i.e., pop songs] as well. But the stuff that moves me, that really moves me, is khazones.[9]

Reliance on their own aesthetic concept places some Hasidic cantorial revivalists in the perilous position of having no congregation to pray for, but also pushes cantors to seek other sites that can serve as venues for sacred performance. These "out of context" sites of performance lean into the cantorial traditions of stage performance and technological mediation. Bypassing the pulpit, Hasidic cantorial revivalists direct their music toward scenes and stages where they can realize their conception of sacred music.

STAGING CANTORIAL MUSIC
IN THE TWENTY-FIRST CENTURY

On January 31, 2018, Yanky and his brother Shulem Lemmer came to Stanford University to perform a concert in the Campbell Recital Hall. This opportunity arose directly out of excitement about their music generated by my research and the presentations I gave during my years as a graduate student at Stanford. I was also involved in the performance as a respondent during a talkback session after the concert, along with Dr. Mark Kligman of UCLA.

For this special event, the Lemmers had hired clarinetist Michael Winograd, an important figure in klezmer music who served for a number of years as the director of KlezKanada, the annual Klezmer music camp, and Yiddish New York, another annual festival dedicated to Yiddish culture. Winograd contracted trumpet player Jonah Levy, an active participant in jazz and klezmer scenes, to fill out the horn section. The band displayed a cultural schism running down the middle of the stage, which was made visual in part by the attire of the performers. On stage left stood Winograd and Levy, neither of whom are religiously observant. On stage right stood the keyboard player Shimmy Markowitz and drummer Yochi Briskman, both Hasidic musicians from Brooklyn. The Lemmer brothers stood center stage. The Hasidic musicians wore long jackets, white shirts, and yarmulkes, typical Hasidic comportment, while Winograd and Levy wore "unmarked" suit jackets. In interviews, Yanky Lemmer has referred to his Hasidic identity as a "look" or "gimmick" that is helpful in establishing his connection to audiences, especially in Europe where, he seems to imply, stereotyped images of Jews are more prevalent.

In his concert appearances, Lemmer typically performs for non-Hasidic Jews with mixed-gender audiences seated together. This was the case at the Stanford concert, where a crowd of mostly older men and women sat in the same auditorium. As a rule, gender segregation in public events is enforced in the Hasidic community. Performing for mixed-gender audiences is controversial for Hasidic singers and has emerged as a source of conflict between rabbis and musicians. The Lemmer brothers have mostly managed to steer clear of explicit conflict around the issue, although Yanky has mentioned that vitriolic comments about his performance for mixed seated audiences in a concert he gave at a non-Orthodox synagogue were a source of discomfort and anxiety for himself and his family.[10] While for non-Hasidic audiences the association of Hasidic Jews with classics of cantorial music may appear natural, even inevitable, singing cantorial music fits uneasily with the Hasidic cultural landscape, in large part because its audiences straddle lines of identity and often include Jews from more liberal backgrounds.

FIGURE 7. Yanky Lemmer. Photo courtesy of the Taube Center for Jewish Studies at Stanford University.

FIGURE 8. Yanky Lemmer, Yochi Briskman, and Shulem Lemmer. Photo courtesy of the Taube Center for Jewish Studies at Stanford University.

FIGURE 9. The Lemmer Brothers and ensemble. Photo courtesy of the Taube Center for Jewish Studies at Stanford University.

The pop-inflected rhythms and synthesizer presets favored by the Orthodox instrumentalists in Yanky and Shulem's backing band reflect the styles and timbres of contemporary Orthodox music, evoking pop song production and the sound of "one man band" wedding musicians who work the Orthodox society circuit performing hit songs on Casio keyboards. The synthesizer pop style was in conflict with the aesthetic presented by Winograd, a folklorist and avant-garde improvising musician. Winograd's playing draws on the sound of early twentieth-century klezmer records and contrasts starkly with the sonic world of the Hasidic players, whose musical terrain mostly hews to drum machine beats and synthesizer pop sounds.

For the opening numbers of the concert, the Lemmer brothers performed nostalgic Yiddish songs such as "Di naye hora" (The new hora) and "Mamele" (Mother), associated with Moishe Oysher (1906–58) and Molly Picon (1898–1992) respectively. While "Di naye hora" is a Zionist song that celebrates the founding of the State of Israel, in this concert setting and arrangement as a klezmer wedding dance number its political meaning was subsumed into an ethos of nostalgia. These pieces were presented in upbeat arrangements that skirted the line between klezmer and pop sounds and served as fitting showcases for the Lemmer brothers' charismatic and energetic stage personas.

For one of Yanky's solo numbers, about twenty minutes into the concert and after the audience had been wooed by a string of entertaining and familiar pieces, the instrumentation and musical style shifted. Winograd switched over to keyboard, replacing Markowitz, and accompanied Yanky in a duo format. Winograd set the keyboard to an acoustic piano setting, removing the stylized synthesizer effects that Markowitz had been using. Yanky introduced the prayer, "Ono Bokoach,"[11] a setting of a centuries-old prayer text of unknown authorship, which Josef Shlisky recorded in 1924, by telling the dramatic story of the cantor's childhood abduction by a choir leader who brought the boy singer to America—a story that has become part of cantorial lore through repetition in liner notes on reissue albums.[12] Yanky then went on to discuss the mystical prayer the piece sets, a poetic and evocative text that calls on God to untie the knots of the spirit. His spoken introduction prepared the audience to hear the cantor's voice as offering a forum for contemplating the experience of pain and an opportunity for mystical introspection. Yanky's speech invited the listeners to hear the music through the prism of the experiences of loss, vulnerability, and the political and economic vicissitudes of Jewish history.

Musically, "Ono Bokoach" was a radical departure from what had preceded it in the concert. Winograd's playing was minimalistic, eschewing flamboyant arpeggios and dance beats for a sparse sound that referenced the kinds of accompaniment heard on early records. On cantorial records, the organ or, less frequently, the piano or the orchestra, provides instrumental accompaniment, mostly played with great restraint, with sustained pedal points and only occasional figuration in imitation of the antiphonal responses that would have been sung by a choir. The austerity of Winograd's choices sounded intentional. His harmonization of the melody was a straightforward transcription from Shlisky's record, bringing to mind other early twentieth-century records that feature sparse and "raw" accompaniment, such as country blues, and Dixieland jazz records. Yanky gradually built up the dynamics of the recitative, exploring its emotional potentials over the course of the five minutes or so he was singing. As the piece gradually moved into the upper register of his voice, the characteristic krekhts accentuating the beginning of phrases became more prominent, matching the idiomatic styling of Shlisky's recorded performance.

Yanky's bodily gestures modeled the responses intended for the audience to experience: eyes closed, face slightly clenched, hands upturned in supplication. Yanky began to sweat. He looked as though he might be about to break into tears. The hall was silent as he sang, the sparse texture of the piano acting as a spotlight drawing Yanky's voice into the center of meditative attention. At the end of the piece, the audience, made up predominantly of older, non-Orthodox Bay Area Jews for whom golden age cantorial music is almost certainly not part of a synagogue-based ritual practice, burst into rapturous applause.

Yanky's emotive concert persona orients the audience to a conception of the cantor as arbiter of aesthetic experience and conduit to pleasure through music. In the concert format, Yanky is able to invoke both the classic sound of the records he loves and the presentational liturgical experience associated with the cantorial

FIGURE 10. Yanky Lemmer. Photo courtesy of the Taube Center for Jewish Studies at Stanford University.

FIGURE 11. The Lemmer Brothers and ensemble. Photo courtesy of the Taube Center for Jewish Studies at Stanford University.

golden age. The concert hall is a forum in which participants are willing to engage in stylized listening practices that cede authority to presentational performers and allow artists to set the parameters for Jewish liturgical experience. Yanky's stage performance connects to a history of cantorial concerts, but unlike cantors of the golden age for whom the pulpit was also a concert-like setting for performance, for Yanky, concerts play a pivotal role as a site for the performance of his concept of cantorial artistry that he can only rarely access in the synagogue.

THE INTERNET AND CANTORIAL CULTURE

Leaders in the Hasidic community have taken a variety of approaches to the internet, with the Chabad embrace of the web as a means of religious outreach representing an extreme liberal stance. A mass event held at Citi Field in 2012 represents a more conservative approach that is well represented among Hasidic leadership. At the 2012 gathering, rabbinic leaders implored their followers to abandon their use of the internet, citing fears about its deteriorative effects on youth and general morality.[13] Despite these qualms, anecdotal evidence suggests that internet use and social media are widespread among Brooklyn Hasidic Jews—both for commerce and entertainment. In the Hasidic cantorial revivalist community, the internet plays a significant role both as a source for learning golden age cantorial repertoire and as a site for performance.

Yanky Lemmer's 2007 video of "Misratzeh B'rachamim," which is based on the 1924 record of Mordechai Hershman, is a live recording of a concert held at the Young Israel Beth El Synagogue in Borough Park Brooklyn, where Yanky was serving as a choir singer for Cantor Benzion Miller.[14] Founded in 1902 and boasting superb acoustics in its cavernous Moorish-style sanctuary, Beth El has an important history as a center for cantorial music, having employed numerous star cantors at its pulpit, including Hershman himself. As I showed in interlude B, Beth El holds a unique position in the liturgical music world of Jewish New York as a holdout of prayer leading in a style that is reminiscent of the golden age presentational approach.

In his Beth El concert video, Yanky, at the time twenty-four years old, sings the piece a whole tone lower than Hershman, rendering his vocal tone darker than Hershman's original. There is a hesitance in his performance, his eyes downcast and his body still throughout (he had not yet developed his showman's bravura). Yet his performance is marked by attention to coloratura and ornamentation that immediately marks his performance as informed by the golden age style. Although the view count of this video has hovered around fifty thousand for over a decade, a modest reach for a "viral" video, Yanky claimed that posting this video on You-Tube led directly to a spate of work as a cantor and ultimately to his being hired at Lincoln Square, thereby giving him one of the most prestigious cantorial positions in New York. Yanky continues to regularly post videos on his Facebook and

Instagram accounts that range in production values from cell phone documentation of concerts to more professional music videos.

For Yoel Kohn, social media has provided his primary forum in which to perform as cantor after leaving the Hasidic community. He describes the role social media played in creating an opportunity for him as a cantor as follows:

> I became nonreligious, and I didn't actually pursue cantorial at all. For some reason I was recorded singing [Pierre Pinchik's 1928 record] "Rozo D'Shabbos" . . . A friend of mine was just pointing a camera at me. And we started recording . . . And suddenly, things started happening. People were contacting me. It became viral . . . So I thought, you know what, I'm gonna start producing, because as soon as I wanted to warm up, it became a big production, I became busy . . . Somebody posted it on Facebook, for friends only, and not just that, with a warning, please do not share, because I didn't want there to be a video of me singing without a yarmulke. I figured if my parents see this, it's gonna hurt them. But by the time it got back to my parents, my mother told me, Oh my God! You're famous! You're viral! I figured, alright. Fuck it. I'll produce some more. I'll put myself out there. Maybe get some work out of it. And that's it. That's the story of me.[15]

The 2015 video performance that altered Kohn's professional prospects was an impromptu cell phone recording that captured a display of virtuosity in the interpretation of old cantorial records.[16] The same is true for early videos of Yanky Lemmer. These raw documentarian videos allow cantors to inhabit the role of "viral" celebrities, using the internet as a venue for their style of sacred music. As cultural critics have noted, video sharing sites like YouTube have a unique capacity to negotiate between commerce and community with content driven by the roughhewn aesthetics of amateur videos.[17] For Yanky, viral internet moments helped stage a major career development. However, in his pulpit position Yanky is extremely limited in performing the kinds of early recorded cantorial repertoire that he initially attained notoriety for and that make up the bulk of his internet videos. For Kohn, the videos helped him frame a space as a cantor who had left his community, paving the way for making a modest "comeback" as a cantor, mostly singing at private events in the Hasidic community, always outside the synagogue ritual context. That his visual appearance is mainstream while he interprets classic cantorial records has been perceived as a paradox and a source of his charisma.[18]

Yanky Lemmer and other Hasidic cantorial revivalists have suggested that the internet helped draw Hasidic singers to cantorial performance by providing access to otherwise difficult to find old records. Aryeh Leib Hurwitz, a cantor who was born in the Brooklyn Chabad community, comments that he does not own any records of his own and listens and learns from cantorial records exclusively online, especially on a cantorial WhatsApp group where fans share mp3 files. Online archives, especially the Florida Atlantic University Recorded Sound Archive Judaic Collection, grant access to an enormous body of historical Jewish records that effectively make individual collections superfluous. The web-based archive contains an estimated 100,000 songs, featuring cantorial records from the earliest gramophone era records through mid-century American cantorial albums, and on into the present. Private collectors have uploaded their cantorial records to streaming sites such as YouTube, making them widely accessible. On file-hosting sites and social media platforms, Hasidic cantorial revivalists interweave uploads of old records with new videos of interpretations of classics, signaling an orientation toward music-making that blurs chronology and a pastiche approach to self-presentation that is well suited to the medium of the internet.

In their online videos, Hasidic cantorial revivalists inhabit the role of the cantor as presentational artist, directing the experience of liturgy through historically informed performances in ways that are rarely possible at the pulpit. With their video productions, cantors present themselves as artists with a relevant musical message, utilizing the most contemporary media platforms to reach a broader public. The artistry demonstrated on these videos serves an overt role as a form of self-promotion, putatively toward the goal of getting jobs as a cantor in concert or in the pulpit. At the same time, making videos functions as an end in itself, affording Hasidic singers a virtual site in which to perform their public identities as cantorial artists in the golden age style. The production of videos connects Hasidic singers to the musical world of the golden age, asserting the role of technological mediation as an expression of cantorial identity. Indeed, for Hasidic cantorial revivalists, the mediated sound of cantorial voices on records are the key source of legitimate knowledge about their art form. Producing recordings of themselves connects Hasidic cantors to a version of the kinds of musical practices typical of the artists they revere.

CANTORIAL *KUMZITS* IN HASIDIC BROOKLYN

The Hasidic kumzits is a music-making party, which, in its essence and aims, can be traced back to the first generation of Hasidim in Eastern Europe. In the early eighteenth century, Hasidic rabbinic leadership cultivated support from their followers through collective singing of paraliturgical music.[19] The term *kumzits* itself derives from Yiddish and literally refers to sitting together. As such, it signifies a central space for collective engagement in music. The khazones kumzits, as these parties are sometimes referred to by participants, differs from typical music parties in the community both in terms of the music being sung and the format of presentation. Instead of Hasidic nigunim, performers sing covers of early twentieth-century cantorial records of liturgical pieces derived from synagogue ritual (not paraliturgical pieces); and, instead of a group vocal texture, soloist voices are featured. As such, the khazones version of the kumzits is a relatively new phenomenon, seeming to have emerged in the twenty-first century. For the new generation of Hasidic cantorial revivalists, such parties are an important outlet for the performance and development of their artistry.

On a hot summer night in 2018, Yoel Kohn sang at a kumzits in the home of a Satmar Hasidic friend of his in Brooklyn, just a few blocks from the Williamsburg Bridge. Like the other men in attendance at the kumzits, Kohn was born and raised in the Satmar community. Despite his break with Orthodoxy, Kohn has maintained his passionate interest in cantorial music and is considered to be a star performer among a small cohort of Hasidic cantorial fans and khazones aficionados. On that summer night, Kohn had been invited to lead a private prayer service and then to participate in a round robin impromptu recital of cantorial classics sung by a small invited group of knowledgeable singers, all Hasidic men. Kohn began the party by leading *mariv*; the focal point of his prayer leading was a rendition of Hashkiveinu, a prayer text in the mariv service, using the setting recorded by Cantor David Roitman in April 1925.[20] Kohn's solo vocal performance was over eight minutes long, mirroring the length of Roitman's double-sided 78-rpm record. His voice captured nuances of Roitman's original with a timbral specificity and fidelity to the intonation and stylistic details captured on the old record.

Yoel, like his peers in the small community of cantors who are committed to historical performance practices, has cultivated coloratura singing techniques that closely follow the models provided by old records, including attention to microtonal inflection and ornamentation. In his performance of Hashkiveinu, Yoel executed a virtuosic falsetto coloratura passage typical of golden age cantorial performance. As in a concert setting, the kumzits attendees sat with eyes focused on the singer, some with looks of intense emotional engagement, mirroring the dynamic arcs of the music, others relaxed, sitting back in their chairs as passive and satisfied audience members. The men present, mostly singers themselves, sang choral responses at appropriate moments in the piece.

Mirroring Roitman's record, which featured a chamber ensemble made up of organ, flute, and string accompaniment, Kohn's rendition also relied on instrumental accompaniment, provided by David Reich, who used the string setting on his synthesizer keyboard, recalling the timbre of the historical performance. Departing from the original, Reich improvised a short passage to "fill in" the space when the 78-rpm record would be turned over to hear its completion on the other side. This mariv service was distinct from norms of Orthodox practice, not only because of the focus on cantorial performance, but also in regard to the use of a musical instrument during prayer. Instrumental accompaniment is forbidden in Orthodox synagogues, but it is a typical element in the sound of early cantorial records. The use of the keyboard in Yoel's prayer leading in this kumzits setting was a notable instance of aesthetic concerns appearing to override or obscure norms of ritual practice.

When Kohn finished, after a confusing and cacophonous interlude of everyone seeming to talk at once, other singers began to perform. One after another, the attendees took turns performing virtuosic vocal pieces recorded by early twentieth-century cantors, at the forefront Yossele Rosenblatt, Samuel Malavsky, and Zawel Kwartin. Some of the singers were youthful and raw; others were seasoned artists who had worked as professional cantors. These included Yossi Pomerantz, who until recently held a pulpit at the prestigious Modern Orthodox Congregation Beth Tikvah in Montreal, and Yoel Pollack, Kohn's cousin and a prominent singer in the Satmar community whose original compositions are sometimes performed at mass gatherings, such as the Satmar Rebbe's Chanukah celebration.

For the final number of the evening, the group sang Israel Schorr's "Yehi Rotzon Sheyibone Beis-Hamikdosh," a ubiquitous favorite originally recorded in 1927 and covered by countless cantors in concert and on record that I discussed above in chapter 1. The end of the piece was approached as an improvisatory jam session, with each of the singers taking a phrase, treating it as a virtuoso improvised cadenza, then passing on the solo to the next singer, and ending with the entire group singing the chorus together, resulting in a roaring, brassy swell of voices as each singer sought to assert his own presence.[21]

The kumzits offered a powerful space for the performance and experience of golden age repertoire, and an outlet for creativity and religious feeling. As such, the kumzits that night had much in common with "classic" Hasidic social music-making parties: it was a homosocial gathering for religious music-making, but with the difference that the musical focus was on the individual not the collective. Rather than reinforcing the social norms of the community, the party made room for the articulation of nonconformist approaches to prayer and aesthetics. The meaning of the party was transformed by the music itself, the presentational performance format, and the ambitions of the artists to reach across time to locate an aesthetic of Jewish prayer that they find to be uniquely compelling.

"KHAZONES IS DEAD": LONG LIVE KHAZONES

After the kumzits party in Williamsburg, a young man who had attended noted with disgust that none of the excellent singers present at the party could get a pulpit position as a cantor, including a few singers who are not so very young and already have substantial experience as professional artists. Switching into English from Yiddish, the young man proclaimed that "khazones is dead," echoing, perhaps intentionally, the old adage from the 1980s that "punk is dead," an articulation of the fear among members of a subculture that the antinormative stance of their music-loving community is at risk of imploding under the social pressures of nonconformity. But unlike punk, which putatively died owing to commercial overexposure and mindless imitation by noncognoscenti, fans of cantorial music fear the death of the genre because its artists are stifled by indifference.

Performance in venues outside the synagogue allows Hasidic cantorial revivalists opportunities to present their desired concept of liturgical expressive culture, pushing against commonly held cantorial narratives of communal indifference to golden age cantorial styles in the synagogue by accentuating other sites of presentation as forums for sacred music. "Out of context" spaces of cantorial performance allow Hasidic cantorial revivalists to connect with the musical past that is the focus of their desires, but with a changed approach to the sociality and function of the music. Whereas cantors of the golden age presented the sacred music style that they developed in synagogue prayer-leading contexts using new mediated technologies and in secular concert spaces, for today's Hasidic cantorial revivalists the opposite is the case. A form of cantorial music they have learned primarily from mediated sources provides the repertoire and stylistic norms of their performance, which is usually conducted outside the synagogue ritual context.

Instead of deriving their sacred music practice from a communally constructed worship music culture, Hasidic cantorial revivalists are focused instead on the aesthetics of their own subculture, invoking a temporally displaced locus of authority that values the music of the past over that of the present while articulating a form of subjectivity that strains limits placed on expressive behavior in their birth community. By singing cantorial music outside the synagogue, Hasidic cantorial revivalists seek to reconcile their alienation from the musical life of the contemporary synagogue by framing cantorial performance as an art experience independent of ritual, but one that is suffused with the spiritual authority of the liturgical roots of their musical offering.

Golden age cantors described their work as serving a variety of functions, including addressing communal desires for cultural preservation, seeking aesthetic elevation of the Jewish community through artistry, and as a means of generating deeply felt experiences of prayer. While contemporary Hasidic cantorial revivalists share these goals as a foundational point of reference, their work points to another set of possibilities for the meaning of cantorial performance and its relationship to the Jewish collective. For Hasidic cantorial revivalists, pursuing aesthetic excellence through khazones is a practice that engages critically with the norms of the Jewish community and surfaces a conception of cantorial music as a nonconforming practice. Khazones offers the cantors a means to articulate artistic impulses and feeling within a Hasidic social context that places limits on expressions of individualism. Their work challenges the norms of multiple Jewish communities, creating a musical experience through repertoires and vocal techniques that are instantly recognizable as markers of difference from the norms of any contemporary synagogue.

Hasidic cantorial revivalists surface an alternative history of cantorial music as an art form that directly addresses and even accelerates points of tension in the Jewish collective response to modernity. The music of golden age cantors attained the status of a recognized representation of the Jewish collective through a system of aesthetics, not through adherence to rabbinic values. The challenges that cantors have posed to religious authority in the past continue to resound in the nonconforming stylistic choices of Hasidic cantorial revivalists. Khazones offers the cantors an alternative to what they perceive as parochialism in synagogue music and challenges the status of normative definitions of Jewish law and custom as the deciding factor in personal comportment in their birth community. By highlighting nonsynagogue sites of performance, whether by choice or necessity, Hasidic cantorial revivalists foreground one possible history of cantorial music that resonates with their own life stories, in which Jewish sacred music is a practice that is dependent on performance outside religious institutions in order to achieve its fullest expression. In this version of cantorial history, new technologies and secular venues allow artists to represent Jewish collectivity in ways that push at the boundaries of rabbinic authority, framing aesthetics, performance, and nonconformity as central organizational values in the music of prayer.

Interlude C

Producing the Revival

Making Golden Ages *the Album*

After experiencing the charismatic talent and powerful sense of community evinced in cantorial kumzits parties, the idea entered my head to produce a record of Hasidic cantorial revivalists. How I brought this idea to fruition was a process that involved strengthening, and at moments straining, my connection to the artists who participated in my research project. Rather than being simply an unusually intense fan who had followed the cantors around for years, I began to take on a role in producing the music. This began with me leveraging my access to the resources of my research institution, Stanford University, to promote the work of the cantors. Already by the time I began pursuing the record project, I had been involved in producing concerts of the Lemmer brothers and Yoel Kohn.

My new, self-nominated role as record producer of the "cantorial revival" involved some negotiations. I was trying to establish a modicum of trust beyond the scope of my relationship with the artists as an academic researcher. My new goal was to engage in dialogue with the artists about what a record of their work should document and how we would go about making it. The process of raising the funds for the recording project, confirming the participants, juggling schedules and engaging the studio that I thought would be best suited to the aesthetic of the performers took the better part of six months. Over this period, I had numerous discussions with the performers about what material they would perform, exploring the classic cantorial records they wanted to create "covers" of, and conversations about which artists to include in this recording project.

Following what I considered to be the organic ethos of a khazones party I had attended in Williamsburg, I organized the recording session around the lineup that had been present that night. I invited David Reich to take the role of accompanist on keyboard. My reasoning was that his knowledge of the cantorial repertoire and comfort with the style would give the cantors the freedom to be able to take their performance in whatever direction they desired. My hope was that the session would provide a degree of openness that would allow the artists to follow their musical fantasies, to improvise, to perhaps create new pieces or sing classic numbers that rose to their mind spontaneously in the context of the music making environment. I focused on Hasidic cantorial revivalists who were participants in my research in deciding who to invite. This decision was not an obvious one, as the cantorial community that these singers interface with embraces cantors from a variety of backgrounds, not only the Hasidic community. The fact that I was crafting a "narrative" about cantors from the Hasidic world did not escape notice and was not approved of by all the participants.

I had hopes that having all the cantors in the studio at the same time would allow for creative interplay and possibly facilitate collaborations. In making decisions about how the session would be carried out I was building on my years of experience making records of my own but was also guided by my fantasies about the kind of record I hoped to listen to in the future. My goals were informed by my personal aesthetics that favor a documentary approach to capturing performances "live" in the studio and that embraces the human "noisiness" of music making, especially the rough edges that are key to the emotive qualities of cantorial performance. While I discussed these aesthetic issues with the participants in advance, I did not predict how my aesthetic choices might conflict with the desires of the artists.

In this Interlude, I will offer some ethnographic vignettes from the recording session that led to the recording of the album "Golden Ages: Brooklyn Chassidic Cantorial Revival Today." I will attend to the problems of aesthetics and artistic control that emerged while working on the album. As I discovered, the cantors were not in agreement with me about some basic decisions I had made in planning the recording. Embracing the situation with its limitation, the cantors and I worked together to create a document that brought out remarkable performances, even if it is not "the final word" on these artists, their work, and their musical self-conceptions. In the dialogue between their musical lives and my own, I was brought into a deeper awareness of the space between my stance of interpretation and reception, positioned outside the Hasidic cantorial revivalist scene, and the inner lives of the artists, which are more textured and complex than any critical perspective can contain.

GETTING STARTED

Seeking to build on the aesthetic of the cantors' musical interests, I sought a sonic counterpoint in the production quality. In hopes of achieving this end, I got in touch with Gabe Roth, the founder of Dap Tone Records, a record label associated with neo soul music. In addition to having worked as a band leader and an entrepreneur, Roth is a lauded recording engineer who has built a reputation as an important exponent of analog recording technologies associated with classic mid-twentieth century records. I was able to engage Roth to take on the project and booked the studio for an extended multiday session. The recording was scheduled to take place from January 13 to 15, 2019.

Dap Tone studio is located in a two-story brownstone building in Bushwick, Brooklyn. It is situated in a part of Brooklyn that has undergone a radical gentrification, although its working-class character as an immigrant neighborhood has not been completely covered over by the thriving economy of businesses catering to young college-educated whites and upper-middle-class professionals. The studio has been in operation since the early 2000s and has a pleasingly ramshackle quality. After entering via the first floor, one sees that there are two rooms: the first is a control room with tape deck, an audio mixing board, and a variety of outboard processing equipment mounted in racks. The room also contains images of Sharon Jones, the late rhythm and blues singer whose work is closely associated with the studio. The second room is the "live room" where the musicians perform. The studio is located just blocks from Williamsburg, where several of the participants in the session grew up or still live. It is literally in their neighborhood; and yet it is a world apart, situated in the realm of secular society and the arts, far outside the perimeters of the Hasidic world. And yet, Dap Tone was not entirely unknown to the cantors. For example, Yanky Lemmer expressed excitement that we would be recording in the same studio where Amy Winehouse made her Grammy-winning 2006 album *Back to Black*.

On the first day of the session, I arrived early with Tatianna McCabe, the videographer I had engaged to document part of the recording session. Gabe Roth and an assistant were in the control room setting up. I walked into the live room where a Hammond organ and an upright piano were set up in a corner opposite each other so that a performer could easily switch from one instrument to the other between songs. The piano looked terrible. Many of the keys were chipped, missing their ivory casing, but it played well and sounded beautiful. The state of the piano was typical of the space. The studio possesses a perhaps intentionally dingy grandeur—it is unarguably shabby in its décor and has many pieces of partly broken music gear lying around.

David Reich arrived first, followed shortly after by Yanky Lemmer. Gabe Roth gave Reich a quick lesson on how to control the organ draw bars to achieve different sounds. David had never played on an actual organ before, the synthesizer being the instrument he has extensive experience with. Yoel Kohn arrived, increasing the intensity and energy in the room with his anxious and, at moments, almost hysterical antics and seemingly uncontrollable impulse to make scandalizing comments. His repartee with Yanky Lemmer was jovial, bordering on manic. The three cantors were in high spirits, joking around. Yoel did a spot-on impersonation of David Roitman's Yiddish-language records, mimicking Roitman's pinched, overly precise vocal approach.

FIGURE 12. David Reich, Yanky Lemmer and Yoel Kohn in front of Daptone Studios. Photo by Tatianna McCabe.

FIGURE 13. David Reich at the organ. Photo by Tatiana McCabe.

We planned to begin with Yanky. In conversations preparatory to the session, I had expressed to Yanky that I wanted him to follow his desires and impulses in choosing what he wanted to sing. For his first piece, he decided to record Zawel Kwartin's "Ribono Shel Olam," an eight-minute-long record that is intensely challenging, both in its technical and its emotional qualities. Choosing this piece was indicative of the seriousness with which Yanky was approaching the project, but it made warming up vocally very challenging and created the sense that recording it would be a difficult task rather than one that would foster a sense of pleasure and satisfaction in the experience. Yanky sang beautifully but got caught on difficult passages. Yoel kept running into the live room from the control room to discuss complex ornamentation patterns. In the control room, Yoel sat in intense concentration listening, frequently singing along and noting whenever Yanky's performance departed from Kwartin's original.

After working through the piece painstakingly for several hours, Yanky was in need of a break. Yoel went in to record; however, like Yanky, he had chosen an incredibly challenging piece, Gershon Sirota's "Hashem Malach," a piece that has been recorded by many cantors over the years, perhaps most famously in a standout performance by Moshe Koussevitzky. Yanky and David worked out a beautiful trio vocal arrangement for the middle section of the piece. Yoel took a variety of approaches to recording, including singing the piece one section at a time. Even with this detailed and methodical process, he was not able to finish a take

FIGURE 14. Yanky Lemmer. Photo by Tatiana McCabe.

FIGURE 15. David Reich and Yanky Lemmer. Photo by Tatiana McCabe.

he felt satisfied with. Both Yanky and Yoel are keenly aware of the possibilities for hyper-perfectionism granted by digital recording technologies that allow micro-editing of performances and a variety of forms of enhancements that smooth out "flaws." They chafed at the absence of these tools. At the same time, Yanky was excited by the beautiful sounds being achieved by the skillful use of recording methods. He seemed to be aware that his voice was being captured with a rich and detailed timbre that was unlike what he had experienced working in other studios.

When Shimmy Miller first walked into the studio, he looked in amazement at the reel-to-reel 24 track tape machine. He said, "I saw something like this when I was a child." Shimmy is no stranger to recording studios, being the son of a cantor who has been making records throughout his life and having done a fair amount of recording of his own as soloist and choir leader.

The idea of not being able to micro-edit performances quickly and seamlessly during the session was an annoyance and challenge for the cantors. My intention in planning the recording session was that the demands of "live" performance would lead the singers to achieve a heightened sensitivity and would elicit committed performances. The idea that some degree of human imperfection would also be documented did not strike me as oppositional to the powerful impact of the cantors' voices that I had heard and been moved by on numerous occasions.

Digital recording platforms have the power to create stylized representations of sound that can effectively manipulate audio signals to produce a sense of sonic smoothness. Digital editing tends to be used to erase a variety of human noises, intentionally blurring into the background "mistakes," including a variety of artefacts of vocal anatomy. This editorial function plays a powerful part in the experience of contemporary music-making and has influenced perceptions of what a professional recording should sound like. Not having access to the digital recording toolkit was perceived as problematic by the cantors. The perceived technical challenge of the analog recording environment was a source of ongoing tension during the sessions. The cantors blamed the analog gear for a variety of problems, ranging from reasonable qualms about the difficulty of editing takes, to more questionable claims, such as blaming beginning a take before the record button had been hit on the tape machine.

Working together with the cantors in the studio, I found that they had their own concept of how they would like to record and a strong grasp of the technical process of recording and recording technologies. The key conflicts that emerged during the session focused on questions about digital versus analog recording technologies, as well as the aesthetic problems of documenting "live" performances, in opposition to sculpting a stylized representation of vocal performances that would be smooth and "flawless." While the cantors spend much of their musical lives listening to old records that are characterized by the mid-range distortion and surface noise of shellac discs and that mostly document unedited performances, perhaps unsurprisingly, their concept of how records should be made is influenced by the mainstream music in the Hasidic community and more broadly in American pop music.

To the extent that the cantors had experiences of recording, they had worked in digital studios where pop-style record producers make music using computer programs that facilitate a cut-and-paste approach to recording. The distinctive creative approach facilitated by computer audio software enables engineers to edit performances to achieve a performance that minimizes human error. The "mistake-free" aesthetic that is attainable using a digital recording platform extends to the use of effects that smooth out dynamics and timbre. In recording the human voice, pop records typically cut out the sound of breathing and many of the vocal mannerisms that draw attention to the embodied presence of the singer.

This digital approach is radically different from the kind of recording that we were set up to do at Dap Tone studio. At the recording session, we recorded live to analog tape, not to a computer program. While editing is not by any means impossible with tape, it is an unwieldy process that cannot be achieved instantly with a few clicks of a button. The cantors did not want to eliminate the distinctively cantorial timbres and vocal effects that might read as "noise" to the ears of pop music listeners, but they did want to be able to have greater control over fine details of performance. They wanted, quite reasonably, to be able to break up phrases and to redo elements of their singing where they felt they had not performed according to their highest standards. This kind of "punching in" was basically impossible because of the setup in the room where all the instruments were bleeding into each other's microphones, reducing the ability to isolate and manipulate individual channels of sound. While I was focused on the particular strengths of the recording aesthetic in the studio and saw this setup as ideal for creating a beautiful document of their work, the cantors had doubts, especially about my goal of documenting complete performances.

The cantors were disturbed by the fact that their recorded performances would be flawed—that is, from the stylized perspective of a recorded music aesthetic. My concept for how to capture their khazones revolved around documenting a performance that a cantor would give, working through a piece of music from start to finish. The cantors understood the value of this approach but generally disagreed with the idea of prioritizing the integrity of a performance over the perfection of the vocal quality being documented. Push and pull over this was a constant issue throughout the recording session and led to the cantors expressing disappointment with the experience.

While I am not concerned with answering the question of who was "correct" from an aesthetic perspective, the issues around representation and defining meaning in the presentation of the work of the cantors present theoretical problems with real ethical resonances. The ethics of control over the public image of Hasidic cantors is a troubling topic for me that brought out self-doubt about the meaning of my role in presenting the work. As scholar and curator, what I do, indeed what I think, has the potential to misrepresent or, worse, do damage to the integrity of the artists and their life's work.

The full story of cantorial revival requires the cantor's authorization in order to be fully articulated. While I have endeavored to act from a place of curiosity and deep respect for the artists, my own aesthetic impulses are always a force in the way I write about the cantors and even more so in the recording process. I am hopeful that the cantors will have the opportunity to produce their own records in the future. At moments during our days in the studio, I imagined that the reason the cantors desired a digital recording platform was to cover for the idiosyncrasy and antinormative qualities of their musical pursuits. The cantors seemed to express the desire that the representation of their work would be ameliorated into a smooth, flawless sound, akin to the norms of Orthodox pop music. Such a representation, while offering fidelity to the desires they expressed during the session, would create a picture that would blur out some of the noisy humanness, conflict, and sonic otherness that are characteristic of their musical lives. It is possible that I value this "noise" quality of their work more than the artists themselves do.

"TIHER RABI YISHMAEL," ANTISEMITISM,
AND THE ABUSE OF THE HASIDIC MYSTIQUE

At the end of the first day of recording, dissatisfied with what he had sung, Yanky asked to be given more time to work than had originally been scheduled for him. We ended up coming in early the next day, before the other artists, and he sang two more pieces, both drawn from the records of Zawel Kwartin. I accompanied him on organ, in a quiet session, free from the raucous energy of the previous day. These two pieces satisfied him to a greater extent than what he sang the first day.

On a break after completing a take of Zawel Kwartin's "Tiher Rabi Yishmael," Yanky and Gabe Roth had an extended conversation. Yanky explained the text of "Tiher Rabi Yishmael," a liturgical prose poem that recounts the persecution and martyrdom of first-century CE rabbis at the hands of the Romans. The text is part of a longer memorial prayer titled Eilo ezkero, which is recited on Yom Kippur and includes gruesome depictions of violence. Yanky spoke about the resonance of the prayer with Holocaust memorial, and with ongoing issues of antisemitism.

Yanky told an anecdote about singing at a Holocaust memorial in Poland and how he felt that his image as a Hasidic man was being used to forward a narrative about Polish heroism during World War II. Ironically, Holocaust memorials have been abused as part of a whitewashing campaign by the right-wing government seeking to present an image of Polish victimization, resistance, and national greatness, obscuring and erasing the role Poles had played as perpetrators of anti-Jewish violence. He felt that his presence had been used propagandistically to present the government as tolerant by manipulating his visual identity to erase the taint of antisemitism.

Concern about the misuse of his image is a recurring theme for Yanky. This is in part the result of the fact that he has become something of a star in Poland, performing primarily to a non-Jewish audience. Yanky has expressed the idea that his Polish fans see in him a vision of authenticity and the Polish past, before the Jewish community of the country was destroyed, and that at times he is employed to perform this past as a kind of reenactment in a theatrical form, perhaps calculated to assuage feelings of guilt Polish people may be troubled by.

I perceived that Yanky's perceptions of the misuse of the image of Hasidic Jews as signifiers of authenticity played a role in his criticisms of the organization of the recording session. Yanky has been involved in numerous productions of internationally known prestigious cantors, usually outside the Hasidic community. He suggested that my selections of personnel and the exclusion of non-Hasidic cantors were part of advancing a "narrative" rather than being motivated by purely aesthetic standards.

Yanky's critique made sense. I took note of the fact that Yanky was alive to my decision-making process and was critical of it. I also noted that Yanky's cantorial community was quite different from that of the other cantors who participated in the project, having expanded through his career to encompass cantors from a variety of communities, including cantors from the liberal movements such as Cantor Azi Schwartz of the Park Avenue Synagogue in Manhattan, whom Yanky views as a friend and peer. While there is a "scene" of Hasidic cantors in Williamsburg and Borough Park who share commonalities in terms of their family backgrounds, education, and musical interests, this is not the only community that Yanky, or any of the cantors for that matter, belong to. It was I, the outsider, who had chosen to group these singers based on this facet of their identity.

Yanky's critique rang true to me; he was showing me the mirror of my gaze and revealing the ways in which my perception is reductionist and perhaps exoticizing. I chose to see him as a Hasidic Jew, categorizing him according to his visual identity and thereby reifying the same form of gaze he and the other cantors face in their day-to-day lives in New York; *this* is how he and they are appraised in daily life by outsiders to his community such as passersby on the street or people on the subway. I foregrounded this identity above other aspects of his public persona, such as his professional identity as a pulpit cantor, an aspect of his life that aligns with the contemporary American cantorate outside Orthodoxy; or simply as a musician—for example, through the lens of his work as a vocal soloist in philharmonic orchestral concerts. Instead, I chose to identify him through the markers of his visible identity.

With the "Hasidic cantorial revivalist" lens that I lean on in this project, my intention was to foreground Yanky's self-proclaimed most keenly held passion: khazones. As Yanky himself has noted, the professional communities that he moves in, especially the synagogue, inhibit this passion and frustrate some of his musical ambitions. My research has been trained on the genre Yanky foregrounded in his self-presentation as an artist. I sought to learn what early twentieth-century cantors and cantorial music meant to him and the possibilities he finds in the music for self-expression and the creation of a musical life. My goal with making a record was to create space for him to do whatever he wants musically. I thought my plan could in some way work in opposition to those aspects of his musical life that have inhibited him from holding agency as an artist. Yanky was aware of this goal.

I have a list of maybe five, ten khazones pieces that literally almost every time I hear them, I just get chills. They do it for me. And these are those pieces and I never really felt ready to record. I still don't feel ready. But I figured I'll give it a shot. Because you're the first producer, so to speak, that told me, just feel what you connect to most. Just sing that. (Yanky Lemmer, January 14, 2019)

And yet even in the context of this recording session, which was designed to integrate artists in the production process, Yanky seemed to feel that the "narrative" or stereotype around his identity played a role in the creative decision making. By foregrounding his connection to Hasidic Jews, I foreshortened and limited other potential formations of identity. As Yanky is well aware, his visual identity works heavy-handedly to create stories in the heads of other people. These stories, in turn, are at times used as the basis for constructing musical or cultural narratives that he is expected to fulfill, usually in the context of concerts for non-Hasidic people.

As philosopher Linda Alcoff notes in her defense of the value of identity as an analytic tool for describing human experience, "Where the salience of identity is affirmed, it is sometimes all too easy to then concretize identity's impact, to assume clear boundaries, and to decontextualize and dehistoricize identity formations."[1] While Yanky is proudly unapologetic for his Hasidic identity, he is aware of the problems of perception and the ways in which he is liable to be reduced to stereotype.

Yanky affirms the importance of his identity and enculturation in giving him tools he needed to approach the cantorial tradition, and audible traces of Hasidic upbringing in his music are part of his appeal to certain audiences. Yet his music also makes problems for him with conservative members of his birth community, which rejects khazones as representative of a different, putatively less "religious" version of Jewishness. At the same time, outsiders to the community are all too happy to collapse Hasidic identity into a public role as a "traditional musician," disregarding the particularities of Yanky's community. In all these narratives, the intense discipline and the personal sacrifices involved in cultivating his craft as a cantor and artist are blurred and disregarded.

"HALLELUYAH": CONFLICT, RESOLUTION AND LEONARD COHEN

After a quiet morning and early afternoon spent with Yanky on the second day of the session, more and more cantors started to arrive. First to appear was Yossi Pomerantz, a cantor with an international biography. He was born into the Israeli Hasidic community and had experience as a choir singer starting in childhood. Yossi worked for some time as a cantor in Montreal and had recently moved to Brooklyn. I met him at a kumsitz party in Brooklyn and had been startled by his unusually powerful, loud, and expressive voice, which Yoel Kohn had described succinctly with the words, "He is God." Pomerantz had suggested that he was in poor voice and expressed nervousness about recording, and yet his performance was extremely strong. Pomerantz recorded "V'al Yedai" by Sholom Katz, a cantor who survived the Holocaust and whose recordings were popular in the years immediately after World War II.

FIGURE 16. David Reich and Yossi Pomerantz in the control room. Photo by Tatiana McCabe.

As Yossi was recording, we were joined by Yoel Pollack and Shimmy Miller. Yoel Pollack is a first cousin of Yoel Kohn, on his mother's side, and unlike his cousin, he has retained his powerful ties to the Satmar community. While most of the other cantors involved in this project have worked in synagogues and performance venues outside the Hasidic world, Yoel Pollack expressed satisfaction with the music-making opportunities he is able to put together within the community. When I asked if he has worked in Modern Orthodox synagogues or only works in Satmar synagogues and community events, he pointedly rejoined, "What do you mean, 'only'?" Yoel Pollack serves as a High Holiday prayer leader and also composes his own pieces, which are sometimes premiered at communal events presided over by the Satmar rebbe. While he shares with his cousin and the other cantors a passionate interest in golden age khazones, his aesthetic pursuits have not led to the kind of crossing of boundaries of identity that typify the cohort of Hasidic revivalist cantors.

Yoel Pollack's presence seemed to delight his cousin Yoel Kohn, and to excite a nervous tension as well. The two men sat with their arms around each other, chatting loudly, joking, and at one point bursting into intense argument. Yoel Kohn at times displays a habit of making provocative comments—sometimes aggressively directed at whomever he happens to be in the room with—which are often characterized by humorous antisanctimony. As someone who has rejected a religiously fundamentalist approach to life, he is given to making comments that mock

FIGURE 17. Yoel Kohn. Photo by Tatiana McCabe.

religious beliefs and ritual acts, often hinging his barbed comments on the puta-tive irrationality of religiously prescribed behaviors, travestying sacred texts and the concept of the divine origin of ritual. These areas make up the basis of the lifestyle of the other participants in the recording session, and I was therefore concerned with how his behavior would impact the others. However, Yoel Kohn was a known quantity to the other cantors present; the cantorial community is fairly small and the singers mostly already knew each other from musical or social events. For the most part they seemed to be willing to countenance his comments without shock, even laughing at him and his scandalous speechifying.

After Yossi Pomerantz finished his first piece, with everyone present packed into the control room to listen back to his performance, a serious argument erupted. Yoel Pollack and Yoel Kohn had been engaging in banter, at first argu-ing about music. Yoel Kohn expressed the controversial opinion that the revered cantor Samuel Malavsky's style of khazones is "boring." He clarified his opin-ion, expressing that while he loved the heartfelt qualities of his parlando style of prayer recitation, sometimes referred to in cantorial discourse as *zogn* (Yiddish, speaking), he thought that these expressive vocal mannerisms were mismatched with a simplistic approach to composition. This playfully contentious conversa-tion about music had somehow gotten out of control, descending into a debate about the validity of obeying the tenets of Orthodox Jewish life. The ensuing argu-ment, fueled by Yoel Kohn making provocative statements, spilled over into open conflict. Yoel Pollack never raised his voice and remained outwardly calm in the face of Yoel Kohn's crescendo of hurried, agitated speech. His cousin's outward tranquility seemed to fluster Kohn and to increase the intensity of his emotions. Raw feelings were expressed. Kohn leapt up from the couch and started yelling, Yiddish interspersed with curses in English. I tried to smooth over the conflict and calm Kohn down, to minimal effect. Yoel Kohn later explained to me that his outburst came in response to comments both his cousin Yoel Pollack and David Reich had been making that he felt were intended to belittle and demean his decision to leave Hasidic life. Their remarks brought to the surface some of the painful ongoing tension that troubles his relationship with his family and old community.

My goal to keep the session running smoothly was interrupted. With some effort I got all the singers back into the live room to begin working on the next piece scheduled. Shimmy Miller was supposed to be accompanied by the whole group singing as a chorus. Yoel Kohn continued to yell at his cousin, and the whole room was discordant with everyone speaking at once, the group overexcited by the fracas. David Reich, an unusually level-headed and calm person, came up to Yoel Kohn and said, "It's not about who's right or wrong in the argument. You are using bully tactics to win and it's not fair." This comment seemed to have some impact.

Then David sat down at the piano and started playing Leonard Cohen's "Hallelujah." All the cantors, including Yoel Kohn, stopped talking or yelling, and began to sing. They all knew the song, and not just the chorus; they sang through multiple verses. David had found a way to tame the anxious roving energy that had been unleashed by the family drama.

Listening to the eruption of tension between the two Yoels, I imagined that their family argument also managed to invoke old controversies around the nature of khazones, with Yoel Kohn embodying the accusations made by critics that cantors and their music are in some ways at odds with traditional Jewish ideals of piety and adherence to communal norms and forms of sociability. The scandal of the disconnect between Yoel Kohn's powerful performance of prayer music and his unapologetic condemnation of the religious context the music emerges from is confusing, potentially upsetting. It occurred to me that perhaps the other cantors see in him a dangerous reflection of how they are perceived by some conservative elements in their community. Words were inadequate to cover the breach in the norms of behavior that was brought into the open by the two cousins' fight; instead, it seemed to me, music was needed to bring the group back into something resembling cohesion.

The music that achieved this repair was not a piece of khazones, the shared musical passion of the group of men and the reason for the gathering, but rather a piece of music with a bicultural identity. "Hallelujah" is the creation of a recognizably Jewish figure, and yet stylistically it is connected to secular popular music, or even Protestant church hymns, not to the Jewish

FIGURE 18. Yoel Kohn, Yoel Pollack, Shimmy Miller, and Zevi Steiger. Photo by
Tatiana McCabe.

musical styles these singers are associated with. Yet the Leonard Cohen song
was acceptable, perhaps even uniquely fitting in that moment to achieve a
modicum of shared communal feeling of purpose that was necessary in order
for the session to proceed. Perhaps the song was fitting because of its broad
approach to the concept of the sacred in music that embraces worlds of feeling
deriving both from art, here conceived as a secular branch of knowledge, and
religious life.

This ecumenical approach was appropriate in the context of the recording session because of Yoel Kohn's critiques of Orthodoxy. His stance in opposition to
his birth community rendered him an outsider, even while his knowledge and
feeling for religious music was acknowledged by all present. Singing "Hallelujah" reconfigured the category of "religious feeling" as something that could fit
into the space of the non-Hasidic world that Yoel Kohn had entered. And at the
same time, the song was welcome in an intimate Jewish space that was recognizable to this group of Hasidic men. The "Jewishness" of the song was achieved
through the identity of its composer, the lyrics that contain recognizable references to images and themes from the Bible, and perhaps some other quality that
is harder to articulate. The cantors were laughing while they sang, acknowledging
the contrivance of the device of foisting a "kumbayah" sing-along moment on the
group to quell an experience of disunity and eruption of long-simmering tensions.
Even while the cantors were too sharp to accept the clumsiness of the musically

FIGURE 19. Yoel Kohn, Shimmy Miller, and Yossi Pomerantz. Photo by Tatiana McCabe.

brokered reconciliation, the tensions in the room were nevertheless calmed to a point where we could continue.

Finally, we got to work on Shimmy's piece, a performance of the Yehi Rotzon prayer for the blessing of the new month. As I discussed in interlude B, this prayer is the center piece of Shimmy's father Benzion Miller's monthly services held at Temple Beth El, a bastion of cantorial culture. Yehi Rotzon is a central part of the cantorial repertoire and exists in countless version with different melodies. Shimmy's take on the piece was partly improvised but included a chorus that recurred twice in the song that the entire cast of cantors sang in a resounding burst of sound. The unmetered recitative sections were lent a special impact by the contrast with the charming waltz metered melody the group sang together in unison. His years of choir leading were put to good effect, and he quickly taught the group the melody and offered easy-to-follow directions to guide the tempo and the dynamics with his hands and even, partly, through his facial expressions. Shimmy was in excellent voice, easily accessing his upper register and executing beautiful and complex coloratura. The engineer Gabe Roth, a staunchly secular Jewish man, offered the opinion, "If it sounded like this in synagogue, I'd go every week."

VULNERABILITY, CONTEMPORARY KHAZONES, AND CONTROL OF THE MEANS OF REPRESENTATION

While the recording session included many moments of excitement and aesthetic success, the moments that were most characteristic of the endeavor involved frustration, especially for two of the lead artists in the project, Yanky Lemmer and Yoel Kohn. For these singers, the high standards of vocal quality and precision in execution of the ornamentation patterns associated with each piece in their repertoire set a bar for performance that they did not feel they had achieved. This frustration created tensions and led to a perception that the technical parameters of the recording were at fault and were stymying the achievement of their desired musical concept.

On the third day of the session, Yoel Kohn's desire for performance excellence effectively derailed the session. He spent many hours working on single pieces and cajoled me into giving him more time than had been scheduled. He tried breaking up a piece in sections, working complex passages one at a time. He sang sections of pieces over and over to try to achieve a completely accurate and fluid line in passages that contained high notes or particularly important coloraturas. In the process, Kohn wore himself out before achieving the sound he wanted. The fact that the organ and voice were being recorded in the same room and bled into each other's track on the multitrack tape recording system was extremely troubling to Kohn. He felt that he should be completely isolated so that he could sing his part over and over without having to rely on the ensemble performance with David Reich's organ.

While Kohn's reasonable critique of the recording process was troubling and, at times, caused distress for multiple members of the group, the intensity and seriousness of his approach were unmistakable and lent a certain heightened state to the undertaking; this had a potent effect. His high emotional register acted as a goad to the entire communal effort, pushing everyone to strain for their highest level of performance achievement.

Kohn's criticism of the studio and my production choices resonated for me as a challenge to some of my ideas about what constitutes a "correct" recording aesthetic. It also pushed me to reexamine how the cantors think about historically informed performance. I was attracted to the idea of producing the album of Hasidic cantors, utilizing vintage recording technologies. My goal was to privilege documentation of "real" performances. I wanted to avoid the digital processing of much of contemporary recording studio work. My approach did not adequately take into consideration the multiple concepts about what constitutes a documentation of the real on record.

Despite my intention to facilitate the documentation of a living musical expression and my goal of giving agency to the artists, my idea of what the Hasidic cantorial revival should sound like played a key role in shaping the project, outweighing the artists' own musical goals. As the producer of this document of the Hasidic cantorial revivalist scene, my aesthetics and musical desires guided the choice of participants, the recording technology employed, and the scheduling and flow of the session. The initial decision to foreground the Hasidic identities of the performers, while growing organically out of the particularities of the music scene, was not a transparent choice simply reflecting reality.

I chose these particular artists based on my assessment that they belong to a cohort of singers whose musical interests are in dialogue with the Jewish musical past in ways that challenge the norms of multiple contemporary musical communities. Their work articulates a conception of prayer that imagines aesthetics as a key constitutive element. They privilege their personal artistic vision over the conventions of synagogue ritual, prioritizing a musical experience based in the work of gramophone-era cantors over the norms of contemporary Jewish American life.

These basic assessments about what the work of these cantors means is not especially controversial among the cantors—it derives from information and opinions they have shared with me. But my intervention by writing about them, and especially by producing the album, has the effect of turning my opinions into fact. I have learned about these artists, about the vulnerability of their antinormative artistic personalities working outside the bounds of convention. My perception of Hasidic cantorial revivalists as nonconformists has now been reified in recorded media and in the public relations campaigns to support performances and the release of recordings. The album that resulted from these sessions, titled *Golden Ages*, was released in 2022, in collaboration with the Krakow Jewish Culture Festival. I produced a record release concert in Krakow featuring Yanky

FIGURE 20. Yanky Lemmer, Jeremiah Lockwood, David Reich, and Yoel Kohn. Photo by Tatiana McCabe.

Lemmer, Yoel Kohn, and Shimmy Miller that played to a sold-out audience and was featured on Polish national television. Over the summer months, the *Golden Ages* album was featured on a segment on NPR's *Morning Edition*, further cementing my narrative about cantorial revival and Hasidic musical nonconformity as the "official" story of the cantors. While these successes are far from mainstream, they have furthered the reach of these artists beyond their usual orbit. The outcome of this collaboration is still in the middle of unfolding. The *Golden Ages* album is a continuation of the cantors' struggle to attain agency and self-expression through music, not a magical answer to their urgent project of self-authoring and musical community building.

In the three interlude sections of this book I have attempted to generate a picture of the lives of the cantors in a manner that is more purely ethnographic and less filtered through my analysis and assessments. And yet at no single moment in this work is my intervention absent. This is especially true with regard to recording the album. The story of this collaboration has brought into focus the ambiguity of my place in the Hasidic cantorial scene and the multiple roles I play as academic, promoter, producer, as well as artistic collaborator and friend. These roles do not always sit easily with each other, but they are motivated by an impulse toward sharing in community with the cantors and offering them something in return for the transformation and inspiration their work has given me. It is my hope that somewhere in all this is a contribution to creating a future in which their outsider approach to the aesthetics of prayer will have a place to live.

Conclusion

Cantors and Their Ghosts

Hasidic cantorial revivalists are representatives of a methodology of research and creative response that has erupted into new life in the past decades, spurred perhaps by the immediacy of access to digitized archival sources. Animating the archive through performance and imaginative forms of research offers a response to a sense of the unnaturalness of the disciplinary divide between performance and the academic study of expressive culture.[1] The approach of the cantors, characterized by an embodied approach to sharing the fruits of archival research and leveraging historical artefacts as the basis for art practices, is shared in different forms across disciplines. Examples of this kind of research have arisen both in the academy and the creative arts, bearing a special appeal for performers and researchers working with the pre-Holocaust world of Ashkenazi musical culture. In this paradigm, research in the archive not only produces knowledge; it also creates new ways of being in the world.

For researchers engaged in creative styles of archival exploration, previously dormant texts, genres, and artistic voices that have been relegated to the immateriality of ghosts are reanimated. Vivid absences are brought into presence as the material to actively construct identities and styles of living. Meaning, as encountered through the artefacts the dead have left behind, is made in collaboration with the dead. These artefacts are chosen carefully, both for their historical significance and for their aesthetic qualities. The perception of value in archival sources is permeable to other forms of fascination, such as erotic desire or perceptions of kinship that bind together researchers and their archival interlocuters. The objects of research are magnetic. They act on the bodies and consciousness of their beholders, enlivening multiple modalities of aesthetics and cultural literacy, sparking ambitions in the researcher to be seen by the world the way they see the archive.

My own work of research is similarly motivated by a magnetic pull of sympathy and excitement—I am looking at artists who are looking at the archive; in the process, my understanding of the archival sources has been transformed. The activating substance that has worked on me and moved me toward a new approach to engaging with the history and sounds of the cantorial golden age is the musical talent and insights of the cantors I have been studying. With this project, I am writing against the idea that exploring the social contexts, histories and political meaning of music is in opposition to its pleasures and embodied experiences. Seeking to know the fullness of where the music has come from, looking closely at how it operates in the lives of musicians and their hearers—these are activities of scholarship that overlap with the experience that occurs in the act of listening.

Music operates in the seams between the senses. It elides and makes light work of the signs and symbols of sedimented cultural meanings. It draws us into deeper communion with a realm of ideas because we are bidden to know through the imperatives of the senses. It invigorates our perception of lineages and histories. The act of listening for me while conducting this research project has opened up histories and sensitized me to problems of learning and cognition.

Khazones is not valuable to young Hasidic singers because it is old, or because of its prestige, or because of an abstract sense of its historical significance. Conversance with the music does not figure as a mark of conventional virtue in the eyes of their birth community, nor does it grant a clear path to fame or employment. The music speaks to its impassioned lovers on its own terms, from a place of expressive power and ritual drama. Interpreting the meanings of the music is something the cantors must undertake on their own, without the scaffolding of institutions. The domain of the encounter with the past is located in old records and in the microcommunities that have gathered around them, in a world that is pointedly apart. The community of khazones revivalists and aficionados reenacts forms of fandom and embodied acts of appreciation of the music that were central to the success of the gramophone-era cantors. Hasidic cantorial revivalists today glean energy and direct their passions toward forms of sociality that were defined in a different time and cultural context and that resonate in a different but parallel form in the present.

Old records document something that cantors in the past had to say about their worlds. They tell a story about persistence of memory, transformations occurring in the context of urban modernity, and conceptions of collectivity shaped by the experiences of economic and political marginalization and state violence. The sound of khazones is inscribed into old records—it is both a sound of prayer and yet something else entirely, given a second skin by its materiality as a technology and a media object. It is akin to the sound of urban modernity, its timbral qualities a close relative to the loudspeaker at a political rally or the urban soundscape of street cars and foot traffic. Cantorial gramophone records offer testimony to the work of Jewish artists in moments when they were heightened in their ability to speak about their lives, communities, and histories. This sound of commentary on the public experiences and inner life of the Jewish community has retained some of its visceral, transgressive pull on the ears of those who know to listen.

Hasidic cantorial revivalists are attuned to the sonic worlds of the music—their characteristic achievement is the transcription of the details of vocal production. Rejecting an approach to cantorial compositions as "pure" musical information or notation that can be detached from a historical performance style, Hasidic cantorial revivalists lean into techniques of embodied transcription. The genius of their style lies in the way the artists master anatomical details of vocal musculature and timbre control they have appropriated from mediated sources. These qualities evoke a physical presence, inviting the world of the gramophone-era cantors into the contemporary scene. Cantorial revival derives grit and substance from the physical strife of Jewish lives of the early twentieth century.

Khazones references a Jewish polyglossia—it is a musical style that speaks multiple languages, invoking the formal Hebrew liturgy, conceptions of the sublime that relate to European art music, the playfulness and flirtation with entertainment characteristic of mediated popular culture, socialist and collectivist political ideologies, and conceptions of the sacred referencing both the Hasidic milieu and the universalizing tendencies of Reform. The gramophone-era cantor's skill lies in the ability to contain multiple worlds of Jewish sonic life within the musical voice of a single performer. Gramophone-era cantors famously were beloved by all strands of the Jewish collective—leftists and rabbis, men and women, Orthodox and secularists. Sounds of khazones were appropriated into Yiddish musicals, the symphonic works of elite Jewish classical composers, and vaudevillians, all of whom were seeking to capture the deep emotive associations of the genre and its ability to paint a picture of Jewish history and community.

Khazones, as described in archival Yiddish press sources and as reimagined by present-day fans, was a performance genre both in the sense of it being a form of expressive culture and as a form of activity in the social world of Jews. Singing khazones had an immediate secondary life as a theatrical script that interpolated listeners as participants in the world of the music. Khazones acts on the bodies of its listeners, inducing embodied responses. Khazones is what film scholar Linda Williams might refer to as a "body genre," a form of art like the horror film or melodrama, which is meant to elicit specific physical responses such as shock, fear, or sorrow.[2] One of the intended responses to the cantor's voice is the shedding of tears.[3] The cantorial vocal style offers the listener specific sonic cues to this scripted response through the repertoire of vocal noises imitative of sobbing or sighing. These sounds engender a mimetic response, gesturing toward practices of introspection, memory, and emotional flooding the listeners are intended to experience.

As Yiddishist and literary critic Zohar Weiman-Kelman notes, there is a particular charge to opening one's own body as a resonant space for the feeling worlds of artists in the past to be rearticulated—there is a powerful eros in aesthetic communion across time.[4] Reanimating texts or bodies of sounds from archival sources opens a variety of questions: Who are you when you allow the voice of a ghost to enter into you and speak? What comment or truth can you offer regarding the present moment if your voice is reinforced by the lineage of bodies that you are in numinous dialogue with?

What becomes of a performance genre with its unique social script when it enters into a marginalized state and disappears into the archive, no longer acting on the bodies of listeners, no longer operational as a performative object that affects the mood and spirit of its audience? Does the unheard gramophone record lie in a mystically suspended state, like the spirits of the dead are sometimes described as doing, awaiting resurrection? Are old records like the Zohar in the centuries between the time of its depicted action in first-century Palestine and its publication to the world in fourteenth-century Spain—a kind of divine immanence awaiting comprehension and integration into the life of the community? What kind of sociality can be retrieved from a text that has gone underground, that is hidden either by intentional obfuscation or insensate neglect?

According to Lurianic kabbalistic traditions, the performance of *mitzvos* (Hebrew, ritual law) can be accompanied by a second layer of meaning beyond the explicitly stated significance of the act. For example, the ritual act of putting on a *talis* (Hebrew, prayer shawl) can be accompanied by a slate of associative concepts relating to the secret meanings of the ritual, binding the body of the worshipper to a conception of the presence of the supernatural—these secondary meanings are thought to reflect the ways in which ritual acts in the divine realm, beyond the explicit meanings and contexts of the visible. These second layers of intentionality are referred to as *kavonos* (Hebrew, intention).

In a folklorized form, the same term references a more generalized sense of heightened feeling in prayer or ritual. A cantor's prayer leading is intended to initiate a state of kavono in the listener. The body of the listener performs its own internal drama, prompted by the sound of the cantor. The dialogue between liturgical text, the emotional script initiated by cantorial performance, and the body of the listener recalls the scripted mystical intentions composed by kabbalists to focus the prayer experience. The sociality of cantorial prayer leading is dependent on a listener who will work with the musical materials that a cantor provides, unspooling the meaning of the musical performance, understanding it as a form of commentary on the liturgy, and transforming it into the material for a heightened state of embodied ritual experience.

The cantor's performance is manifold. The cantor performs by singing. Simultaneously, the music proposes a script performed together by cantor and listener. The musical object, the sound of the cantor, initiates both the ritual and a theatrical presentation of the imagined Jewish folkloric past. Cantors are not only themselves when they sing khazones—they sing with the voices of a cast of characters.

This was already the case for cantors of the gramophone era, when their work was concerned with the preservation of the memory of Jewish life in premodern circumstances, as Kwartin, Vigoda, and other cantor/authors made explicit in their writings. Cantors sing as praying bodies resonating through and with their listeners. They are representatives of a Jewish collectivity.

In the context of the rapid rise of anti-Jewish violence in the early twentieth century, the cantorial imperative toward ethnographic memorialization took on new urgency and new power as a means of representation. Their work of cultural preservation no longer referenced an existing form of Jewish life in the small towns of the Pale of Settlement. It now took on a singular reality as the only means of accessing an imagined authenticity of Jewish life that no longer existed. It is easy to see how this image of a singular cultural memory of Jewish prayer that cantors were thought to have access to could be leveraged as the basis for the establishment of a professional class of synagogue professionals in the aftermath of the Holocaust.

Rather than continuing the work of khazones as an art performance genre, the role of the professional cantor changed, taking on a new set of meanings as a communal functionary in the post-World War II American synagogue. The cantorial gramophone stars were rapidly rendered obsolete by new conceptions of Jewish American liturgical aesthetics perpetuated by synagogues and educational institutions, but they did not disappear entirely. Their work was preserved on reissued albums marketed mostly to elder Jews; these served as useful totems of liturgical authenticity to be occasionally referenced by the newly established American professionalized cantorate. But their presence as a musical force shifted away from their previous status as a mass media phenomenon; this change has usually been interpreted as a decline. Questions about the reality of the lachrymose narrative of Jewish culture aside, the communal function and the stylistic elements of Jewish liturgical music underwent a profound shift, both in the liberal movements and in the Orthodox world.

The Hasidic cantorial revivalists of the current generation gesture toward an absence in the texture of Jewish musical culture. Their focus on reenactment of compositions, vocal techniques, and timbral specifics of gramophone-era cantors creates a living image of something that is popularly conceived of as lost. They offer a recreation of an artifact from the past, an aspect of Jewish heritage as produced by cantors of the early twentieth century who were themselves grappling with how to represent the Jewish collective in a time of radical political instability and social change. But what are Hasidic cantorial revivalists really creating with this work of genre revival?

As Yoel Kohn and Shimmy Miller hastened to tell me, Hasidic cantorial revivalists are speaking a language that is no longer broadly comprehended, or at least no longer holds pride of place as a form of communication in the context of ritual exchange. The project of Hasidic cantorial revivalists, focused on embodying the techniques and mastering the repertoires of the golden age, can be read as an exercise in self-deception. In this view, their effort to achieve mastery of virtuosic skills functions only as a memento mori of absences inscribed by the Holocaust, as well as the cultural losses associated with assimilation and Zionism but that offers no breach to these losses. Their music only further accentuates the extent to which Jewish bodies have lost their facility with culturally specific uses of the sense of hearing.

Or their work can be understood in a different light. The purported futility of their work can instead be seen as a refusal to accept the parameters of their hier-archically bounded world. Singing khazones pushes at the political organization of music, the "regime of listening,"[5] which Hasidic cantorial revivalists encounter in their multiple social worlds of Jewishness, masculinity, and music. In this line of reasoning, singing khazones stands as a utopian gesture that directs listeners to a model of sacred experience and a style of communication that is obscured in the present moment but that can, perhaps, be reanimated through the medium of performance. Khazones, performed as a staged art form, provides a scaffolded structure, a cultural pedagogy of Jewish sacred listening.

According to this logic, Hasidic cantorial revivalists have developed skills toward the goal of focusing their hearers on a spiritual music practice associated with transport and transcendence, presented through the familiar behavioral modality of consumption of the arts. This methodology of performance, in which the sacred is recreated for the stage or the internet, radically democratizes access and allows for the formation of communities that defy the borders of contem-porary Jewish life. The performance model offered by the old stars of khazones reawakens the possibilities of mass consumption of the sacred that were charac-teristic of the gramophone era.

Deep listening to khazones crossed boundaries of community in an era when "It would seem now that Yossele Rosenblatt takes the place of Karl Marx" in the affec-tions of radical Jews, and cantorial modernist Leib Glantz vituperated that kha-zones "has its greatest enemies amongst the ranks of assimilationists, among the ranks of the upper bourgeoisie."[6] Khazones activated the crossing of boundaries—between religious Orthodoxy and radical political engagements, and between images of tradition and engagement with modernity.

These areas of slippage between seemingly irreparable breaks in the Jewish collective have a heightened significance in an era when questions about the for-mation of identity are of keenly felt significance for Jews of many communal affili-ations. The question of what a Jew is and what commitments he or she must hold resonate on multiple sides of the cultural chasm between separatist Orthodoxy, the Jewish "mainstream," and leftist radicalism.

Trying to answer, *what is a Jew?* is a near relative to another perennial question, *what does a Jew sound like?* The process of delving in the archive to reanimate Jew-ish texts, sounds, and lifeways has found adherents among individuals drawn from a broad range of identities and backgrounds. Animators of the archive drawn from divergent identity formations are perhaps motivated by similar urges to deconstruct hierarchies of access to knowledge, to deepen the aesthetics of Jewish life, and to sensitize the community to its internal diversity.

Hasidic cantorial revivalists have located a power in old records of khazones, but what purpose they can put this power to is yet to be seen. Possibilities inhere in the fact of their self-cultivation and skill. The changes they have wrought in themselves, in the powers of their own bodies, indicate an ambition to make changes in the world as they have found it. Singing khazones is a method to achieve some kind of social magic, to create a glue that will hold together individuals of various backgrounds in a collective. Being a singer of khazones implies a specific form of personhood, but what this identity consists of is attenuated differently in each of the social spheres that I have discussed in this book. The deep listener alone with old records or in the company of aficionados is a different person than the student of professional nusakh, or the pulpit cantor, or the stage performer. In each of these social settings of music-making, the history of khazones as the sound of a Jewish radicalism and a key to nonconformist identity building is operational. Khazones is a sound that presents the internal diversity and contradictions of Jewish life, both vertically in the strata of the different communities that live today, and horizontally across the axis of history.

By performing khazones, Hasidic cantorial revivalists are manifesting a fantasy about the creation of a meeting place where the polyphony of Jewish experience can resound. In the act of performance, histories of difference and points of commonality across communal boundaries are activated. Experimentation with the creation of a new listening community is brought into focus by a sound, by a stance of passionate and heightened dramatic performance of sacred text, and by an indelible aesthetic rooted in an imagined ethnography of Jewish expressive forms. The ambition to unite multiple historical moments of Jewishness and multiple conflicting forms of contemporary identity is inherently unstable and is liable to be censured and chastised from a variety of viewpoints. Yet the power the music grants its adherents in their performances is undeniable and uncontainable, at least at moments.

How this rupture of the bounds of contemporary norms of Jewish comportment will play out is painfully ambiguous and tethered to technology—the internet is the primary ground for the expression of khazones performance today. Like the gramophone at the turn of the twentieth century, the internet is often construed by conservative voices as a site of immorality or degradation. Yet it is in the realm of media, once again, that the unique qualities of khazones as a sacred listening experience has the potential to change the world. Cantorial revivalists gesture toward an absence, but at the same time their work creates possibilities. Whether their work is an act of delusion or prophecy is not, for the moment, important; what can be seen and known is that the singers have made transformations in themselves.

The formation of new styles of personhood through the animation of the archive is real and will continue to unfold with unknown and perhaps unexpected outcomes for the multiple communities where the singers work, pressing them against the limits of history and community. What a community built around a radical aesthetic of prayer as performance would look like is a striking and provocative question. Such a community would be guided by the prophecy/ delusion of artists driving them to some new and unknowable style of experience. This chapter of the story of the Hasidic cantorial revival scene is yet to be written and may never come to pass, but the work of the singers featured in this book opens up onto just such a vista of fantasy. In that unknown future, history and the needs of the present moment are locked in a tight dialogue, given voice by the passions of artists.

INTRODUCTION: "I DIDN'T KNOW WHAT I WAS CRAVING
UNTIL I FOUND IT"

1. Ari Klein is a cantor from a Hasidic background; he is a generation older than the singers profiled in this study. Klein was part of a first wave of Hasidic cantorial revivalists who emerged around the turn of the last century, drawing attention to the existence of the early twentieth-century cantorial style among younger Hasidic singers. For a report on the first stirrings of cantorial star careers emerging from the Hasidic community at the turn of the twenty-first century, see Akiva Zimmermann, "The Hasidic World's Attitude towards Hazzanut," *Journal of Synagogue Music* 34, no. 10 (2009): 148–50.

2. Mostly Music is a well-known record store in Borough Park, Brooklyn that sells exclusively Jewish records and other media. Up until a decade ago it had a well-stocked cantorial section. Its cantorial selection is more limited today; the store's stock focuses its offerings on Orthodox pop music.

3. The interview quotations from David Reich that follow in this chapter are from the same 2019 interview, except where noted.

4. Peter Narvaez calls this a "revelatory moment" in his discussion of blues revival. See Peter Narváez, "Paradoxical Aesthetics of the Blues Revival," in *Transforming Tradition*, ed. Neil V. Rosenberg (Urbana: University of Illinois Press, 1993), 245.

5. See Anthony F. C. Wallace, "Revitalization Movements," *American Anthropologist* 58, no. 2 (1956): 264–81; Peter Narváez, "Paradoxical Aesthetics"; Tamara Livingston, "Music Revivals: Towards a General Theory," *Ethnomusicology* 43, no. 1 (Winter 1999): 66–85; Mark Slobin, *Fiddler on the Move: Exploring the Klezmer World* (Oxford: Oxford University Press, 2000); Barbara Kirschenblatt-Gimblett, "Sounds of Sensibility," in *American Klezmer: Its Roots and Offshoots*, ed. Mark Slobin (Berkeley: University of California Press, 2002).

6. Recent histories of the Hasidic movement that critically outline its emergence, ideologies, and the political processes by which the establishment of Hasidic dynasties was achieved include David Biale et. al., *Hasidism: A New History* (Princeton, NJ: Princeton University Press, 2018); Glenn Dynner, *Men of Silk: The Hasidic Conquest of Polish Jewish Society* (New York: Oxford University Press, 2006); David Assaf, *Untold Tales of the Hasidim: Crisis and Discontent in the History of Hasidism* (Waltham, MA: Brandeis University Press, 2010).

7. For a discussion of demographics in contemporary American Orthodoxy, see Samuel C. Heilman, *Sliding to the Right: The Contest for the Future of American Jewish Orthodoxy* (Berkeley: University of California Press, 2006), 62–77.

8. See Gordon A. Dale, "Music in Haredi Jewish Life: Liquid Modernity and the Negotiation of Boundaries in Greater New York," PhD diss., City University of New York, 2017, 47–94; Ari Y. Kelman and Shaul Magid, "The Gate to the Village: Shlomo Carlebach and the Creation of American Jewish Folk," *American Jewish History* 100, no. 4 (2016): 511–40.

9. See Ellen Koskoff, *Music in Lubavitcher Life* (Urbana: University of Illinois Press, 2001); André Hajdu and Yaakov Masur "The Musical Traditions of Hasidism," in *Encyclopedia Judaica* (Jerusalem: Keter, 1971).

10. See Mark Kligman, "Contemporary Jewish Music in America," *American Jewish Year Book* 101 (2001).

11. See Haym Soloveitchik, "Rupture and Repair: The Transformation of Contemporary Orthodoxy," *Tradition* 28, no. 4 (1994).

12. See Abigail Wood, "Pop, Piety and Modernity: The Changing Spaces of Orthodox Culture," *Routledge Handbook to Contemporary Jewish Cultures*, ed. Laurence Roth and Nadia Valman (New York: Routledge, 2014), 286–96. While Woods focuses on controversies over the limits of Orthodox pop and attempts by rabbis to censor the music, my ethnography and interviews with Hasidic singers suggest that the music is pervasive and in general unmarked. High profile exceptions periodically crop up, such as the well-known case of Lipa Shmelzer, a controversy-embracing Orthodox pop star. See Dale, "Music in Haredi Jewish Life," 123–58.

13. In the early 2000s, some early twentieth-century cantorial records were further mediated and publicized by what Jason Stanyek and Benjamin Piekut have called *intermundane collaborations* between living and dead artists—in this case, old cantorial record stars and contemporary producers in the Orthodox music world. The cantorial gramophone era has been given more recognizability in the Orthodox world by recording efforts such as the work of the late Israeli conductor Mordechai Sobol who, starting in 2004, released a series of symphonic remixes of old cantorial records that digitally sampled the vocals of early twentieth-century star cantors, or the *Od Yosef Chai* record series that offered a similar conceptual treatment of the extracted vocals of Rosenblatt records with a new accompaniment featuring synthesizers and choir in an Orthodox pop style. Mordechai Sobol and his son Ofir Sobol also regularly produce orchestral concerts in Israel featuring cantors performing a "standard repertoire" of pieces drawn from the recorded cantorial archive. Some of the Brooklyn Hasidic cantors I worked with in this study have been featured in concerts produced by the Sobols. Khazones as an "elite" concert genre has a salience in Israel that does not have a parallel in the US scene, although some high-profile philharmonic concerts of cantorial music have been produced over the years—notably, the collaborations of Cantor Yitzchak Meir Helfgot and violinist James Levine. See Sol Zim, "Remembering

My Friend, Maestro Mordechai Sobol, z"l," *New York Jewish Week*, September 26, 2018, https://jewishweek.timesofisrael.com/remembering-my-friend-maestro-mordechai-sobol-zl/; Joseph Berger, "Bit by Bit a Cantor's Voice is Restored," *New York Times*, June 20, 2010; Jason Stanyek and Benjamin Piekut, "Deadness: Technologies of the Intermundane," *Drama Review* 54, no. 1 (2010): 14–38.

14. See Lewis Glinert, "Toward a Social Study of Ashkenazi Hebrew," *Jewish Social Studies* 2, no. 4 (1996): 85–114.

15. Alternate pronunciations of the term *khazones* using Israeli Hebrew phonology, rather than the Yiddish pronunciation generally used by Hasidic Jews, render the word as *hazzanut*, a spelling that occurs occasionally in this book in the context of quotations.

16. See Tina Frühauf, *Salomon Sulzer: Reformer, Cantor, Icon* (Berlin: Hentrich & Hentrich Verlag, 2012).

17. For a history of the cantorial golden age, see Velvel Pasternak, "The Golden Age of Cantors," *Journal of Synagogue Music* 31, no. 1 (September 2006): 160–64; Mark Slobin, *Chosen Voices: The Story of the American Cantorate* (Chicago: University of Illinois Press, 1989), chapter 1.

18. Roland Gelatt, *The Fabulous Phonograph, 1877–1977* (New York: Macmillan, 1977), 114–29.

19. See Ari Kelman, *Station Identification: A Cultural History of Yiddish Radio in the United States* (Berkeley: University of California Press, 2009), 128–73.

20. See Asya Vaisman, "'Hold on Tightly to Tradition': Generational Differences in Yiddish Song Repertoires among Contemporary Hasidic Women," in *Choosing Yiddish: New Frontiers of Language and Culture*, ed. Lara Rabinovitch, Shiri Goren, and Hannah S. Pressman (Detroit: Wayne State University Press, 2013).

21. See Samuel C. Heilman, *Sliding to the Right*.

22. Ayala Fader, *Mitzvah Girls: Bringing Up the Next Generation of Hasidic Jews in Brooklyn* (Princeton, NJ: Princeton University Press, 2009), 48.

23. Examples of popular representations of "ultra" Orthodox Jews include the 2017 Netflix documentary *One of Us*, the 2020 Netflix limited series *Unorthodox*, and memoir literature such as Shulem Deen, *All Who Go Do Not Return: A Memoir* (Minneapolis: Graywolf Press, 2015). See also a commentary on the "liberal gaze" in pop culture treatments of Orthodoxy in Naomi Seidman, "My Scandalous Rejection of Unorthodox," *Jewish Review of Books*, May 4, 2020, https://jewishreviewofbooks.com/articles/7564/telling-the-otdtale-or-my-scandalous-rejection-of-unorthodox/.

24. See Saba Mahmood, *Politics of Piety* (Princeton, NJ: Princeton University Press, 2005).

25. See Orit Avishai, "'Doing Religion' In a Secular World," *Gender & Society* 22, no. 4 (2008): 409–33; Lea Taragin-Zeller, "A Rabbi of One's Own? Navigating Religious Authority and Ethical Freedom in Everyday Judaism," *American Anthropologist* 123, no. 4 (December 2021): 833–45; Tsipy Ivry and Elly Teman, "Shouldering Moral Responsibility: The Division of Moral Labor among Pregnant Women, Rabbis, and Doctors," *American Anthropologist* 121 no. 4 (2019): 857–69; Nechumi Malovicki Yaffe, Melissa McDonald, Eran Halperin, and Tamar Saguy, "God, Sex, and Money among the Ultra-Orthodox in Israel: An Integrated Sociocultural and Evolutionary Perspective," *Evolution and Human Behavior* 39, no. 6 (2018): 622–31; Jessica Roda, *For Women and Girls Only: The Arts, the Digital, and Jewish Orthodoxy* (New York: New York University Press, 2024).

26. See Fader, *Mitzvah Girls*, 47; David Lehmann and Batia Siebzehner, "Power, Boundaries and Institutions: Marriage in Ultra-Orthodox Judaism," *European Journal of Sociology* 50, no. 2 (2009): 273–308.

27. See Hussein Ali Agrama, "Ethics, Tradition, Authority: Toward an Anthropology of the Fatwa," *American Ethnologist* 37, no. 1 (February 2010): 2–18.

28. Dorothy Holland, ed., *Identity and Agency in Cultural Worlds* (Cambridge, MA: Harvard University Press, 2001), 8.

29. Yehoshua Kahana, "When Hasidic Singers Perform in a Litvish Accent," *Forverts*, September 10, 2019, https://forward.com/yiddish/431118/when-hasidic-performers-sing -in-a-litvish-dialect/.

30. See Jeremiah Lockwood, "House of Friendly Ghosts Vol. 1" (liner notes), JDub Records, 2011.

31. See Owe Ronström, "Traditional Music, Heritage Music," in *The Oxford Handbook of Music Revival*, ed. Caroline Blithell and Juniper Hill (New York: Oxford University Press, 2014); Barbara Kirschenblatt-Gimblett, "Theorizing Heritage," *Ethnomusicology* 39, no. 3 (1995): 367–80.

32. See Zohar Weiman-Kelman, "Touching Time: Poetry, History, and the Erotics of Yiddish," *Criticism* 59, no. 1 (2017): 99–121.

33. See Kirschenblatt-Gimblett, "Sounds of Sensibility," in *American Klezmer*; Alicia Svigals, "Why We Do This Anyway: Klezmer as Jewish Youth Subculture," in *American Klezmer*.

34. See Jeffrey A. Summit, *The Lord's Song in a Strange Land: Music and Identity in Contemporary Jewish Worship* (New York: Oxford University Press, 2000), 117–25.

35. See Dorothy Holland and Jean Lave, eds., *History in Person: Enduring Struggles, Contentious Practice, Intimate Identities*, 1st. ed., (Santa Fe, NM: SAR Press, 2001).

1. ANIMATING THE ARCHIVE: OLD RECORDS AND YOUNG SINGERS

1. See Édouard Glissant, *Poetics of Relation* (Ann Arbor: University of Michigan Press, 1997). I am indebted to Ioanida Costache's discussion of Glissant in the context of Roma studies. See Ioanida Costache, "Reclaiming Romani-Ness," *Critical Romani Studies* 1 (2018): 30–43.

2. See Linda Alcoff, *Visible Identities: Race, Gender, and the Self* (New York: Oxford University Press, 2006)

3. Samuel Rosenbaum, "Surviving Future Shock," *Journal of Synagogue Music* 9, no. 2 (June 1979): 26.

4. Nate Wooley, "Cantor Joshua Breitzer on Nusach in Jewish Life and Tradition," *Sound American: The Ritual Issue* SA11 (2015), accessed June 11, 2023. http://archive.soundamerican .org/sa_archive/sa11/sa11-the-interviews.html.

5. See E. J. Hobsbawm and T. O. Ranger, *The Invention of Tradition* (Cambridge: Cambridge University Press, 1983).

6. See Michael Herzfeld, *Cultural Intimacy: Social Poetics and the Real Life of States, Societies and Institutions* (New York: Routledge, Taylor & Francis, 2016).

7. The term "named system" was coined by Neil Rosenberg to describe the proliferation of music scenes and subcultures based in music styles often drawn from early twentieth-century recorded vernacular music. See Neil V. Rosenberg, ed. *Transforming Tradition: Folk Music Revivals Examined* (Urbana: University of Illinois Press, 1993).

8. See Philip Vilas Bohlman, *Jewish Music and Modernity* (Oxford: Oxford University Press, 2008); Tina Fruhauf, *Salomon Sulzer: Reformer, Cantor, Icon* (Berlin: Hentrich & Hentrich Verlag, 2012); Edwin Seroussi, "The Jewish Liturgical Music Printing Revolution: A Preliminary Assessment," in *Textual Transmission in Contemporary Jewish Cultures*, ed. Avriel Bar-Levav and Uzi Rebhun (New York: Oxford University Press, 2020), 100–136.

9. Samuel Vigoda, *Legendary Voices: The Fascinating Lives of the Great Cantors* (New York: S. Vigoda, 1981), 22–23.

10. See James Loeffler, *The Most Musical Nation: Jews and Culture in the Late Russian Empire* (New Haven, CT: Yale University Press, 2010).

11. Ibid., 56–93.

12. See Dan Miron, *The Image of the Shtetl and Other Studies of Modern Jewish Literary Imagination* (Syracuse, NY: Syracuse University Press, 2000).

13. See Samuel Spinner, *Jewish Primitivism* (Stanford, CA: Stanford University Press, 2021).

14. See entries on Novakovsky and Leow in Elias Zaludkovsky, *Kulturtreger fun der Idisher litugiye*, (Detroit: S. N., 1930), 193–94, 305–7.

15. See Ashot Arakelyan, "Forgotten Opera Singers: Selmar Cerini (Tenor) (Poland, Wólka 1861—Poland, Breslau 1923)," *Forgotten Opera Singers* (blog), November 21, 2014, http://forgottenoperasingers.blogspot.com/2014/11/selmar-cerini-tenor-poland-1861 -breslau.html.

16. See Issachar Fater, "Gershon Sirota: An Appreciation," *Journal of Synagogue Music* 2, no. 3 (1968): 16–21.

17. Zevulun Kwartin, *Mayn leben* (Philadelphia: Self-published, 1952), 294.

18. Ibid., 148.

19. See Mark Slobin, *Chosen Voices: The Story of the American Cantorate* (Urbana: University of Illinois Press, 1989), 54; Annie Polland, *Landmark of the Spirit: The Eldridge Street Synagogue* (New Haven, CT: Yale University Press, 2009), 49–63.

20. Chaim Zhitlowsky, *Der sotsializm un di natsionale frage* (New York: A. M. Evalenko, 1908), 35.

21. See Leib Glantz, "Khazones—der 'shir ha shirim' fun di idishe masn," in *Khazonim zhurnal*, ed. Mordechai Yardeini (New York: Jewish Ministers Cantors' Association of America, 1950), 13–14; Gershon Ephros, "The Hazzanic Recitative: A Unique Contribution to our Music Heritage," *Journal of Synagogue Music* 6, no. 3 (1976): 23–28.

22. Pinchas Minkovsky, *Moderne liturgia in unsere synagogen* [= *Modern Liturgy in Our Synagogues in Russia*], 1910, reproduced in Akiva Zimmermann, *Perakim Be-Shir: Sefer Pinkhas Minkovski* (Tel Aviv: Sha'are Ron, 2011), 228.

23. Ibid, 223–24.

24. Critical assessments of popular cantors were a feature of Yiddish-language criticisms and ran parallel to the castigation of lowbrow *shund* (Yiddish, trash) literature and theater. See Jeremiah Lockwood, ""Prayer and Crime: Cantor Elias Zaludkovsky's Concert Performance Season in 1924 Poland," *In Geveb: A Journal of Yiddish Studies* (2022): https://ingeveb.org/articles/prayer-and-crime.

25. See Herzfeld, *Cultural Intimacy*.

26. Representative anthologies of cantorial recitatives include Noah Schall, *Yossele Rosenblatt: Classic Cantorial Recitatives* (New York: Tara, 2015); Zawel Kwartin, *Smiroth Zebulon: Recitative für Kantoren* (New York: self-pub., 1928).

27. Descriptions of cantorial prayer-leading services in the soloist presentational style abound in the Yiddish press. For example, see Pinchos Jassinowsky, "In der velt fun khazones un idisher negina," *Der morgn zhurnal*, January 23, 1948. This article describes the hypnotic effect of Samuel Vigoda on a congregation. Bootleg recordings of "star" cantors, made in the 1960s or after and frequently documenting star cantors in their elder years, have survived through a network of circulation among fans, originally on homemade cassette tapes, and today accessible on YouTube and file sharing sites. See "Chazzanut For All," Mediafire, accessed June 11, 2023, http://www.mediafire.com/?u8j92uzbihc30.

28. Leib Lange, "Dos alte khazones—der shlisel tsu der idisher neshome," in *Di shul un di khazanim velt*, ed. Pinchas Sherman, 33, no. 52 (July 1939): 9–10.

29. Samuel Rosenblatt, *Yossele Rosenblatt: The Story of His Life* (New York: Farrar, Straus and Young, 1954), 233.

30. See Jeffrey Shandler, *Jews, God and Videotape: Religion and Media in America* (New York: New York University Press, 2009).

31. From an undated press clipping in Berele Chagy's archive titled "Ma'asim onshtot reyd," bearing Chagy's byline, probably from the New York Yiddish newspaper *Morgn zhurnal* (ca. 1930), YIVO Archives, RG 1278.

32. See Judah M. Cohen, "Professionalizing the Cantorate—and Masculinizing It? The Female Prayer Leader and Her Erasure from Jewish Musical Tradition," *Musical Quarterly* 101, no. 4 (2018): 455–81.

33. See Arianne Brown, "The Khazntes—The Life Story of Sophie Kurtzer, Bas Sheva, Sheindele the Khaznte, Perele Feig, Goldie Malavsky and Frayedele Oysher," *Journal of Synagogue Music* 32 (2007): 51–79; Henry Sapoznik, "The Promiscuous World of Jewish Music Series, Lecture 18: Kol Isha: The Pioneering Women Cantors 1923–1975" (public lecture on Zoom, September 14, 2020).

34. See Israel Goldfarb, "An Analysis of the Hazanic Styles of Kwartin, Roitman and Rosenblatt," *Proceedings of the Seventh Annual Conference-Convention of The Cantors Assembly of America* (New York: Jewish Theological Seminary, 1954), 26, https://archive.org/stream/CantorsAsssemblyConferenceProceedings/1954_djvu.txt. Addressing the newly established organization of Conservative cantors, Goldfarb asserted, "In the future the Kwartins, the Roitmans and the Rosenblatts will be listened to as a novelty by lovers and connoisseurs of the old hazanic style. They will also be studied by students of Hazanut as the basic sources of our liturgic music of past generations. But there will be no place for them in our modern synagogue of the present or the future."

35. See Riv-Ellen Prell, *Prayer and Community: The Havurah in American Judaism* (Detroit: Wayne State University Press, 1989), 30–68.

36. As was stated in note 26 above, numerous examples of bootleg recordings of prayer services that were formerly in the hands of private collectors have begun to circulate online. While these recordings were intended to immortalize the prayer leading of cantorial artists, they also document the noisiness and presence of the praying congregation. For a representative example, see Cantorial Legends, "Cantor David Koussevitzky Live Shabbos Shacharis and Musaf Rosh Chodesh Bentching," April 26, 2012, YouTube video, 1:20:00, https://www.youtube.com/watch?v=ze3O-Bp6nBU.

37. See Biale, ed., *Hasidism*, 209–16. Glen Dynner refers to Hasidic approaches to communal singing as a form of "propaganda" that helped draw new followers to the movement. See Dynner, *Men of Silk*, 197–226.

38. See Gershom Scholem, "Isaac Luria and His School," in *Major Trends in Jewish Mysticism* (New York: Schocken Books, 1995), 244–86.

39. See Dynner, *Men of Silk*, 224.

40. See Mordekhai Shtrigler, "Vi azoy darf oyszehn di moralishe geshtalt fun a khazn," *Di shul un di khazonim velt* 33, no. 52 (July 1939): 7–9.

41. See Chani Haran Smith, "Music as a Spiritual Process in the Teachings of Rabbi Nahman of Bratslav," *Journal of Synagogue Music* 34 (2009): 8–47.

42. See Hanoch Avenary, "The Hasidic Nigun: Ethos and Melos of a Folk Liturgy," *Journal of the International Folk Music Council* 16 (1964): 60–63.

43. See Ellen Koskoff, *Music in Lubavitcher Life* (Urbana: University of Illinois Press, 2001). A variety of adaptations and transformations of Hasidic nigunim have influenced other strands of contemporary Jewish life that have little contact with the extent Hasidic community. These "non-Hasidic" nigunim repertoires include the Israeli Hasidic Song Festival, founded in the 1970s, as well as the broad popularity of neo-Hasidic nigunim, which are often composed by professional singer-songwriters, in liberal Jewish movements in the United States. See Motti Regev and Edwin Seroussi, *Popular Music and National Cultures In Israel* (Berkeley: University of California Press, 2004), 126–29; Ari Y. Kelman and Shaul Magid, "The Gate to the Village: Shlomo Carlebach and the Creation of American Jewish Folk," *American Jewish History* 100, no. 4 (2016): 511–40.

44. See Leo Landman, "The Office of the Medieval 'Hazzan,'" *Jewish Quarterly Review* 62, no. 3 (January 1972), 156–87; Wayne Allen, *The Cantor: From the Mishna to Modernity* (Eugene, OR: Wipf & Stock, 2019).

45. Akiva Zimmerman, "The Hasidic World's Attitude towards Hazzanut," *Journal of Synagogue Music* 34, no. 10 (2009): 149.

46. See Martin Buber, *Tales of the Hasidim* (New York: Schocken Books, 1991), 61–63.

47. Samuel Vigoda, *Legendary Voices*, 318.

48. See Abraham Rechtman, Nathaniel Deutsch, and Noah Barrera, *The Lost World of Russia's Jews: Ethnography and Folklore in the Pale of Settlement* (Bloomington: Indiana University Press, 2021), 225–34; Paul Radensky, "The Rise and Decline of a Hasidic Court: The Case of Rabbi Duvid Twersky of Tal'noye," in *Holy Dissent: Jewish and Christian Mystics in Eastern Europe*, ed. Glenn Dynner (Detroit: Wayne State University Press, 2011), 131–68.

49. See Helen Winkler, "Hazzanut in a Hasidic Court Between the Two Wars," *Journal of Synagogue Music* 34 (Fall 2009): 151–57.

50. See Vigoda, *Legendary Voices*, 199–202.

51. See Samuel Rosenblatt, *Yossele Rosenblatt*, 56–61.

52. See "Sacred Sabbath: Cantor Ben Zion Kapov-Kagan," LP liner notes, Collectors Guild CG618 (1962).

53. See Joseph A. Levine, "The Glantz / Pinchik Conundrum," *Journal of Synagogue Music* 34 (Fall 2009): 76–100.

54. See Leib Glantz, "*Khazones—der "shir ha shirim" fun di idishe masn*," in *Khazonim Zhurnal*, ed. Mordechai Yardeini (New York: Jewish Ministers Cantors' Association of America, 1950), 13–14.

55. Many versions of Rozo D'Shabbos by Hasidic artists circulate online. For an illustrative example, see the collaboration of Haredi pop star Motti Steinmetz and elder Belz Hasidic bal tefile, Yermiah Damen. See Shneor Shif, "Raza D'Shabat'-Yirmiyah Damen

Motti Steinmetz Mikahlat Neranena," July 22, 2016, YouTube video, 08:58, https://www
.youtube.com/watch?v=oDiyEq4OCfo.

56. See "Chazan Moshe Teleshevsky, 85 OBM," COLlive, October 2, 2016, https://collive
.com/chazan-moshe-teleshevsky-85-obm/; *Cantor Moshe Teleshevsky*, LP record, (n.d., ca.
1960s), no label listed; *Chabad Nigunim Volume 5*, LP record (1964), Nichoach N-5724.

57. Zimmerman, "The Hasidic World's Attitude towards Hazzanut," 150.

58. See Hana Levi Julian, "Renowned Cantor Moshe Teleshevsky, OBM," *Israel National
News*, October 4, 2012, https://www.israelnationalnews.com/news/160537.

59. Zimmerman, "The Hasidic World's Attitude towards Hazzanut," 150.

60. See "Charlie's Bio," Two Hours of Jewish Social Music—Hosted by Charlie Bernhaut, accessed June 11, 2023, http://www.charliebernhaut.com/about.html.

61. See Regula Burckhardt Qureshi, "His Master's Voice? Exploring Qawwali and
'Gramophone Culture' in South Asia," *Popular Music* 18, no. 1 (Jan 1999): 63–98.

INTERLUDE A. THE LEMMER BROTHERS:
MUSIC AND GENRE IN ORTHODOX NEW YORK LIFE

1. For journalistic accounts of the Lemmer brothers' music and career, see Yisroel Besser, "Dear Shulem," *Mishpacha Jewish Family Weekly*, July 25, 2018, https://mishpacha.com
/dear-shulem/; Curt Schleier, "The Musician Shulem on Being the First Artist Raised Hasidic
to Sign with a Major Record Label," *Jewish Telegraph Agency* (April 23, 2020) https://www
.jta.org/2020/04/23/culture/the-musician-shulem-on-being-the-first-artist-raised-hasidic
-to-sign-with-a-major-record-label; Steve Lipman, "New Cantor, New Look," *New York Jewish Week*, September 17, 2013, https://jewishweek.timesofisrael.com/new-cantor-new-look/.

2. See Abigail Woods, "Pop, Piety and Modernity: The Changing Spaces of Orthodox
Culture," in *The Routledge Handbook to Contemporary Jewish Cultures*, ed. Lawrence Roth
and Nadia Valman (New York: Routledge, 2014), 286–96.

3. See Roger Bennett and Josh Kun, *And You Shall Know Us by the Trail of Our Vinyl:
The Jewish Past as Told by the Records We Have Loved and Lost* (New York: Crown, 2008).

4. See "Helen Stambler Latner's Oral History," Yiddish Book Center, , June 5, 2015,
https://www.yiddishbookcenter.org/collections/oral-histories/interviews/woh-fi-0000704
/helen-stambler-latner-2015.

5. See Lubavitcher Chorus and Instrumental Ensemble, *"Nichoach" Chabad Melodies*,
Collectors Guild CGL 615, recorded 1960, LP; Velvel Pasaternak, *Behind the Music: Stories,
Anecdotes, Articles & Reflections* (Cedarhurst, NY: Tara, 2017).

6. See Mark Kligman, "Contemporary Jewish Music in America," *American Jewish Year
Book* 101 (2001): 88–141; Gordon A. Dale, "Music in Haredi Jewish Life"; Abigail Woods,
"Pop, Piety and Modernity."

7. In an Orthodox Jewish magazine, David Olivestone offers a popular history of
golden age cantors—namely, that voices the perceived ethical problems with the genre.
See David Olivestone, "Shul or Show?" *Segula: The Jewish History Magazine* 54 (September
2020): 30–39. For a more strident expression of condemnation of golden age cantors, see
Yehoshua Kahana, "When Hasidic Singers Perform in a Litvish Accent," *Forverts*, September 10, 2019, https://forward.com/yiddish/431118/when-hasidic-performers-sing-in-a
-litvish-dialect/.

8. See Haym Soloveitchik, "Rupture and Reconstruction: The Transformation of Contemporary Orthodoxy," *Tradition* 28, no. 4 (1994): 64–130.

9. See Asya Vaisman, "'Hold on Tightly to Tradition': Generational Differences in Yiddish Song Repertoires among Contemporary Hasidic Women," in *Choosing Yiddish: New Frontiers of Language and Culture*, ed. Lara Rabinovitch, Shiri Goren, and Hannah S. Pressman (Detroit: Wayne State University Press, 2013); Jeremiah Lockwood, "Ira Temple and the Williamsburg Senior Center," *Conversations: Words and Music from the American Jewish Experience* (blog), August 30, 2021, https://schoolofmusic.ucla.edu/conversations -dispatches-from-brooklyn/.

10. Interview with Yanky Lemmer.

11. Note here the use of the term *hazzanut*; this is a modern Hebrew pronunciation of the same word for cantorial music that is rendered as *khazones* in Yiddish pronunciation. *Hazzanut* is the so-called modern Hebrew pronunciation, modeled after the form of Hebrew used in Israel. The language politics around the pronunciation of Hebrew among American Jews is complex. The sounds of Hebrew pronunciation invoke issues, including Hasidic cultural maintenance of Yiddish and traditional Ashkenazi liturgical Hebrew, or the adoption of a modified form of Israeli Hebrew pronunciation in liturgical contexts by the liberal Jewish movements as part of a general turn toward a Zionist orientation in mid-century Jewish American life. In the interview clip quoted here, Yanky was in a public conversation with me and ethnomusicologist Mark Kligman in front of an audience of mostly non-Orthodox American Jews in a secular concert hall environment. In this context, I speculate, Yanky felt that the modern Hebrew pronunciation would be more legible to his audience than the Yiddish pronunciation that he usually used in our private conversations. In addition to being multilingual (he speaks Yiddish, Hebrew, and English fluently, although he has stated that he feels most comfortable speaking in English), he is also able to code switch in his pronunciation of liturgical Hebrew, moving between Hasidic Yiddish pronunciation, "standard" Orthodox Ashkenazi Hebrew, and "modern" Hebrew modeled on Israeli pronunciation. Each of these systems has distinct, and, to insiders, instantly recognizable sounds and cultural associations. For discussions of the politics of Hebrew phonology, see Benjamin Harshav, *Language in Time of Revolution* (Stanford, CA: Stanford University Press, 1999); Lewis Glinert, ed. *Hebrew in Ashkenaz: A Language in Exile* (New York: Oxford University Press, 1993).

12. For an example of Yanky Lemmer's forays into pop music, see his recent duet with his brother Shulem, "The Man from Vilna—Shulem and Yanky Lemmer," December 20, 2021, YouTube video, 06:15, https://www.youtube.com/watch?v=Nmei13H16aI.

13. See B. Shelvin, "Di tsukunft fun khazones in amerike," in *Di geshikhte fun khazones*, ed. Aaron Rosen (New York: Jewish Ministers Cantors Association of America, 1924), 77–78.

14. See Mark Slobin, *Chosen Voices: The Story of the American Cantorate* (Urbana: University of Illinois Press, 1989), chapter 4.

15. For an overview of the cantorial decline narrative, see Wayne R. Allen, *The Cantor: From the Mishnah to Modernity* (Eugene, OR: Wipf & Stock, 2019), 261–68.

16. See Ben Kenigsberg, "'The Song of Names' Review: A Prodigy, a War and a Mystery," *New York Times*, December 24, 2019.

2. LEARNING *NUSAKH*: CULTIVATING SKILL AND IDEOLOGY
IN THE CANTORIAL TRAINING STUDIO

1. For an account of Zeidel Rovner's life, see Samuel Vigoda, *Legendary Voices: The Fascinating Lives of the Great Cantors* (New York: S. Vigoda, 1981).

2. Noah Schall's publications include *Hazzanut for the High Holy Days* (New York: Tara, 1969); *Hazzanic Thesaurus*, 3 vols. (New York: Tara, 1970); *Yossele Rosenblatt: Classic Cantorial Recitatives* (New York: Tara, 2015); *Sefer Shel Nusach T'hilot Netsach: Nusach Improvisations for Shabbat Morning* (Self-published, 2017).

3. As Judah Cohen notes, this periodization is not absolute and there were unsuccessful efforts to form cantorial schools in the United States prior to World War II. See Judah M. Cohen, "Embodying Musical Heritage in a New–Old Profession: American Jewish Cantorial Schools, 1904–1939," *Journal of the Society for American Music* 11, no. 1 (2017): 25–52. In Germany, where the Jewish community was legally incorporated into the state, various forms of institutionalization of cantorial training had been established beginning in the mid-nineteenth century. See Geoffrey Goldberg, "The Training of Hazzanim in Nineteenth-Century Germany," *Yuval* 7 (2002): 307–14. Goldberg notes that institutional training of cantors led to discontinuities in cantorial repertoires and that some graduates of cantorial training schools found it necessary to hire elder cantors as tutors to train them to sing in a way that would be stylistically familiar to their congregations. A handful of cantors in Poland and Russia, including Abraham Ber Birnbaum in Czestechova, Poland, ran semiformal cantorial training programs in Europe that foreshadowed the curriculum of the American cantorial schools. For a description of the Birnbaum cantorial program, see Pinchos Sherman, "Fun mayn yugend . . ." *Di Khazonim Velt* 14 (December 1934): 9–11.

4. See Jean Lave and Etienne Wenger, *Situated Learning: Legitimate Peripheral Participation* (Cambridge: Cambridge University Press, 1991).

5. For descriptions of the culture of *meshoyrer* cantorial apprentice singers, see Michl Gelbart, *Fun Meshoyrerim Lebn* (New York: M. S. Shklarski, 1942); Kevin Plummer, "Historicist: Torn Between the Synagogue and the Concert Hall," *Torontoist*, December 13, 2014, https://torontoist.com/2014/12/historicist-torn-between-the-synagogue-and-concert-hall/; David Roitman, "Autobiography of David Roitman" (unpublished manuscript, n.d.); Mark Slobin, *Tenement Songs: The Popular Music of the Jewish Immigrants* (Urbana: University of Illinois Press, 1982), 21, 31–47.

6. See the biographies of cantors in Aaron Rosen, ed., *Di Geshikhte Fun khazones: Aroysgegeben Tsum 30 Yohrigen Yubileum Fun Agudat Hazonim Di-Amerikah ve-Kanadah, Zuntog Dem 3ten Februar, 1924*, ed. (New York: Jewish Ministers Cantors Association of America, 1924); Elias Zaludkovsky, *Kultur-treger fun der Idisher liturgye* (Detroit: S. N., 1930).

7. Interviews with elder cantors, Noah Schall and Robert Kieval.

8. See Mark Slobin, *Chosen Voices: The Story of the American Cantorate* (Urbana: University of Illinois Press, 1989), 72; Leibele Waldman, *A Song Divine: An Autobiography* (New York: Saravan House, 1941). Dyadic lessons in which European-born cantorial pedagogues taught American novice cantors have been described to me in interviews I have conducted with elder cantors including Robert Kieval, Julius Blackman, and Rabbi Michael Roth.

9. Personal correspondence with Cantor Nancy Abramson, the director of the H. L. Miller Cantorial School.

10. See Adolph Katchko, *Services for Sabbath Eve and Morning* (New York: Hebrew Union School of Education and Sacred Music, 1951); Judah M. Cohen, *The Making of a Reform Jewish Cantor*, (Bloomington: Indiana University Press, 2009), 42.

11. For examples of the musical philosophy of Belz School instructors, see Bernard Beer, "How the Traditional Chants of the Synagogue Create Continuity in Tefilah," YU Torah Online, Yeshiva University, October 6, 2008, https://www.yutorah.org/lectures /lecture.cfm/728260/cantor-bernard-beer/how-the-traditional-chants-of-the-synagogue -create-continuity-in-tefilah/; Bernard Beer, "The Importance of Nusach in Tefillah," YU Torah Online, Yeshiva University, April 3, 2011, https://www.yutorah.org/lectures/lecture .cfm/759649/cantor-bernard-beer/the-importance-of-nusach-in-tefillah/.

12. See Boaz Tarsi, "The Early Attempts at Creating a Theory of Ashkenazi Liturgical Music," in *Jüdische Musik als Dialog der Kulturen*, ed. Jascha Nemtsov (Wiesbaden: Harrassowitz, 2013): 59–69; Joseph A. Levine, "Toward Defining the Jewish Prayer Modes With a Particular Emphasis on the Adony Malakh Mode," *Musica Judaica* 3, no. 1 (1980–81): 13–41.

13. See H. Weintraub, *Schire beth Adonai oder Tempelgesänge für den Gottesdienst der Israeliten* (Leipzig: Breitkopf & Härtel, 1859).

14. See Daniel S. Katz, "A Chestnut, a Grape, and a Pack of Lions: A Shabbos in Płock with a Popular Synagogue Singer in the Early Nineteenth Century," in *Polin: Studies in Polish Jewry Volume 32: Jews and Music-Making in the Polish Lands*, ed. François Guesnet, Benjamin Matis, and Antony Polonsky, 15–30 (Liverpool: Liverpool University Press, 2020).

15. See Abraham Baer, *Baal T'fillah oder Der practische Vorbeter* (Gothenburg: n.p., 1877); Anders Hammerlund, *A Prayer For Modernity: Politics and Culture in the World of Abraham Baer (1834–1894)*, Musikverket, accessed June 12, 2023. https://musikverket.se /svensktvisarkiv/files/2013/06/Online_publ_A_Prayer_for-Modernity.pdf.

16. Associations of cantorial performance with the shedding of tears is noted in classic works on Jewish music including A. Z. Idelsohn, *Jewish Music in Its Historical Development* (New York: Schocken Books, 1967), 194; Zaludkovsky, *Kultur-treger*, 11. The trope of a cantor causing tears to be shed was so ingrained as to be the subject of cartoon caricatures; see "In shul baym unsane tokef," *Der groyse kibitser*, October 3, 1913. In this newspaper comic, a cantor needs an umbrella to protect himself from a literal rainstorm of tears as he sings one of the most important prayers in the High Holiday liturgy.

17. Competition between cantors was especially fierce in the area of the *probe*, or cantorial audition. See Slobin, *Chosen Voice*, 55–60. The probe was represented to comic effect in Yiddish cinema. See Ilya Motyleff, dir. *The Cantors Son*, Eron Pictures (1937).

18. There are numerous examples of liturgical melodies that exist in very similar versions across the Ashkenazi diaspora. A classic example is the Kol Nidre melody sung on the eve of Yom Kippur; it is sung with a fixed set of motifs across a broad array of geographic and communal settings.

19. See Elias Zaludkovsky, *Kultur-treger*. Zaludkovsky uses the term *nusakh* throughout the book in the expected modern cantorial sense to refer to knowledge of traditional melodies for prayer recitation.

20. See Jonathan L. Friedmann, "From Text to Melody: the Evolution of the Term Nusach Ha-tefillah," *Journal of Modern Jewish Studies* 20, no. 3 (2021): 339–60; Tarsi, "Early Attempts at Creating a Theory" Friedman's study misses the use of nusakh in earlier

Yiddish language writings, partly undermining his thesis that the musical sense of the term is essentially a coinage of mid-twentieth-century cantorial institutional pedagogues.

21. See Riv-Ellen Prell, *Prayer and Community: The Havurah in American Judaism* (Detroit: Wayne State University Press, 1989), chapter 1.

22. See Geoffrey Goldberg, "The Development of Congregational Song in the American Conservative Synagogue: 1900–1955," *Journal of Synagogue Music* 44, no. 1 (2019): 35–88; Israel Goldfarb, "An Analysis of the Hazanic Styles of Kwartin, Roitman and Rosenblatt," *Proceedings of the Seventh Annual Conference-Convention of The Cantors Assembly of America* (New York: Jewish Theological Seminary, 1954), 27. https://archive.org/stream/Cantors AsssemblyConferenceProceedings/1954_djvu.txt.

23. Merrill Fisher, "Committee on Standards," *Proceedings of the Fourth Annual Conference Convention of the Cantors Assembly and The Department of Music of The United Synagogue of America* (1951): 6, https://archive.org/stream/CantorsAssemblyConvention Proceedings/1951.

24. See Boaz Tarsi, "Observations on Practices of Nusach in America," *Asian Music* 33, no. 2 (2002), 175–219; Mark Slobin, *Chosen Voices: The Story of the American Cantorate* (Chicago: University of Illinois Press, 1989), 265–69; Cohen, *The Making of a Reform Jewish Cantor*.

25. For example, Joey Weisberg, a popular Jewish liturgical song writer and prayer leader, trumpets his connection to Schall as a source of his connection to tradition. See Leonard Felson, "A Brooklyn-Based Prayer Leader Heralds a Revolution in Jewish Music," *Tablet*, June 4, 2013, https://www.tabletmag.com/sections/belief/articles/joey-weisenberg -revolution-in-jewish-music.

26. See Aleida Assman, *Cultural Memory and Western Civilization: Arts of Memory* (Cambridge: Cambridge University Press, 2011); Jan Assman, *Cultural Memory and Early Civilization: Writing, Remembrance and Political Imagination* (Cambridge: Cambridge University Press, 2011).

27. See Maurice Halbwachs, *On Collective Memory*, ed. and trans. Lewis A. Coser (Chicago: University of Chicago Press, 1992); Erving Goffman, *Frame Analysis: An Essay on the Organization of Experience* (Evanston, IL: Northwestern University Press, 1974).

28. See Jeremiah Lockwood and Ari Kelman, "From Aesthetics to Experience: How Changing Conceptions of Prayer Changed the Sound of Jewish Worship," *Religion and American Culture: A Journal of Interpretation* 30, no. 1 (2020), 26–62.

29. See Israel Goldfarb, "An Analysis of the Hazanic Styles."

30. See "Historical Collection of Jewish Musical Folklore 1912–14, Volumes 10–11: Cantorial Compositions and Yiddish Folk Songs from the An-Ski Expeditions (1912–14)," National Academy of Sciences of Ukraine Vernadsky National Library of Ukraine, Institute for Information Recording (2020), http://audio.ipri.kiev.ua/CD10.html.

31. For a discussion of heterogeneity and individual style in prayer leading in the Eastern European Jewish context, see Judit Frigyesi, "The 'Ugliness' of Jewish Prayer—Voice Quality as the Expression of Identity." *Musicology* 7 (2007): 99–117.

32. Early attempts at building a Jewish music theory were driven by ideological motivations to defend Jews from the antisemitic accusation that Jews have no music, seeking to fit synagogue music into the prestigious theoretical structures of Western art music. Creating a Jewish music theory would "normalize" Jews and their music, downplaying the noisy and chaotic qualities of Jewish liturgical practices that were radically different from those

of Christian Europeans. The recent work of musicologist Boaz Tarsi has taken up a critical reevaluation of the concept of mode in Jewish musicology. Judit Frigyesi has proposed an analytical work on Ashkenazi Jewish prayer music based on her field recordings, offering promising new directions in this area of study. For classic studies that base theoretical analysis of Jewish prayer music on textual transcriptions, see Josef Singer, "Die Tonarten des traditionellen Synagogengesanges (Steiger), ihr Verhältnis zu den Kirchentonarten und den Tonarten der vorchristlichen Musiken periode," in *Sammlung kantoral-wissenschaftlicher Aufsätze*, ed. Aron Friedmann (Berlin: C. Boas, 1922), 90–100; A. Z. Idelsohn, *Jewish Music*, 72–91; Baruch Joseph Cohon, "The Structure of the Synagogue Prayer-Chant," *Journal of the American Musicological Society* 3, no. 1 (1950): 17–32.

33. See Marc Bregman, "Pseudopigraphy in Rabbinic Literature," in *Pseudopigraphic Perspectives: The Apocrypha and Pseudopigrapha in Light of the Dead Sea Scrolls* (Leiden, E. J. Brill, 1999), doi: https://doi.org/10.1163/9789004350328_004.

34. See Cohen, *The Making of a Reform Jewish Cantor*, 68–112.

35. See Brigid Barron, "Interest and Self-Sustained Learning as Catalysts of Development: A Learning Ecology Perspective," *Human Development* 49 (2006), 193–224.

36. See Cantor Moshe Teleshefsky, *T'filoh L'Moshe*, Cantorphone, FRS 113, LP (ND); Hana Levi Julian, "Renowned Cantor Moshe Teleshevsky, OBM," Israel National News, April 10, 2012, https://www.israelnationalnews.com/news/160537.

3. CANTORS AT THE PULPIT: THE LIMITS OF REVIVALIST AESTHETICS

1. The popularity of "You Raise Me Up" in the Haredi context has been mentioned to me by Lemmer and other cantors.

2. For discussions of change in the musical life of twentieth-century synagogues in the second half of the twentieth century, see Mark Slobin, *Chosen Voices: The Story of the American Cantorate* (Urbana: University of Illinois Press, 1989), 195–212. For a discussion of Reform cantorial education and the changes in synagogue practice see Judah M. Cohen, *The Making of a Reform Jewish Cantor* (Bloomington: Indiana University Press, 2009). For a discussion of American liturgical practices in the late twentieth and early twenty-first centuries, see Jeffrey A Summit, *The Lord's Song in a Strange Land: Music and Identity in Contemporary Jewish Worship* (New York: Oxford University Press, 2000); Sarah M. Ross, *A Season of Singing: Creating Feminist Jewish Music in the United States* (Waltham, MA: Brandeis University Press 2016).

3. Zev Muller, interview July 13, 2016. Zev Muller is the only participant in this research project who was not born into the Hasidic community. Muller was raised in a style of Orthodoxy often referred to as *Litvish* or *Yeshivish*. Both of these terms convey the centrality of traditional Jewish textual learning to the community, the former referring to the institutions of learning in northeastern Europe, and the latter simply meaning of the Yeshivah (rabbinic training academy). Litvish and Hasidic Jews are often grouped together under the umbrella term *Haredi*, a word used in Israel to connote separatist Orthodox Jewish communities.

4. Yanky Lemmer, interview March 21, 2016.

5. Diana Taylor, *The Archive and the Repertoire: Performing Cultural Memory in the Americas* (Durham, NC: Duke University Press, 2003), 20.

6. Ibid., 19.

7. Kohn recorded the service himself and shared the recording with me.

8. See Cohen, *The Making of a Reform Jewish Cantor*, 42; Adolph Katchko, *Services for Sabbath Eve and Morning* (New York: Hebrew Union School of Education and Sacred Music, 1951).

9. Cantorial discourse has taken on a permanent narrative of embattled decline, often presented in dramatic and unambiguous terms. See the revealingly titled edition of the Conservative cantorial journal, *"Nusach Wars," Journal of Synagogue Music* 40, no. 1 (March 2015).

10. See Peter Szendy, *Listen: A History of our Ears*, trans. Charlotte Mandell (New York: Fordham University Press, 2008).

11. See Jacque Ranciére, *The Politics of Aesthetics: The Distribution of the Sensible*, trans. Gabriel Rockhill (London: Continuum, 2004).

12. Sophia Rosenfeld, "On Being Heard: A Case for Paying Attention to the Historical Ear," *American Historical Review* 116, no. 2 (April 2011): 318.

13. Pinchos Jassinowsky, "In der velt fun khazones un idisher negina," *Der morgn zhurnal*, January 23, 1948.

14. Live davenings can be heard on YouTube, uploaded by collectors. Many examples of live davenings have been digitized and compiled on a file sharing site by an anonymous collector: see "Chazzanut For All shared by 'CantorEsq,'" Mediafire, accessed June 12, 2023, http://www.mediafire.com/?u8j92uzbihc30.

15. Yanky Lemmer, interview July 10, 2018. See interlude B for a discussion of Benzion Miller's work. Moshe Stern (born in 1937 in Hungary) continued to practice in the Eastern European cantorial tradition until late in the twentieth century.

16. Personal conversation with Rabbi Michael Wolk.

17. For a discussion of Ashkenazi liturgical Hebrew, see Lewis Glinert, ed., *Hebrew in Ashkenaz: A Language in Exile* (New York: Oxford University Press, 1993); for a discussion of cantorial discourse around Ashkenazi Hebrew pronunciation see Cohen, *The Making of a Reform Jewish Cantor*, 136–41.

18. See Milken Archive, "Conversations with Moshe Ganchoff," May 22, 2019, YouTube video, 05:28, https://www.youtube.com/watch?v=SC-Mt5qKuSQ.

19. Samuel Rosenbaum, "Prayer: The Lost Art," *Journal of Synagogue Music* 1, no. 2 (September 1967): 4.

20. Riv-Ellen Prell, *Prayer and Community: The Havurah in American Judaism* (Detroit: Wayne State University Press, 1989).

21. See Jeremiah Lockwood and Ari Kelman, "From Aesthetics to Experience: How Changing Conceptions of Prayer Changed the Sound of Jewish Worship," *Religion and American Culture: A Journal of Interpretation*, 30, no. 1 (2020): 26–62.

22. See Ari Y. Kelman and Shaul Magid, "The Gate to the Village: Shlomo Carlebach and the Creation of American Jewish Folk," *American Jewish History* 100, no. 4 (2016): 511–40; Judah M. Cohen, "Sing unto God: Debbie Friedman and the Changing Sound of Jewish Liturgical Music," *Contemporary Jewry* 35, no. 1 (2015): 13–34.

23. Judah Cohen, *Jewish Religious Music in Nineteenth-Century America: Restoring the Synagogue Soundtrack* (Bloomington: Indiana University Press, 2019).

24. See Geoffrey Goldberg, "The Development of Congregational Song in the American Conservative Synagogue: 1900–1955," *Journal of Synagogue Music* 44, no. 1 (2019): 35–88.

25. See Slobin, *Chosen Voices*, 213–55; Thomas Turino, *Music as Social Life: The Politics of Participation* (Chicago: University of Chicago Press, 2008).

26. For a discussion of prayer music in a representative Modern Orthodox synagogue, see Summit, *The Lord's Song*, 117–25. The research participants Summit interviews specifically note that they reject the idea of a trained cantor as being overly grand and showy and improper for the needs of their community.

27. Asya Vaisman, "Haredi Women's Musical Creativity," in "Contemporary Jewish Music in America 2000–2020: A Symposium," curated by Mark Kligman and Judah M. Cohen, *Journal of Synagogue Music* 46, no. 1 (September 2021): 10–11. See also Ross, *A Season of Singing* on the role of women prayer leaders in the liberal movements.

28. Yisroel Lesches, interview, July 11, 2018.

29. See Daniel Schley, "Sherwood Goffin Interview," Dartmouth Jewish Sound Archive, accessed June 12, 2023, https://djsa.dartmouth.edu/pages/goffin; David Olivestone, "Fifty Years of Neshama: Cantor Sherwood Goffin," *Jewish Action: The Magazine of the Orthodox Union* (Winter 2016): https://jewishaction.com/profile/fifty-years-neshama-cantor-sherwood-goffin/.

30. Yanky Lemmer, interview July 10, 2018.

31. A note on methodology is in order here. As a rule, I do not record the sacred music performances of cantors in synagogues out of respect for local custom, even though there is a tradition of recording services surreptitiously that the cantors benefit from, per my discussion above of "live davenings." Instead, after services, I write field notes that include musical examples transcribed from memory—a highly limiting form of transcription. This particular service conducted by Yanky and Shulem Lemmer was recorded by the cantors themselves and posted online. During the period of the COVID-19 quarantine many synagogues, including Lincoln Square, began hosting services by Zoom streaming video services. This special service led by the Lemmers from Yanky's living room was streamed on a variety of platforms, including Facebook Live and Instagram, where it is archived.

32. See "Shulem," accessed June 12, 2023, www.iamshulem.com. The text citing the influence of Michael Jackson has since been removed from the website.

33. See Samuel C. Heilman and Menachem Friedman, *The Rebbe: The Life and Afterlife of Menachem Mendel Schneerson* (Princeton, NJ: Princeton University Press, 2010).

34. See Jack Wertheimer, "Orthodox Outreach: Nourishing the Jewish World," in *The New American Judaism: How Jews Practice Their Religion Today* (Princeton, NJ: Princeton University Press, 2018), 211–32.

35. See Goldberg, "The Development of Congregational Song," 50.

36. Zevy Steiger, interview July 25, 2017.

INTERLUDE B. FRAGMENTS OF CONTINUITY:
TWO CASE STUDIES OF FATHERS AND SONS IN THE CHANGING
LANDSCAPE OF AMERICAN ORTHODOX JEWISH LITURGY

1. See "Young Israel Beth El of Borough Park," Orthodox Union, accessed June 9, 2023, https://www.yibethel.org/.

2. See "Charles Davidson & Noah Schall," interview by Mark Slobin," Wesleyan University, Digital Collections, 1986, https://digitalcollections.wesleyan.edu/object/cantorate-1097.

3. Geoffrey Goldberg, "The Development of Congregational Song in the American Conservative Synagogue: 1900–1955," *Journal of Synagogue Music* 44, no. 1 (2019): 41.

4. See Sarah G. Golden, "Richard Tucker in Chicago," *Chicago Jewish History* 38, no. 3 (Summer 2014).

5. See Arianne Brown, "The Khazntes—The Life Story of Sophie Kurtzer, Bas Sheva, Sheindele the Khaznte, Perele Feig, Goldie Malavsky and Frayedele Oysher," *Journal of Synagogue Music*. Vol. 32, 2007; Henry Sapoznik, "The Promiscuous World of Jewish Music Series, Lecture 18: Kol Isha: The Pioneering Women Cantors 1923–1975," Public lecture, September 14, 2020.

6. See B. Shelvin, "*Di tsukunft fun khazones in Amerike*," In *Di Geshikhte Fun khazones: Aroysgegeben Tsum 30 Yohrigen Yubileum Fun Agudat Hazonim Di-Amerikah ve-Kanadah, Zuntog Dem 3ten Februar, 1924*, ed. Aaron Rosen (New York: Jewish Ministers Cantors Association of America, 1924), 77–78.

7. I am aware of no scholarship on Helen Stambler's role in shaping the direction of recorded Jewish music in the second half of the twentieth century. Interviews with Stambler are available on the website of the Yiddish Book Center. See "Helen Stambler Latner's Oral History," Yiddish Book Center, accessed June 12, 2023, https://www.yiddishbookcenter.org /collections/oral-histories/interviews/woh-fi-0000704/helen-stambler-latner-2015.

8. The music of the Malavsky Family Choir offers a stylistic model for the development of contemporary Orthodox choirs, accentuating metered melodies, and embracing "mainstream" American pop culture elements in its rhythmic tendencies and instrumentation.

9. This move away from cantorial soloistic prayer services was already noted by cantors in the liberal Conservative and Reform movements when Mark Slobin was conducting research on the American cantorate in the 1980s.

10. See Roman Jakobson, "Closing Statements: Linguistics and Poetics," in *Style in Language*, ed. Thomas A. Sebeok (Cambridge, MA: MIT Press, 1960).

11. See J. L. Austin *How to Do Things with Words* (Cambridge, MA: Harvard University Press, 1962).

12. See Erving Goffman, "Response Cries," *Language* 54, no. 2 (1978): 800.

13. See Michel Foucault, "Des espaces autres: Cercle d'études architecturales" (Paris lecture to architecture students, 1967), *Architecture, Mouvement, Continuité* 5 (1984): 46–49. Translated by Jay Miskowiec as "Of Other Spaces: Utopias and Heterotopias," http://web .mit.edu/allanmc/www/foucault1.pdf.

4. CONCERT, INTERNET, AND KUMZITS: STAGES OF SACRED LISTENING

1. David Reich, in discussion with the author, January 13, 2019.

2. See Tina Frühauf, *Salomon Sulzer: Reformer, Cantor, Icon* (Berlin: Hentrich & Hentrich, 2012), 54–55.

3. See Philip Vilas Bohlman, *Jewish Music and Modernity* (Oxford: Oxford University Press, 2008), 73–104.

4. Elias Zaludkovsky, "Der khazonisher matzev," *Der morgn-zhurnal*, November 17, 1926.

5. Jeremiah Lockwood, "Prayer and Crime: Cantor Elias Zaludkovsky's Concert Performance Season in 1924 Poland," *In Geveb: A Journal of Yiddish Studies* (May 2022): https://ingeveb.org/articles/prayer-and-crime.

6. Henry Sapoznik, *Klezmer! Jewish Music from Old World to Our World* (New York: Schirmer Books, 1999), 83.

7. See Joachim Stutschewsky, *Der Vilner Balebesl (1816–1850)* (Tel Aviv: Y. L. Perets, 1968).

8. Samuel Rosenblatt, *Yossele Rosenblatt: The Story of His Life* (New York: Farrar, Straus and Young, 1954), 261–62.

9. Yanky Lemmer, in discussion with the author, July 16, 2019.

10. Yanky Lemmer, in discussion with the author, July 16, 2019.

11. The spelling employed on Shlisky's 1928 Victor records release is listed incorrectly as "Ono behoach." This typographic carelessness is typical of early cantorial records, mixing German spelling conventions with idiosyncratic phonetic spelling of Ashkenazi liturgical Hebrew, and sometimes overt errors.

12. Benedict Stambler and Helen Stambler, *Cantor Joseph Shlisky: Faith Eternal*, Collectors Guild, CG619 (1962), LP, liner notes.

13. See Biale et al., *Hasidism: A New History* (Princeton, NJ: Princeton University Press, 2018), 783–87.

14. Yaakov Lemmer, "Chazzan Yaakov Lemmer-Beth E-l," March 25, 2007, YouTube video, 04:08, https://youtu.be/tWrXQv19-kQ.

15. Yoel Kohn, in discussion with the author, January 15, 2019.

16. Yoel Kohn's video of Rozo D'Shabbos, originally posted in 2015, was deleted. Another account holder reposted the video. See Seth N, "Ruzu D'Shabbos Kohn," September 22, 2016, YouTube video 06:10, https://youtu.be/-6MbS2DybAE.

17. See Pelle Snickars and Patrick Vonderau, eds., *The YouTube Reader* (Stockholm: National Library of Sweden, 2009).

18. Sarah-Rachel Shechter, "Stirring Yiddish Singing by an Ex-Hasid," *The Yiddish Daily Forward*, November 27, 2015, http://yiddish.forward.com/articles/192080/stirring-yiddish -singing-by-an-ex-hasid/ (accessed April 28, 2021).

19. Biale et al., *Hasidism*, 209–11.

20. Bluechazzan, "Cantor Yoel Kohn: Hashkiveinu (Roitman)," August 19, 2019, YouTube video, 8:20, https://youtu.be/S5yXzJjjLRU.

21. Chazonus.com, "Sheyibone—Yoely Kohn, Yossi Pomerantz," June 28, 2018, YouTube video, 6:41, https://youtu.be/sa35i-Rfco0.

INTERLUDE C. PRODUCING THE REVIVAL:
MAKING *GOLDEN AGES* THE ALBUM

1. Linda Alcoff, *Visible Identities: Race, Gender, and the Self* (New York: Oxford University Press, 2006), 85.

CONCLUSION: CANTORS AND THEIR GHOSTS

1. Examples of creative or experimental research reportage that I consider relevant to the work of the cantors profiled in this book are found in the parallel scene of Jewish instrumental folk musicians who are also academic researchers or have collaborated with academics. Examples of this would include the work of the klezmer bands Veretski Pass, Tsibele, and the recent work of violinist Alicia Svigals, among others. Relevant experimental

research reportage emanating from the academy that has inspired my research project include Saidiya V. Hartman, *Wayward Lives, Beautiful Experiments: Intimate Histories of Social Upheaval* (New York; London: W. W. Norton, 2019); Ianna Hawkins Owen, "Still, Nothing: Mammy and Black Asexual Possibility," *Feminist Review* 120, no. 1 (November 2018): 70–84; and especially the unfinished collaboration of Jewlia Eisenberg and David Shneer, "Art is My Weapon: The Radical Musical Life of Lin Jaldati."

2. Linda Williams, "Film Bodies: Gender, Genre, and Excess," *Film Quarterly* 44, no. 4 (1991): 2–13.

3. In a passage from the classic work of Jewish musicology, A. Z. Idelsohn cites the special ability of Eastern European khazones to inspire tears, quoting a rabbinic source that reads, "it frequently happened that people who did not cry even when their parents died and had no desire to pray, were moved to tears and to repentance." See A. Z. Idelsohn, *Jewish Music in Its Historical Development* (New York: Schocken Books, 1967), 194. My grandfather, Cantor Jacob Konigsberg, once related an anecdote to me about the special value of tears as a proof of the value of cantorial music, transcending its ethical position in the Jewish community. He told me an anecdote about his grandfather, a Rabbi, who said of the famed Cantor Mordechai Hershman, who was well-known to be less than fully Orthodox, "That damned apikoros [heretic] made me cry." Despite his condemnation of secularizing Jews, the value of a cantor being able to elicit tears was more important for my great-great-grandfather, and perhaps other religious Jews of his generation, than conformity to normative religious comportment.

4. See Zohar Weiman-Kelman, "Touching Time: Poetry, History, and the Erotics of Yiddish," *Criticism* 59, no. 1 (2017): 99–121.

5. See Peter Szendy, *Listen: A History of Our Ears*, trans. Charlotte Mandell (New York: Fordham University Press, 2008).

6. See Samuel Rosenblatt, *Yossele Rosenblatt: The Story of His Life* (New York: Farrar, Straus and Young, 1954), 233; Leib Glantz, "*Khazones—der 'shir ha shirim' fun di idishe masn*," *Khazonim Zhurnal*, ed. Mordechai Yardeini (New York: Jewish Ministers Cantors' Association of America, 1950), 13–14.

GLOSSARY

bal tefile	Hebrew and Yiddish, prayer leader, pl. bal tefiles.
chazzonut haregesh	Hebrew, feelingful cantorial music; a term found in the writings of cantors to contrast florid and improvisatory cantorial chant with the more "rational" choral cantorial style; this idiosyncratic spelling, with its Modern Hebrew phonology, is used in Samuel Vigoda's *Legendary Voices*.
davenen	Yiddish, chanting prayer texts.
davening	Yinglish, cantorial prayer leading, used both as a verb and noun.
eilo ezkero	Hebrew, these I will remember; the title of a memorial prayer recited on Yom Kipur.
el maleh rachamim	Hebrew, God full of mercy; a memorial prayer recited by cantors.
farbrengen	Yiddish, social gathering; typically, of a devotional nature, featuring religious teachings and/or group singing of paraliturgical songs.
fray	Yiddish, free; used in the contemporary Hasidic community to refer to someone who is not religious, especially a Hasidic person who has left the community.
freygish	Yiddish, a variant on the musical term Phrygian; used to describe the major-sounding pitch group with a characteristic augmented 2nd interval that is used in many Jewish melodies.
gesise	Aramaic, dying gasp.
goyim	Hebrew and Yiddish, nation; used to refer to non-Jewish people, often with a pejorative overtone.

goyish	Yiddish, non-Jewish.
gust	Yiddish, mode; used in early cantorial discourse to discuss the melodic systems of Jewish prayer.
halacha	Hebrew, religious law.
haredi	Hebrew, orthodox; a term used in Israel to connote separatist Orthodox Jewish communities.
hazzanut	Hebrew, cantorial music; this is the same word as the Yiddish khazones, used more frequently by Hasidic cantors, but pronounced with the Modern Hebrew (i.e., Israeli) phonological system as opposed to the Ashkenazi liturgical Hebrew phonology employed by Hasidim and other Jews of Ashkenazi heritage, especially in present-day American Orthodox settings.
hefker	Hebrew, a term found in the Talmud to refer to property that has been abandoned.
hefker khazones	Yiddish, wanton cantorial music; used to denote cantorial music that has been cheapened or commercialized, especially in the writings of Elias Zaludkovski.
kadish	Hebrew, the mourner's prayer.
khasidishe velt	Yiddish, the Hasidic world; i.e., the Hasidic community.
khazente	Yiddish, the wife of a cantor; the term was used to refer to women performers of cantorial music, starting by the 1910s.
khazn	Hebrew and Yiddish, cantor, pl. khazonim.
khazones	Hebrew and Yiddish, cantorial music.
khidush	Hebrew and Yiddish, an innovation.
krekhts	Yiddish, sob; used to refer to vocal techniques in cantorial performance that are imitative of the sounds of crying.
kumzits	Yiddish, music-making party; derived from the words for *come sit*.
kvetsh	Yiddish, whine; used to refer to a vocal technique in cantorial performance that can be described as an ornament or a stylized vocal break that imitates the sound of crying.
litvish	Yiddish, Lithuanian; a term to described non-Hasidic separatist Orthodox Jews; the terms conveys the centrality of traditional Jewish textual learning to the religious community by referring to the institutions of learning in North Eastern Europe.
mamish	Hebrew and Yiddish, an intensifier.
mariv	Hebrew, the evening prayer service.
meshoyrer	Yiddish, cantorial choir singer; pl. *meshoyrerim*.
minyan	Hebrew, the required minimum of ten (men in the Orthodox rite) needed to conduct a prayer service.
mitre	a ceremonial cantorial hat, often with an angled peak, derived from Lutheran priestly vestments.

nigun	Hebrew and Yiddish, melody; pl. nigunim; in the Hasidic context nigun is used to describe a genre of devotional melodies, frequently sung without words.
nusakh ashkenaz	Hebrew, German version; used to refer to the "standard" prayer text of European Jews, which was mostly fixed by the seventeenth century.
nusakh hatefilah	Hebrew, manner of prayer; used to refer to the professional musical knowledge of cantors of the different musical forms used for the various elements of the Jewish liturgical cycle; often shortened to *nusakh*.
nusakh sefard	Hebrew, Sephardic version; used to describe the variant of the prayer book adopted by Hasidic Jews in the eighteenth century, influenced by the kabbalistic rabbis of Safed, in Palestine. In a confusing terminological palimpsest, although the Hasidic liturgy is called sefard, in reference to Sephardic Kabbalists, this liturgical variant is distinct from the version of the prayer book that is used by Sephardic Jews (i.e., the Jews with roots in the Iberian peninsula, exiled during the Inquisition in the fifteenth century, and later taking up residence across the Mediterranean world and in other international diasporic locations).
omud	Hebrew, the reader's lectern in synagogue; symbolically associated with cantors, the Yiddish phrase *daven farn omud*, or the Yinglish variant, *daven* for the *omud*, refers to a cantor leading prayer services.
rebbe	Yiddish, a familiar term for rabbi; used to refer to the leader of a Hasidic sect, used interchangeably with *tsadik*.
rebbes tish	Yiddish, the rabbi's table; a gathering at which a Hasidic leader gathers together with his disciples in gender-segregated all-male spaces for a shared devotional experience typically including singing of nigunim.
rebishe layt	Yiddish, the class of people drawn from elite rabbinic lineages.
recitative	Yiddish, a musical term borrowed from opera to refer to cantorial compositions in a heavily ornamented vocal style that does not have a clear pulse-based meter.
ribono shel olam	Hebrew, master of the universe; the opening formula of address to God in many prayers, and thus the title of many cantorial pieces, including a classic recitative by Pierre Pinchik sung by many cantors.
rosh khodesh bentshn	Hebrew and Yiddish, the blessing of the new moon; a special prayer that is added to sabbath services the week before a new month begins and that receives special musical treatment from cantors.

rov	Hebrew and Yiddish, rabbi, communal leader.
shakhris	Hebrew, the morning prayer service.
schmoozing	Yinglish, chatting.
shokhein ad	Hebrew, he dwells forever; the beginning of the *shakhris* Sabbath morning service; typically, earlier parts of the service are led by a nonprofessional community member and the cantor begins their part of the service with this text.
shtetl	Yiddish, small town.
shtibl	Yiddish, small Hasidic prayer house.
shtikl	Yiddish, a little piece; used to refer informally to a cantorial composition.
siddur	Hebrew, order; the term for the Jewish prayer book.
siman tov umazel tov	Hebrew, good fortune, good luck; the title of a song performed at celebratory life cycle events.
simchas	Hebrew and Yiddish, festive occasions such as weddings.
skarbove nigun	Yiddish, sacred melody; used by cantors to describe a set of melodies that are used throughout the Ashkenaz diaspora and are considered to be very old and especially representative of the liturgical music tradition.
ta'amey hamikra	Hebrew, Torah cantillation notation.
tallis	Hebrew, prayer shawl worn by Jews during specific prayer services.
trop	Yiddish, the traditional Jewish system of musical notation for scriptural chanting.
tsadik	Hebrew, righteous one, pl. *tsadikim*; term used interchangeably with *rebbe* to describe leaders of Hasidic sects.
ur alte	Yiddish, ancient; used in early cantorial discourse to describe the older strands of Jewish prayer music in use before choral music reforms were introduced in the nineteenth century.
vunderkind	Yiddish, child prodigy; used in Jewish musical contexts to describe a child singer who performs professionally in a synagogue or on stage.
yehi rotzon	Hebrew, may it be your will; the opening formula of address to God in many prayers, including the blessing for the new month that is a specially marked part of cantorial repertoire.
yeshivah	Hebrew and Yiddish, an institution of Jewish traditional religious learning; a training academy for rabbis.
yeshivish	Yiddish, of the yeshivah; this term is used to describe non-Hasidic separatist Orthodox Jews; it conveys the centrality of traditional Jewish textual learning to the community.

BIBLIOGRAPHY

Agrama, Hussein Ali. "Ethics, Tradition, Authority: Toward an Anthropology of the Fatwa." *American Ethnologist* 37, no. 1 (February 2010): 2–18.

Alcoff, Linda. *Visible Identities: Race, Gender, and the Self.* New York: Oxford University Press, 2006.

Allen, Wayne. *The Cantor: From the Mishna to Modernity.* Eugene, OR: Wipf & Stock, 2019.

Arakelyan, Ashot. "Selmar Cerini (Tenor) (Poland, Wólka 1861—Poland, Breslau 1923)." *Forgotten Opera Singers* (blog). November 21, 2014. http://forgottenoperasingers.blogspot .com/2014/11/selmar-cerini-tenor-poland-1861-breslau.html.

Assaf, David. *Untold Tales of the Hasidim: Crisis and Discontent in the History of Hasidism.* Waltham, MA: Brandeis University Press, 2010.

Assman, Aleida. *Cultural Memory and Western Civilization: Arts of Memory.* Cambridge: Cambridge University Press, 2011.

Assman, Jan. *Cultural Memory and Early Civilization: Writing, Remembrance and Political Imagination.* Cambridge: Cambridge University Press, 2011.

Austin, J. L. *How to Do Things with Words.* Cambridge, MA: Harvard University Press, 1962.

Avenary, Hanoch. "The Hasidic Nigun: Ethos and Melos of a Folk Liturgy." *Journal of the International Folk Music Council* 16 (1964): 60–63.

Avishai, Orit. "'Doing Religion' In a Secular World." *Gender & Society* 22, no. 4 (2008): 409–33.

Baer, Abraham. *Baal T'fillah oder Der practische Vorbeter.* Gothenburg: n.p., 1877.

Barron, Brigid. "Interest and Self-Sustained Learning as Catalysts of Development: A Learning Ecology Perspective." *Human Development* 49 (2006): 193–224.

Beer, Bernard. "How the Traditional Chants of the Synagogue Create Continuity in Tefilah, "YU Torah Online. Yeshiva University. October 6, 2008. https://www.yutorah.org /lectures/lecture.cfm/728260/cantor-bernard-beer/how-the-traditional-chants-of-the -synagogue-create-continuity-in-tefilah/.

———. "The Importance of Nusach in Tefillah." YU Torah Online. Yeshiva University April 3, 2011. https://www.yutorah.org/lectures/lecture.cfm/759649/cantor-bernard-beer/the-importance-of-nusach-in-tefillah/.

Bennett, Roger, and Josh Kun. *And You Shall Know Us by the Trail of Our Vinyl: The Jewish Past as Told by the Records We Have Loved and Lost.* New York: Crown, 2008.

Berger, Joseph. "Bit by Bit a Cantor's Voice Is Restored." *New York Times*, June 20, 2010.

Besser, Yisroel. "Dear Shulem." *Mishpacha Jewish Family Weekly*, July 25, 2018. https://mishpacha.com/dear-shulem/.

Biale, David, ed. *Hasidism: A New History.* Princeton, NJ: Princeton University Press, 2018.

Bluechazzan. "Cantor Yoel Kohn: Hashkiveinu (Roitman)." August 19, 2019. YouTube video, 8:20. https://youtu.be/S5yXzJjjLRU.

Bohlman, Philip Vilas. *Jewish Music and Modernity.* Oxford: Oxford University Press, 2008.

Bregman, Marc. "Pseudopigraphy in Rabbinic Literature." In *Pseudopigraphic Perspectives: The Apocrypha and Pseudopigrapha in Light of the Dead Sea Scrolls*: 27–41. Leiden: E. J. Brill, 1999.

Brown, Arianne. "The Khazntes—The Life Story of Sophie Kurtzer, Bas Sheva, Sheindele the Khaznte, Perele Feig, Goldie Malavsky and Frayedele Oysher." *Journal of Synagogue Music* 32 (2007): 51–79.

Buber, Martin. *Tales of the Hasidim.* New York: Schocken Books, 1991.

Cantor Moshe Teleshevsky. LP record (n.d. ca. 1960s), no label listed.

Cantorial Legends. "Cantor David Koussevitzky Live Shabbos Shacharis and Musaf Rosh Chodesh Bentching." April 26, 2012. YouTube video, 1:20:00. https://www.youtube.com/watch?v=ze3O-Bp6nBU.

Cantwell, Robert, Archie Green, Bruce Jackson, Ellen J. Stekert, Kenneth S. Goldstein, Sheldon Posen, Pauline Greenhill, et al. *Transforming Tradition: Folk Music Revivals Examined.* Urbana: University of Illinois Press, 1993.

Chabad Nigunim Volume 5. LP record (1964). Nichoach N-5724.

Chagy, Berele. "Ma'asim onshtot reyd." Undated press clipping. YIVO Archives, RG 1278.

"Charles Davidson & Noah Schall." Interview by Mark Slobin. Wesleyan University, Digital Collections, 1986. https://digitalcollections.wesleyan.edu/object/cantorate-1097.

"Charlie Bernhaut's Volunteer 'Radio Career' Began in 1977 When He Introduced the Friday Morning Pre-Shabbos Segment on Larry Gordon's 'Jewish and Hebrew Sound' at WFMU." About Charlie Bernhaut—Two Hours of Jewish Music. Accessed June 12, 2023. http://www.charliebernhaut.com/about.html.

Chazonus.com. "Sheyibone—Yoely Kohn, Yossi Pomerantz." June 28, 2018. YouTube video, 6:41. https://youtu.be/sa35i-Rfcoo.

"Chazzanut For All." Mediafire. Accessed June 12, 2023. http://www.mediafire.com/?u8j92uzbihc30.

Cohen, Judah M. "Embodying Musical Heritage in a New–Old Profession: American Jewish Cantorial Schools, 1904–1939." *Journal of the Society for American Music* 11, no. 1 (2017): 25–52.

———. *Jewish Religious Music in Nineteenth-Century America: Restoring the Synagogue Soundtrack.* Bloomington: Indiana University Press, 2019.

———. *The Making of a Reform Jewish Cantor.* Bloomington: Indiana University Press, 2009.

———. "Professionalizing the Cantorate—and Masculinizing It? The Female Prayer Leader and Her Erasure from Jewish Musical Tradition." *Musical Quarterly* 101, no. 4 (2018): 455–81.

———. "Sing unto God: Debbie Friedman and the Changing Sound of Jewish Liturgical Music." *Contemporary Jewry* 35, no. 1 (2015): 13–34.

Cohon, Baruch Joseph. "The Structure of the Synagogue Prayer-Chant." *Journal of the American Musicological Society* 3, no. 1 (1950): 17–32.

COLlive News and COLlive. "Chazan Moshe Teleshevsky, 85 OBM." COLlive, October 3, 2012. https://collive.com/chazan-moshe-teleshevsky-85-obm/.

Costache, Ioanida. "Reclaiming Romani-Ness." *Critical Romani Studies* 1 (2018): 30–43.

Dale, Gordon A. "Music in Haredi Jewish Life: Liquid Modernity and the Negotiation of Boundaries in Greater New York." PhD diss., City University of New York, 2017.

Deen, Shulem. *All who go do not return: a memoir.* Minneapolis, MN: Graywolf Press, 2015.

Dynner, Glenn. *Men of Silk: The Hasidic Conquest of Polish Jewish Society.* New York: Oxford University Press, 2006.

Eisenberg, Jewlia, and David Shneer. "Art is My Weapon: The Radical Musical Life of Lin Jaldati." Performance/public talk. 2018.

Ephros, Gershon. "The Hazzanic Recitative: A Unique Contribution to our Music Heritage." *Journal of Synagogue Music* 6, no. 3 (1976): 23–28.

Ewing, Heidi, and Rachel Grady. *One of Us.* Netflix, 2017.

Fader, Ayala. *Mitzvah Girls: Bringing Up the Next Generation of Hasidic Jews in Brooklyn.* Princeton, NJ: Princeton University Press, 2009.

Fater, Issachar. "Gershon Sirota: An Appreciation." *Journal of Synagogue Music* 2, no. 3 (1968): 16–21.

Felson, Leonard. "A Brooklyn-Based Prayer Leader Heralds a Revolution in Jewish Music." *Tablet*, June 4, 2013. https://www.tabletmag.com/sections/belief/articles/joey-weisenberg-revolution-in-jewish-music.

Fisher, Merrill. "Committee on Standards." *Proceedings of the Fourth Annual Conference Convention of the Cantors Assembly and The Department of Music of The United Synagogue of America* (1951): 6. https://archive.org/stream/CantorsAssemblyConvention Proceedings/1951.

Foucault, Michel. "Des espaces autres: Cercle d'études architecturales" (Paris, lecture to architecture students, 1967). In *Architecture, Mouvement, Continuité*, 5 (1984): 46–49. Translated by Jay Miskowiec as "*Of Other Spaces: Utopias and Heterotopias.*" http://web .mit.edu/allanmc/www/foucault1.pdf.

Friedmann, Jonathan L. "From Text to Melody: the Evolution of the Term Nusach Ha-tefillah." *Journal of Modern Jewish Studies* 20, no. 3 (2021): 339–60.

Frigyesi, Judit. "The 'Ugliness' of Jewish Prayer—Voice Quality as the Expression of Identity." *Musicology* 7 (2007): 99–117.

Frühauf, Tina. *Salomon Sulzer: Reformer, Cantor, Icon.* Berlin: Hentrich & Hentrich Verlag, 2012.

Gelatt, Roland. "A Musical Instrument." In *The Fabulous Phonograph, 1877–1977*, 114–29. New York: Macmillan, 1977.

Gelbart, Michl. *Fun Meshoyrerim Lebn*. New York: M. S. Shḵlarsḵi, 1942.

Glantz, Leib. "Khazones—der 'shir ha shirim' fun di idishe masn." In *Khazonim zhurnal*, edited by Mordechai Yardeini, 13–14. (New York: Jewish Ministers Cantors' Association of America, 1950).

Glinert, Lewis, ed. *Hebrew in Ashkenaz: A Language in Exile*. New York: Oxford University Press, 1993.

———. "Toward a Social Study of Ashkenazi Hebrew." *Jewish Social Studies* 2, no. 4 (1996): 85–114.

Glissant, Édouard. *Poetics of Relation*. Ann Arbor: University of Michigan Press, 1997.

Goffman, Erving. *Frame Analysis: An Essay on the Organization of Experience*. Evanston, IL: Northwestern University Press, 1974.

———. "Response Cries." *Language* 54, no. 2 (1978): 787–815.

Goldberg, Geoffrey. "The Development of Congregational Song in the American Conservative Synagogue: 1900–1955." *Journal of Synagogue Music* 44, no. 1 (2019): 35–88.

———. "The Training of Hazzanim in Nineteenth-Century Germany." *Yuval* 7 (2002): 307–14.

Golden, Sarah G. "Richard Tucker in Chicago." In *Chicago Jewish History* 38, no. 3 (Summer 2014).

Goldfarb, Israel. "An Analysis of the Hazanic Styles of Kwartin, Roitman and Rosenblatt." *Proceedings of the Seventh Annual Conference-Convention of The Cantors Assembly of America*. New York: Jewish Theological Seminary, 1954. https://archive.org/stream /CantorsAsssemblyConferenceProceedings/1954_djvu.txt.

Hajdu, André, and Yaakov Masur. "The Musical Traditions of Hasidism." In *Encyclopedia Judaica*. Jerusalem: Keter Publishing House; New York: Macmillan Publishers, 1971.

Halbwachs, Maurice. *On Collective Memory*. Edited and translated by Lewis A. Coser. Chicago: University of Chicago Press, 1992.

Hammerlund, Anders. *A Prayer for Modernity: Politics and Culture in the World of Abraham Baer (1834–1894)*. Stockholm: Svenskt visarkiv/Statens musikverk, 2013.

Harshav, Benjamin. *Language in Time of Revolution*. Stanford, CA: Stanford University Press, 1999.

Hartman, Saidiya V. *Wayward Lives, Beautiful Experiments: Intimate Histories of Social Upheaval*. New York; London: W. W. Norton, 2019.

Heilman, Samuel C., and Menachem Friedman. *The Rebbe: The Life and Afterlife of Menachem Mendel Schneerson*. Princeton, NJ: Princeton University Press, 2010.

Heilman, Samuel C. *Sliding to the Right: The Contest for the Future of American Jewish Orthodoxy*. Berkeley: University of California Press, 2006.

"Helen Stambler Latner's Oral History." Yiddish Book Center. June 5, 2015. https://www .yiddishbookcenter.org/collections/oral-histories/interviews/woh-fi-0000704/helen -stambler-latner-2015.

Herzfeld, Michael. *Cultural Intimacy: Social Poetics and the Real Life of States, Societies and Institutions*. New York: Routledge, Taylor & Francis, 2016.

"Historical Collection of Jewish Musical Folklore 1912–14, Volumes 10–11: Cantorial Compositions and Yiddish Folk Songs from the An-Ski Expeditions (1912–14)." National Academy of Sciences of Ukraine Vernadsky National Library of Ukraine, Institute for Information Recording (2020). http://audio.ipri.kiev.ua/CD10.html.

Hobsbawm, E. J., and T. O. Ranger. *The Invention of Tradition.* Cambridge: Cambridge University Press, 1983.

Holland, Dorothy and Jean Lave, eds. *History in Person: Enduring Struggles, Contentious Practice, Intimate Identities.* Santa Fe, NM: SAR Press, 2001.

Holland, Dorothy, William S. Lachiotte Jr., Debra Skinner, and Carole Cain, eds. *Identity and Agency in Cultural Worlds.* Cambridge, MA: Harvard University Press, 2001.

Idelsohn, A. Z. *Jewish Music in Its Historical Development.* New York: Schocken Books, 1967.

"In shul baym unsane tokef." *Der groyse kibitzer,* October 3, 1913.

Ivry, Tsipy, and Elly Teman. "Shouldering Moral Responsibility: The Division of Moral Labor among Pregnant Women, Rabbis, and Doctors." *American Anthropologist* 121, no. 4 (2019): 857–69.

Jakobson, Roman. "Closing Statements: Linguistics and Poetics." In *Style in Language,* edited by Thomas A. Sebeok, 350–77. Cambridge, MA: MIT Press, 1960.

Jassinowsky, Pinchos. "In der velt fun khazones un idisher negina." *Der morgn zhurnal,* January 23, 1948.

Julian, Hana Levi. "Renowned Cantor Moshe Teleshevsky, OBM." Israel National News. October 4, 2012. https://www.israelnationalnews.com/news/160537.

Kahana, Yehoshua. "When Hasidic Singers Perform in a Litvish Accent." *Forverts,* September 10, 2019. https://forward.com/yiddish/431118/when-hasidic-performers-sing-in-a-litvish-dialect/.

Katchko, Adolph. *Services for Sabbath Eve and Morning.* New York: Hebrew Union School of Education and Sacred Music, 1951.

Katz, Daniel S. "A Chestnut, a Grape, and a Pack of Lions: A Shabbos in Płock with a Popular Synagogue Singer in the Early Nineteenth Century." In *Polin: Studies in Polish Jewry Volume 32: Jews and Music-Making in the Polish Lands,* edited by François Guesnet, Benjamin Matis, and Antony Polonsky, 15–30. Liverpool: Liverpool University Press, 2020.

Kelman, Ari Y. "An Acoustic Community, 1936–1941." In *Station Identification: A Cultural History of Yiddish Radio in the United States,* 128–73. Berkeley: University of California Press, 2009.

Kelman, Ari Y., and Shaul Magid. "The Gate to the Village: Shlomo Carlebach and the Creation of American Jewish Folk." *American Jewish History* 100, no. 4 (2016): 511–40.

Kenigsberg, Ben. "'The Song of Names' Review: A Prodigy, a War and a Mystery." *New York Times,* December 24, 2019.

Kirschenblatt-Gimblett, Barbara. "Sounds of Sensibility." In *American Klezmer: Its Roots and Offshoots,* edited by Mark Slobin, 129–73. Berkley: University of California Press, 2002.

———. "Theorizing Heritage." *Ethnomusicology* 39, no. 3 (1995): 367–80.

Kligman, Mark. "Contemporary Jewish Music in America." *American Jewish Year Book* 101, (2001): 88–141.

Koskoff, Ellen. *Music in Lubavitcher Life.* Urbana: University of Illinois Press, 2001.

Kwartin, Zawel. *Smiroth Zebulon: Recitative für Kantoren.* New York: Self-published, 1928.

Landman, Leo. "The Office of the Medieval 'Hazzan.'" *Jewish Quarterly Review* 62, no. 3 (January 1972): 156–87.

Lange, Leib. "Dos alte khazones—der shlisel tsu der idisher neshome." In *Di shul un di khazanim velt* 33, no. 52, edited by Pinchas Sherman (July 1939): 9–10.

Lave, Jean, and Etienne Wenger. *Situated Learning: Legitimate Peripheral Participation.* Cambridge: Cambridge University Press, 1991.

Lehmann, David, and Batia Siebzehner. "Power, Boundaries and Institutions: Marriage in Ultra-Orthodox Judaism." *European Journal of Sociology / Archives Européennes de Sociologie / Europäisches Archiv Für Soziologie* 50, no. 2 (2009): 273–308.

Lemmer, Yaakov. "Chazzan Yaakov Lemmer-Beth E-l." March 25, 2007. YouTube video, 4:08. https://youtu.be/tWrXQv19-kQ.

Levine, Joseph A. "The Glantz / Pinchik Conundrum." *Journal of Synagogue Music* 34 (Fall 2009): 76–100.

———. "Nusach Wars," *Journal of Synagogue Music* 40, no. 1 (March 2015).

Levine, Joseph A. "Toward Defining the Jewish Prayer Modes With a Particular Emphasis on the Adony Malakh Mode." *Musica Judaica* 3, no. 1 (1980–81): 13–41.

Lipman, Steve. "New Cantor, New Look." *New York Jewish Week*, September 17, 2013. https://jewishweek.timesofisrael.com/new-cantor-new-look/.

Livingston, Tamara. "Music Revivals: Towards a General Theory." *Ethnomusicology* 43, no. 1 (Winter 1999): 66–85.

Lockwood, Jeremiah. "House of Friendly Ghosts Vol. 1," Liner notes, JDub Records (2011).

———. "Ira Temple and the Williamsburg Senior Center." *Conversations: Words and Music from the American Jewish Experience* (blog). August 30, 2021. https://schoolofmusic.ucla.edu/conversations-dispatches-from-brooklyn/.

———. "Prayer and Crime: Cantor Elias Zaludkovsky's Concert Performance Season in 1924 Poland." *In Geveb: A Journal of Yiddish Studies* (2022): https://ingeveb.org/articles/prayer-and-crime.

Lockwood, Jeremiah, and Ari Kelman. "From Aesthetics to Experience: How Changing Conceptions of Prayer Changed the Sound of Jewish Worship." *Religion and American Culture: A Journal of Interpretation* 30, no. 1 (2020), 26–62.

Loeffler, James. *The Most Musical Nation: Jews and Culture in the Late Russian Empire.* New Haven, CT: Yale University Press, 2010.

Lubavitcher Chorus and Instrumental Ensemble. *"Nichoach" Chabad Melodies.* Collectors Guild CGL 615, recorded 1960, LP.

Mahmood, Saba. *Politics of Piety.* Princeton, NJ: Princeton University Press, 2005.

Milken Archive. "Conversations with Moshe Ganchoff." May 22, 2019. YouTube video, 5:28. https://www.youtube.com/watch?v=SC-Mt5qKuSQ.

Minkovsky, Pinchas. *Moderne liturgia in unsere synagogen* (1910). Reproduced in Akiva Zimmermann, *Perakim Be-Shir: Sefer Pinkhas Minkovski* (Tel Aviv: Sha'are Ron, 2011).

Miron, Dan. *The Image of the Shtetl and Other Studies of Modern Jewish Literary Imagination.* Syracuse, NY: Syracuse University Press, 2000.

Motyleff, Ilya, dir. *The Cantors Son.* 1937; Pennsylvania: Eron Pictures, 2006.

N, Seth. "Ruzu D'Shabbos Kohn." September 22, 2016. YouTube video, 6:10. https://youtu.be/-6MbS2DybAE.

Narváez, Peter. "Paradoxical Aesthetics of the Blues Revival." In *Transforming Tradition,* edited by Neil V. Rosenberg, 241–57. Urbana: University of Illinois Press, 1993.

Olivestone, David. "Fifty Years of Neshama: Cantor Sherwood Goffin." *Jewish Action: The Magazine of the Orthodox Union* (Winter 2016): https://jewishaction.com/profile/fifty-years-neshama-cantor-sherwood-goffin/.

———. "Shul or Show?" *Segula: The Jewish History Magazine* 54 (September 2020): 30–39.

Owen, Ianna Hawkins. "Still, Nothing: Mammy and Black Asexual Possibility." *Feminist Review* 120, no. 1 (November 2018): 70–84.

Pasternak, Velvel. *Behind the Music: Stories, Anecdotes, Articles & Reflections*. Cedarhurst, NY: Tara, 2017.

———. "The Golden Age of Cantors." *Journal of Synagogue Music* 31, no. 1 (September 2006): 160–64.

Plummer, Kevin. "Historicist: Torn Between the Synagogue and the Concert Hall." *Torontoist*, December 13, 2014. https://torontoist.com/2014/12/historicist-torn-between-the-synagogue-and-concert-hall/.

Polland, Annie. *Landmark of the spirit: The Eldridge Street Synagogue*. New Haven, CT: Yale University Press, 2009.

Prell, Riv-Ellen. *Prayer and Community: The Havurah in American Judaism*. Detroit: Wayne State University Press, 1989.

Qureshi, Regula Burckhardt. "His Master's Voice? Exploring Qawwali and 'Gramophone Culture' in South Asia." *Popular Music* 18, no. 1 (January 1999): 63–98.

Radensky, Paul. "The Rise and Decline of a Hasidic Court: The Case of Rabbi Duvid Twersky of Tal'noye." In *Holy Dissent: Jewish and Christian Mystics in Eastern Europe*, edited by Glenn Dynner, 131–68. Detroit: Wayne State University Press, 2011.

Ranciére, Jacque. *The Politics of Aesthetics: The Distribution of the Sensible*. Translated by Gabriel Rockhill. London: Continuum, 2004.

Rechtman, Abraham, Nathaniel Deutsch, and Noah Barrera. *The Lost World of Russia's Jews: Ethnography and Folklore in the Pale of Settlement*. Bloomington: Indiana University Press, 2021.

Regev, Motti, and Edwin Seroussi. *Popular Music and National Cultures In Israel*. Berkeley: University of California Press, 2004: 126–29.

Roda, Jessica. *For Women and Girls Only: the Arts, the Digital, and Jewish Orthodoxy*. New York: New York University Press, 2024.

Roitman, David. "Autobiography of David Roitman." Unpublished manuscript, n.d.

Ronström, Owe. "Traditional Music, Heritage Music." In *The Oxford Handbook of Music Revival*, edited by Caroline Bithell and Juniper Hill, 43–59. New York: Oxford University Press, 2014.

Rosen, Aaron, ed. *Di Geshikhte Fun khazones: Aroysgegeben Tsum 30 Yohrigen Yubileum Fun Agudat Hazonim Di-Amerikah ve-Kanadah, Zuntog Dem 3ten Februar, 1924*. New York: Jewish Ministers Cantors Association of America, 1924.

Rosenberg, Neil V., ed. *Transforming Tradition*. Urbana: University of Illinois Press, 1993.

Rosenbaum, Samuel. "Surviving Future Shock." *Journal of Synagogue Music* 9, no. 2 (June 1979): 26.

———. "Prayer: The Lost Art," *Journal of Synagogue Music* 1, no. 2 (September 1967): 3–8.

Rosenblatt, Samuel. *Yossele Rosenblatt: The Story of His Life*. New York: Farrar, Straus and Young, 1954.

Rosenfeld, Sophia. "On Being Heard: A Case for Paying Attention to the Historical Ear." *American Historical Review* 116, no. 2 (April 2011): 316–34.

Ross, Sarah M. *A Season of Singing: Creating Feminist Jewish Music in the United States*. Waltham, MA: Brandeis University Press, 2016.

"Sacred Sabbath: Cantor Ben Zion Kapov-Kagan." LP liner notes. Collectors Guild CG618 (1962).

Sapoznik, Henry. *Klezmer! Jewish Music from Old World to Our World.* New York: Schirmer Books, 1999.

———. "The Promiscuous World of Jewish Music Series, Lecture 18: Kol Isha: The Pioneering Women Cantors 1923–1975." Public lecture on Zoom, September 14, 2020.

Schall, Noah. *Hazzanut for the High Holy Days.* New York: Tara, 1969.

———. *Hazzanic Thesaurus.* 3 vols. New York: Tara, 1970.

———. *Yossele Rosenblatt: Classic Cantorial Recitatives.* New York: Tara, 2015.

———. *Sefer Shel Nusach T'hilot Netsach: Nusach Improvisations for Shabbat Morning.* N.p.: Self-published, 2017.

Shechter, Sarah-Rachel. "Stirring Yiddish Singing by an Ex-Hasid." *Yiddish Daily Forward.* November 27, 2015. http://yiddish.forward.com/articles/192080/stirring-yiddish-singing-by-an-ex-hasid/.

Sherman, Pinchos. "Fun mayn yugend . . ." *Di Khazonim Velt* 14 (December 1934): 9–11.

Schleier, Curt. "The Musician Shulem on Being the First Artist Raised Hasidic to Sign with a Major Record Label." *Jewish Telegraph Agency,* April 23, 2020. https://www.jta.org/2020/04/23/culture/the-musician-shulem-on-being-the-first-artist-raised-hasidic-to-sign-with-a-major-record-label.

Schley, Daniel. "Sherwood Goffin Interview." Dartmouth Jewish Sound Archive. Accessed June 12, 2023. https://djsa.dartmouth.edu/pages/goffin.

Scholem, Gershom. "Isaac Luria and His School." In *Major Trends in Jewish Mysticism,* 244–86. New York: Schocken Books, 1995.

Schrader, Maria. *Unorthodox.* Netflix, 2020.

Seidman, Naomi. "My Scandalous Rejection of Unorthodox." *Jewish Review of Books,* Summer 2020.

Seroussi, Edwin. "The Jewish Liturgical Music Printing Revolution: A Preliminary Assessment." In *Textual Transmission in Contemporary Jewish Cultures,* edited by Avriel Bar-Levav and Uzi Rebhun, 100–136. New York: Oxford University Press, 2020.

Shandler, Jeffrey. *Jews, God and Videotape: religion and media in America.* New York: New York University Press, 2009.

Shelvin, B. "Di tsukunft fun khazones in amerike." In *Di geshikhte fun khazones,* edited by Aaron Rosen, 77–78. New York: Jewish Ministers Cantors Association of America, 1924.

Shif, Shneor. "Raza D'Shabat'—Yirmiyah Damen Motti Steinmetz Mikahlat Neranena." July 22, 2016. YouTube video, 8:58. https://www.youtube.com/watch?v=oDiyEq4OCfo&ab _channel=%D7%A9%D7%A0%D7%99%D7%90%D7%95%D7%A8%D7%A9%D7%99 D7%A3.

Shtrigler, Mordekhai. "Vi azoy darf oyszehn di moralishe geshtalt fun a khazn." *Di shul un di khazonim velt* 33, no. 52 (July 1939): 7–9.

Shulem. "The Man from Vilna—Shulem and Yanky Lemmer." December 20, 2021. YouTube video, 6:15. https://www.youtube.com/watch?v=Nme1I3H16aI.

"Shulem." Accessed June 12, 2023. www.iamshulem.com.

Singer, Josef. "Die Tonarten des traditionellen Synagogensgesanges (Steiger), ihr Verhältnis zu den Kirchentonarten und den Tonarten der vorchristlichen Musiken periode." *Sammlung kantoral-wissenschaftlicher Aufsätze,* edited by Aron Friedmann, 90–100. Berlin: C. Boas, 1922.

Slobin, Mark. *Chosen Voices: The Story of the American Cantorate*. Chicago: University of Illinois Press, 1989.

———. *Fiddler on the Move: Exploring the Klezmer World*. Oxford: Oxford University Press, 2000.

———. *Tenement Songs: The Popular Music of the Jewish Immigrants*. Urbana: University of Illinois Press, 1982.

Smith, Chani Haran. "Music as a Spiritual Process in the Teachings of Rabbi Nahman of Bratslav." *Journal of Synagogue Music* 34 (2009): 8–47.

Snickars, Pelle, and Patrick Vonderau. *The YouTube Reader*. Stockholm: National Library of Sweden, 2009.

Soloveitchik, Haym. "Rupture and Reconstruction: The Transformation of Contemporary Orthodoxy." *Tradition* 28, no. 4 (1994): 64–130.

Spinner, Samuel. *Jewish Primitivism*. Stanford, CA: Stanford University Press, 2021.

Stambler, Benedict, and Helen Stambler. *Cantor Joseph Shlisky: Faith Eternal*. Collectors Guild, CG619 (1962), LP, liner notes.

Stanyek, Jason, and Benjamin Piekut. "Deadness: Technologies of the Intermundane." *TDR* 54, no. 1 (2010): 14–38.

Stutschewsky, Joachim. *Der Vilner Balebesl (1816–1850)*. Tel Aviv: Y. L. Perets, 1968.

Summit, Jeffrey A. *The Lord's Song in a Strange Land: Music and Identity in Contemporary Jewish Worship*. New York: Oxford University Press, 2000.

Svigals, Alicia. "Why We Do This Anyway: Klezmer as Jewish Youth Subculture." In *American Klezmer*, edited by Mark Slobin, 211–20. Berkley: University of California Press, 2002.

Szendy, Peter. *Listen: A History of our Ears*. Translated by Charlotte Mandell. New York: Fordham University Press, 2008.

Taragin-Zeller, Lea. "A Rabbi of One's Own? Navigating Religious Authority and Ethical Freedom in Everyday Judaism." *American Anthropologist* 123, no. 4 (December 2021): 833–45.

Tarsi, Boaz. "The Early Attempts at Creating a Theory of Ashkenazi Liturgical Music." In *Jüdische Musik als Dialog der Kulturen*, edited by Jascha Nemtsov, 59–69. Wiesbaden: Harrassowitz, 2013.

———. "Observations on Practices of Nusach in America." *Asian Music* 33, no. 2 (2002): 175–219.

Taylor, Diana. *The Archive and the Repertoire: Performing Cultural Memory in the Americas*. Durham, NC: Duke University Press, 2003.

Teleshefsky, Moshe. *T'filoh L'Moshe*. Cantorphone. FRS 113. LP (ND).

Turino, Thomas. *Music as Social Life: The Politics of Participation*. Chicago: University of Chicago Press, 2008.

Vaisman, Asya. "Haredi Women's Musical Creativity." In "Contemporary Jewish Music in America 2000–2020: A Symposium," curated by Mark Kligman and Judah M. Cohen, *Journal of Synagogue Music* 46, no. 1 (September 2021): 10–11.

———. "'Hold on tightly to tradition': Generational Differences in Yiddish Song Repertoires among Contemporary Hasidic women." In *Choosing Yiddish: New Frontiers of Language and Culture*, edited by Lara Rabinovitch, Shiri Goren, and Hannah S. Pressman, 339–57. Detroit: Wayne State University Press, 2013.

Vigoda, Samuel. *Legendary Voices: The Fascinating Lives of the Great Cantors*. New York: S. Vigoda, 1981.

Waldman, Leibele. *A Song Divine: An Autobiography*. New York: Saravan House, 1941.

Wallace, Anthony F. C. "Revitalization Movements." *American Anthropologist* 58, no.2 (1956): 264–81.

Weiman-Kelman, Zohar. "Touching Time: Poetry, History, and the Erotics of Yiddish." *Criticism* 59, no. 1 (2017): 99–121.

Weintraub, H. *Schire beth Adonai oder Tempelgesänge für den Gottesdienst der Israeliten.* Leipzig: Breitkopf & Härtel, 1859.

Wertheimer, Jack. "Orthodox Outreach: Nourishing the Jewish World." In *The New American Judaism: How Jews Practice Their Religion Today*, 211–32. Princeton, NJ: Princeton University Press, 2018.

Williams, Linda. "Film Bodies: Gender, Genre, and Excess." *Film Quarterly* 44, no. 4 (1991): 2–13.

Winkler, Helen. "Hazzanut in a Hasidic Court Between the Two Wars." *Journal of Synagogue Music* 34 (Fall 2009): 151–57.

Wood, Abigail. "Pop, Piety and Modernity: The Changing Spaces of Orthodox Culture." In *The Routledge Handbook to Contemporary Jewish Cultures*, edited by Laurence Roth and Nadia Valman, 286–96. New York: Routledge, 2014.

Wooley, Nate. "Cantor Joshua Breitzer on Nusach in Jewish Life and Tradition." *Sound American: The Ritual Issue* SA11 (2015). Accessed June 11, 2023. http://archive .soundamerican.org/sa_archive/sa11/sa11-the-interviews.html.

Zim, Sol. 2018. "Remembering My Friend, Maestro Mordechai Sobol, z"l." *New York Jewish Week*, September 26, 2018. https://jewishweek.timesofisrael.com/remembering-my -friend-maestro-mordechai-sobol-zl/.

Yaffe, Nechumi Malovicki, Melissa McDonald, Eran Halperin, and Tamar Saguy. "God, Sex, and Money among the ultra-Orthodox in Israel: An Integrated Sociocultural and Evolutionary Perspective." *Evolution and Human Behavior* 39, no. 6 (2018): 622–31.

Young Israel Beth El of Borough Park. Accessed June 12, 2023. https://www.yibethel.org/.

Zaludkovsky, Elias. "Der khazonisher matzev." *Der morgn zhurnal*, November 17, 1926.

———. *Kultur treger fun der idisher liturgye.* Detroit: S. N., 1930.

Zevulun, Kwartin. *Mayn leben*. Philadelphia: Self-published, 1952.

Zhitlowsky, Chaim. *Der sotsializm un di natsionale frage*. New York: A. M. Evalenko, 1908.

Zimmermann, Akiva. "The Hasidic World's Attitude towards Hazzanut." *Journal of Synagogue Music* 34, no. 10 (2009): 148–50.

INDEX

aesthetics: and Jewish particularism, 19, 91; as alternative to rabbinic authority, 128; as basis of ritual experience, 2, 50, 52; of contemporary American synagogue, 80, 155; Hasidic approaches to, 37, 104; of recording technology, 131, 148

antisemitism, 139

archive and repertoire, 82

"Avinu Shebashamayim," 94–95

Baal Shem Tov, 3, 48, 50

bal tefiles, 5–6, 8, 61, 102–3; in contrast to cantors, 104

Beimel, Jacob, 90, 91, 97

Belz Hasidism, 54

Belz School of Jewish Music at Yeshiva University, 60–61

Bobov Hasidism, 106, 109

bodily gesture: in cantorial performance, 43–44, 121 ; in Jewish prayer, 82, 109

Borough Park, Brooklyn, 1, 49, 50, 51, 70, 103, 107, 108, 123, 140, 159n2

Breitzer, Josh, 24

cantorial training seminaries, 59, 60–61, 168n3

Carlebach, Shlomo, 4, 90–91, 93–98

Chabad (Lubavitch) Hasidism, 40–41, 72, 92, 123

Chabad houses, 41, 73, 96

Chagy, Berele, 34, 107

choirs: at Beth El Young Israel of Borough Park, 50, 70, 107, 109–10; cantorial, 8, 26, 32, 35, 49, 59; Hasidic/Orthodox pop, 5, 51, 110–11, 160n13, 174n8. *See meshoyrerim*

Cohen, Judah, 34, 66, 70, 79, 168n3

Cohen, Leonard, 96, 144–45

coloratura, 104, 30, 43, 69, 77, 104–5, 126

concerts, 13, 30, 35, 50, 53, 64, 116–23; and cantorial ethics, 33–34, 116; and gender mixing, 54, 10, 105; history of cantorial concerts, 116–17

contrafact, 52, 78, 85, 93, 95

cultural intimacy, 9, 26, 27, 30, 33, 90

cultural memory, 66–68

creativity, 28, 67–68, 87

davenen, 8

Debbie Friedman School of Sacred Music at Hebrew Union College-Jewish Institute of Religion, 60, 69–70

decline narrative, 35, 79, 86, 101, 106, 110, 111–13

decorum as American synagogue ideal, 90

digital recording technology, 136–38, 148, 160n13

dyadic lessons, 60, 168n8

Engel, Joel, 29

embodied response to cantorial music, 53, 153–54

folk-pop liturgy, 21, 90–91

Friday night *mariv*, 83–85

Founded in 1893,
UNIVERSITY OF CALIFORNIA PRESS
publishes bold, progressive books and journals
on topics in the arts, humanities, social sciences,
and natural sciences—with a focus on social
justice issues—that inspire thought and action
among readers worldwide.

The UC PRESS FOUNDATION
raises funds to uphold the press's vital role
as an independent, nonprofit publisher, and
receives philanthropic support from a wide
range of individuals and institutions—and from
committed readers like you. To learn more, visit
ucpress.edu/supportus.